Ovid: *Metamorphoses X*

Bloomsbury Latin Texts

Other titles in the series:
Ovid: *Metamorphoses I*, edited by A. G. Lee
9780862921446
Ovid: *Metamorphoses III. An Extract: 511–733*, edited by
John Godwin
9781472508508
Ovid: *Metamorphoses VIII*, edited by H. E. Gould & J. L. Whiteley
9781853997228
Ovid: *Metamorphoses XI*, edited by G. M. H. Murphy
9780906515402
Two Centuries of Roman Poetry, edited by E. C. Kennedy &
A. R. Davis
9781853995279

Ovid: *Metamorphoses X*

Edited by Lee Fratantuono

B L O O M S B U R Y

LONDON · NEW DELHI · NEW YORK · SYDNEY

Bloomsbury Academic

An imprint of Bloomsbury Publishing Plc

50 Bedford Square	1385 Broadway
London	New York
WC1B 3DP	NY 10018
UK	USA

www.bloomsbury.com

BLOOMSBURY and the Diana logo are trademarks of Bloomsbury Publishing Plc

First published 2014

© Lee Fratantuono, 2014

Lee Fratantuono has asserted his right under the Copyright, Designs and Patents Act, 1988, to be identified as Editor of this work.

British Library Cataloguing-in-Publication Data
A catalogue record for this book is available from the British Library.

ISBN: PB: 978–1–47252–290–0
ePub: 978–1–47253–064–6
ePDF: 978–1–47253–305–0

Library of Congress Cataloging-in-Publication Data
Ovid, 43 B.C.–17 A.D. or 18 A.D., author.
Metamorphoses X / Ovid; edited by Lee Fratantuono.
pages cm
Latin text with English commentary.
Includes bibliographical references and index.
ISBN 978-1-4725-2290-0 (pbk.)
1. Ovid, 43 B.C.–17 A.D. or 18 A.D. Metamorphoses. Liber 10.
I. Fratantuono, Lee, 1973– II. Title.
PA6519.M6A10 2014
873′.01–dc23
2014030605

Typeset by RefineCatch Limited, Bungay, Suffolk
Printed and bound in Great Britain

Contents

Preface

The present volume has a deceptively simple goal: to provide a commentary for student and scholar on the tenth book of Ovid's epic of transformation, *Metamorphoses*.[1]

For anglophone students of Book 10, two very different commentaries are available: Anderson's Oklahoma volume on Books 6–10 (1972), and Hill's set of editions in the Aris and Phillips series (with translations and brief annotations).[2] Bömer and (more recently) Reed offer significantly more advanced commentaries for scholars. In comparison to its English language predecessors, the present volume offers lengthier and more detailed notes (not necessarily virtues *in ipsis*) than its English language predecessors, with a plan to offer the user material for consideration of the place of Book 10 in Ovid's epic, and in particular the special status of the book at the close of the second third of the poem.

No student or teacher is likely ever to be satisfied with what is provided by that odd genre still sometimes called a "schoolboy commentary," that is, one intended for the perhaps always somewhat

---

[1] Most commentaries of this sort reproduce another text (the Oxford *vel sim.*), with or without its full critical apparatus, and this is no exception. The best text of the *Metamorphoses* currently available is Tarrant's in the *OCT* (*Oxford Classical Texts*) series, and this is the text I essentially use, with some quibbles here and there as discussed in the notes; Anderson's Teubner retains its value (the Loeb edition, despite the best efforts of George Goold as series editor, is out of date). I do, however, offer something of a novel arrangement of the text and notes. Lines of Latin are printed with annotations below each verse, thus eliminating the need for constant flipping back and forth in the volume, and allowing for appreciation of the verse as a discrete unit, rather than as a source of dismembered *lemmata*. Having the full text ahead of the commentary still permits reading from a "clean text," though there is no *apparatus*—particularly significant textual problems are addressed in the notes. The most accessible introduction to the manuscript tradition of *Metamorphoses* is probably that provided by Anderson in the introduction to his edition of Books 6–10.

[2] Anderson's edition of Books 1–5 was published a quarter century later, in 1997; Garth Tissol is preparing Books 11–15 to complete the set. There are scattered volumes devoted to individual books of the poem in other series; e.g., the Cambridge *Greek and Latin Classics* library includes Books 13–14.

mythical "undergraduates and sixth formers"; the notes nevertheless try, as always in works of this sort, to address issues that seem to me likely to occasion difficulty for first time readers of Ovid. At the same time, I have also endeavored to offer something of interest to more advanced devotees of the poet, especially in the absence of a separate, standalone treatment of the book. I have refrained deliberately from offering yet another primer on how to scan dactylic hexameters, or on the history of Augustan Rome and Ovid's place therein, and (most especially) a vocabulary; while there is undeniable convenience in having everything one might conceivably need to read a book of Ovid within one volume, I think the value of encouraging the use of dictionaries (especially the *Oxford Latin* and the Lewis and Short) and other works of reference alongside a commentary outweighs such a consideration.[3] Some may find that there are notes that give rather obvious aids to the student; other lemmata may contain details (and references) that seem beyond the ability or desired range of younger students. Throughout, an attempt has been made to strike a balance between competing aims and audiences, especially in the absence of another standalone treatment of the book.

Commentaries (especially on relatively well studied authors and works) are inevitably indebted to the scholarship of predecessors. In the notes of this volume, when a commentator such as Anderson or Reed is cited it is usually an implicit reference that his particular edition has especially full and useful consideration of a problem (i.e., not necessarily that the note represents the first treatment of a given issue). I have also not refrained from offering consideration of both

[3] So, too, I have downplayed the "division" of the book into separate sections in accord with the progress of the stories (though the notes do offer brief introductions to each), so as to mitigate against the all too frequent tendency to view the epic and its books as a mere collection of more or less loosely connected tales. It is to be hoped that any resultant inconvenience will be offset by the chance to appreciate better the book as a whole. The Latin text has been presented without divisions of paragraph and indeed without quotations, so as to provide a clean text that allows for different interpretations of certain passages (as noted where relevant in the commentary).

fairly technical points that include reference to work in foreign languages. This is in part because no serious work can be done on Ovid's *Metamorphoses* in particular without some reference to the standard German and Italian language commentaries (and because beginning and intermediate Latin students may lack access to these works, either because of language barriers or library resources, and should not, in my opinion, be unaware of the riches and wisdom they contain).[4] But it is also because I think that students from even an early stage of scholarly training should become aware of larger issues, especially if said issues sometimes (hopefully) inspire them to seek out dictionaries and other reference works. The result may seem a bit chimerical, as one note may record an identification of how *uti* takes an ablative object, while another may reference a German note that a first-time reader of Ovid is (perhaps) unlikely ever to consult. Again, not everyone may be happy at this response to the oft-asked question, "What intended audience?." For in the case of the present volume the answer would be any lover of Latin and Ovid.[5]

It is always a pleasure to record the help of colleagues in the production of scholarly works. I am indebted to Jay Reed for his unfailing generosity and help in exploring the enigmas and treasures of Ovidian verse, in particular as evinced by his own masterful edition of *Metamorphoses* 10–12 for the Fondazione Lorenzo Valla series. My

---

[4] Lexical and syntactical references are likelier to be to *OLD* (the *Oxford Latin Dictionary*) and Allen and Greenough, though, than to *TLL* (*Thesaurus Linguae Latinae*) and Hofmann-Szantyr, for the sake of student convenience; nor are there citations of the *Real-Encyclopädie der classischen Altertumswissenschaft*. Students should note throughout that the abbreviation "c." = *carmen* = poem or lyric (in reference to the works of Latin poets; e.g., Horace, c. 1.35 = Horace's first book of odes, poem 35. Occasionally, there are references in the notes of this commentary to the standard commentaries of scholars on works of classical literature (e.g., "Dodds on Euripides, *Bacchae*"); these citations are meant both for scholars and more advanced students.

[5] Space, too, is a very real consideration; I have consciously sought to avoid duplicating material that can more or less easily be found elsewhere, striving to balance user convenience with the exigencies of volume size and a desire to avoid excessive citation by quoting and referencing at length the work of others in matters in which I find no reason to disagree.

Ovidian colleague Erika Nesholm has been a constant source of help and inspiration in the composition of these notes, and to her I owe a special debt of gratitude. I am particularly indebted to Alice Reid for her superb editorial assistance, and to the helpful and welcome suggestions of the anonymous readers for the press.

Most especially, the process of completing this volume would not have been nearly as enjoyable without the wit and wisdom offered by my musical colleague Jennifer Jolley, composer and professor, whose own work and devotion to her craft and the arts never fails to inspire.

My classics students are a constant source of grace and help in my work. The "tetrarchs" of the departmental student board of 2013–2014 have been especially delightful members of the Department of Classics during the writing of this book: Marissa Popeck; Elizabeth Simmons; Selena Ross; and Sarah Lucas; so also my two Ovid tutorial students in Spring, 2014: Margaux Erilane and Kathryn Pickens. My former student and research assistant Cynthia Susalla has continued to be a most welcome collaborator in scholarly enterprises during the years of her graduate training.

For some time now (and together with my friend and biochemical colleague Dan Vogt) I have been privileged to serve as an adviser to my college's Delta Upsilon chapter of the Delta Delta Delta sorority. This brief reflection on a breathtaking book of Latin verse is offered in sincere appreciation to the sisters of Tri-Delta at Ohio Wesleyan, in gratitude and appreciation for all that they do for so many. *Let us steadfastly love one another.*

Lee Fratantuono
31 March, 2014
Delaware, Ohio

Introduction

Ovid's epic *Metamorphoses* is one of the longest and most perennially popular poems to survive from classical antiquity.[1] At least some of the contents of its fifteen books are familiar through the retelling, abridgment, and sometimes bowdlerization of popular surveys of mythology such as those of a Bulfinch or an Edith Hamilton.[2] Latin students not infrequently encounter Ovid relatively early in the study of the language, through excerpted stories in readers and intermediate textbooks; more advanced students (both undergraduate and graduate) read more or less extensively from the epic as a regular part of classics curricula at colleges and universities. And scholarship on the *Metamorphoses* remains a lively and vigorous field of academic inquiry, as evidenced by the steady stream of monographs and articles on various aspects of its art and mystery.

---

[1] The life and works of Publius Ovidius Naso (43 B.C.–A.D. 17) are conveniently surveyed in such standard reference works as *The Oxford Classical Dictionary* (now in its fourth edition); and *The Cambridge History of Classical Literature*. Introductory studies of the *Metamorphoses* include Elaine Fantham's 2004 *Ovid's Metamorphoses* in the "Oxford Approaches to Classical Literature" series; Nikolas Holzberg's *Ovid: The Poet and His Work* (Ithaca: Cornell University Press, 2002—a translation of the author's *Ovid: Dichter und Werk*, München, 1997); and my own *Madness Transformed: A Reading of Ovid's Metamorphoses* (Lanham, Maryland: Lexington Books, 2011). The *Metamorphoses* was likely underway in A.D. 1 (certainly by 3); it was likely largely "finished" by the time of the poet's mysterious exile in 8. We have no record of when the epic was released/published, or of any particular literary (or other) figure who was entrusted with the duty of seeing the work through to its audience. The Age of Augustus can be said to have ended in A.D. 17, the year that saw the death of both Ovid and Livy. Ovid complains more than once in his *Tristia* that he was not able to put the final touch on the *Metamorphoses*; the poet in exile may be playing something of a literary game with response to the Virgilian *Aeneid* and the poet's alleged wish that his work be burned.

[2] I first read Ovid's epic in the verse translation of Horace Gregory, though it was Edith Hamilton's wonderful introductions to his stories (with comment on his style and even psychology) that first introduced me to him. Students have a wide range of English translations from which to choose; the *Oxford World's Classics* edition of Melville is both reliable and equipped with a useful introduction and fairly detailed explanatory notes, after the fashion of that series.

The present volume—devoted as it is to a single book of the epic—is in one important respect seemingly at variance with my general introduction to the poem, *Madness Transformed: A Reading of Ovid's Metamorphoses*. That book complained that Ovid's epic had suffered from a deleterious practice of selection and culling of passages for study—a product, at least in part, of the impossibility of reading the entire epic in Latin in most classes. While such abridgment may be understandable, the result is oftentimes a lack of appreciation of the unity of Ovid's epic achievement—a lack of perception of the whole. Ovid's epic is a vast compendium of myths and lore, with an astonishingly diverse structure and stunningly varied array of poetic treasures—but it also has a definite structure and deliberate arrangement of its component parts, indeed a structure that is formidably tripartite, with a distinct division of its material into the three act drama of Books 1–5; 6–10; and 11–15.[3] This threefold division into groups of five books may have been inspired by the original five book arrangement of Ovid's first published work, his *Amores*, which was later altered into the three book edition that has survived; it may also have been inspired by the threefold arrangement of Horace's original collection of odes, what we know of as "Books 1–3" (the fourth was added later). Virgil's *Aeneid*, too, can be understood as a three-act drama, where Books 1–4, 5–8, and 9–12 are discrete units of poetic reflection.[4]

[3] On this arrangement of books/divisions of the epic into thirds see especially N. Holzberg, "*Ter Quinque Volumina* as *Carmen Perpetuum:* The Division Into Books in Ovid's *Metamorphoses*," in *Materiali e discussioni per l'analisi dei testi classici* 40 (1998), 77–98. In the *Tristia* Ovid more than once refers to the "thrice five" division of his *Metamorphoses*; the number *quindecim* or "fifteen" does not readily lend itself to Latin verse, of course—but the metrical convenience does allow the poet to highlight the fact that his epic is divided most especially into three discrete units of five books each.

[4] Many studies of Ovid's epic give consideration of the structure of the poem; useful further reading here include Brooks Otis' *Ovid as an Epic Poet* (Cambridge, 1966; second edition 1970); Karl Galinsky's *Ovid's Metamorphoses: An Introduction to the Basic Aspects* (Berkeley-Los Angeles: The University of California Press, 1975); Joseph Solodow, *The World of Ovid's Metamorphoses*, Chapel Hill-London: The University of North Carolina Press, 1988; and Stephen Wheeler, *Narrative Dynamics in Ovid's Metamorphoses*, Tübingen: Narr, 2000.

But this threefold arrangement does not offer merely a balanced and aesthetically pleasing structure that evokes the poet's first work and the storied achievement of a predecessor. Rather, it allows for something of a response to Horace, in particular, who closed his last book of odes with a statement about poetic immortality that Ovid echoes at the end of his epic of metamorphosis.[5] In Horace, the statement is bold and unqualified: the poet "will not wholly die" (*non omnis moriar*), and his immortality will come in virtue of his poetic masterpiece and achievement. In Ovid, similar language closes the last book with a declaration of the undying aspects of the poet and the poetic craft—*if the predictions of poets have anything of truth in them* (15.879 *siquid habent veri vatum praesagia*). This qualifier about the ability of verse to confer immortality is Ovid's response to Horace's more direct pronouncement; it relates, too, to the idea of truth and falsehood, especially as reflected in poetic song. This theme of falsehood is of central concern to Ovid elsewhere in his epic, and in particular, we shall see, in his depiction of Orpheus in Book 10.[6] This question of truth *vs.* mendacity was also of paramount importance to Virgil at the end of his underworld book (*Aeneid* 6), where his hero exits the realm of the dead through the Ivory Gate of false dreams—a book where Orpheus, too, plays a part in the Virgilian drama of Aeneas' descent to Elysium, a journey that is replete with eschatological concerns (i.e., exploration of the "last things" and the world of the dead and the afterlife). Ovid adds a qualifier at the close of his epic on the matter of eternal life through verse; his work, and by extension his very self, will live forever—provided that the *praesagia vatum* have something of truth in them.

---

[5]   cf. the language of Horace, c. 3.30 *Exegi monumentum aere perennius* and the closing verses of the *Metamorphoses*.

[6]   "Ovid presents a *lying* Orpheus, a figure who promises resurrection but does not deliver, a singer who says he will tell of youths loved by the gods and of women given over to loves not granted them, only to tell of Pygmalion and his ivory statue; Orpheus is a liar, as he himself admits before he sings of Myrrha." (Fratantuono 2011: 298).

The question of the possibility of immortality (poetic or otherwise) relates most intimately to the problem of the fate of the human soul after death—and here the poet finds a rationale for the division of his epic into three parts, the first third of which closes in a book that tells of the abduction of Persephone (*Metamorphoses* 5); the second third of which is focused on Orpheus, who would harrow hell, as it were, to seek the rescue of his lost wife (10); the final third of which will center on Pythagoras and his teachings, and reach its climax in the dramatic epiphany of the apotheosis of the assassinated Julius Caesar, with the poet's own aforementioned reflection on the possibility of *his* attainment of some form of immortality appended as a coda to the whole enterprise (15). If there is a fundamental concern that is explored in Ovid's epic, it might well be this problem of eternal life *vs.* the permanence and inevitability of the grave. The exploration of that issue can be pursued through particular attention to the last books of the three thirds of the poem: Books 5, 10, and 15.

The present commentary, then, focuses in particular on the closing book of the second third of Ovid's epic. Certainly that decision was partly made because Book 10 contains some of Ovid's most enduring and popular stories, despite a relative dearth of treatments, especially for younger Latinists—and Ovid is always and ever a poet to be cherished for the enjoyment and pleasure of a good story that is well told.[7] Herein the stories of Pygmalion's statue and Atalanta's race vie for attention with the more sordid story of Myrrha and the tragedy of her doomed son Adonis. Book 10 is one of the more familiar sections of the epic in terms of the relative dissemination of the stories contained therein; it also offers something of a balanced sampling of Ovidian narrative, with an especially rich variety of stories of different

---

[7]   There is also no other single treatment of the book of which I am aware, though I have not made an exhaustive survey of Victorian and other school editions. The Allyn and Bacon Latin series, one of the finest for an introduction to Latin in its earlier editions and incarnations, offered fairly extensive extracts from the book.

length and focus.[8] In terms of the *Nachleben* or "afterlife" of Ovid, few stories have been as enduring as Pygmalion and Adonis; from Shakespeare to Shaw, *Metamorphoses* 10 has cast its spell.[9]

But on a level of concern more fundamental than aesthetic appreciation of artfully composed tales that have endured, Book 10 is key to the study of Ovid's epic as a *trilogy*. The fifth book of the epic, the close of its first third, closes with the victory of the Muses in a music competition; Calliope, the muse of epic verse, tells the story of the abduction of Proserpina, the daughter of Ceres who undergoes something of a metamorphosis from carefree girl of spring to queen of the underworld. The eschatology or "study of the last things" that is represented by the Proserpina/Persephone story is complex; on the one hand there is the traditional enough underworld of, say, Homer— an underworld that serves as a permanent place of diverse rewards and punishments, from Tartarus to Elysium—while on the other hand, we have the association of Persephone and the story of her yearly return to the upper world with the Elysian mystery religion and a theology of rebirth and renewal. Put another way, the story of Ceres' daughter and her descent and ascent from the underworld speaks powerfully to the dream of mortals to be immortal, at least in some way and after some fashion. Ceres' daughter, immortal goddess though she was, was able to be ransomed from the underworld—even if, interestingly enough, she seems often enough if not always to be in the underworld when some myth demands her presence (as if Greek heroes travel to the infernal regions only in winter).

---

[8] One might compare the very different case of Book 15, which is less suitable as an introduction to the poet or a sampling of the poem's contents.

[9] An increasingly formidable bibliography has been devoted to the reception of Ovid's work; Shakespeare's *Venus and Adonis* and Shaw's *Pygmalion* are probably the most famous reinventions of the narratives found in *Metamorphoses* 10. The present volume does not engage extensively with the vast array of literary, visual, and musical works of virtual *hommage* to Ovid; the *Oxford Guide to Classical Mythology in the Arts* provides a convenient survey.

Book 10 presents a different composer of music, the celebrated poet and singer Orpheus—the son of the Muse Calliope and Apollo, the patron god of the poetic arts and the craft of versifying. The second third of the epic closes with *Orpheus'* song, or, more accurately, series of songs—a cycle that is vastly different from that of his mother and her sisters in Book 5. In a sense the song of Orpheus begins with Proserpina, as the poet is compelled to enter the lower regions to seek the rescue of his wife Eurydice—in other words, to do something of what Ceres had tried to do for her daughter in the narrative of Book 5. Ceres was only partially successful in her quest; she regained her daughter, but not entirely; the girl who once roamed over Sicilian meadows in search of flowers would forever be associated with the lord of the dead as his bride and co-ruler.

Calliope's son Orpheus would be *entirely* unsuccessful in rescuing his wife, and in consequence would lament his loss in something of a parallel to the dark emotions of Ceres as she sought her daughter for so long in vain. Orpheus will in some sense sing of the exceedingly fleeting and fragile world of *flowers*—appropriately enough once we learn how many trees gather to hear his melodic strains—and he will sing a song cycle that is not entirely unlike the first third of the epic plus the bulk of its second—the loves of the immortals plus the questionable actions of humans in matters of love and lust. And Orpheus is no mere poet, no mere musician of strains of sound already familiar from nearly two thirds of a long epic. No, Orpheus is also associated with his own system of eschatological investigation of the fate of the soul after death and the question of immortality—a system in which rebirth and renewal are not at all impossible concepts, notwithstanding the utter failure of the bard to save his own wife (let alone his own life, in the end). Orpheus' song will in some sense be devoted to flowers in testament to the exceedingly fragile world they represent, one where death may come with the slightest breeze—as mirrored more or less in the stories of a Hyacinthus or an Adonis.

Book 15, the last in the epic, will open with yet another song, this time a work of music that introduces the shadowy Pythagoras, the mysterious sixth century B.C. (?) philosopher and theologian. The Pythagorean song of the poet's last book focuses in part on the problem of metempsychosis and the transmigration of souls; this material links the end of Ovid's epic directly to the problems of the great revelation of Anchises to his son Aeneas in the underworld of *Aeneid* 6, a book that stands forth as a vast compendium of the epic poet's absorption, amalgamation and adaptation of sometimes seemingly contradictory and inconsistent patterns of philosophical and theological thought: Stoic; Platonic; Orphic-Pythagorean; Orphic-Bacchic; Homeric (in no particular order).[10] Both "Orpheus" and "Pythagoras" were associated with a richly complex and even confused array of theological and philosophical concepts that relate to the afterlife and the "last things." And despite the inability of Orpheus to save Eurydice in the familiar myth, both names were associated with the idea that death is not necessarily the end, and that there may be something of a chance for life beyond the shadows of the grave.

Book 10, as aforementioned, opens with the failed achievement of Orpheus to rescue his wife. Here, too, the poet of transformation responds to his Virgilian predecessor, who told the story of the loss of Eurydice at length as the climactic tale of his four books of *Georgics*. The failure of Orpheus in Virgil to save his wife amounts to something of a perversion of the misty magic of the promises of *Aeneid* 6 and the

---

[10] The absence of a separate, standalone commentary on the last book of the epic is to be lamented; a good start for investigation of the problems of Pythagoreanism in *Metamorphoses* 15 = Philip Hardie's "The Speech of Pythagoras in Ovid, *Metamorphoses* 15: Empedoclean Epos," in *The Classical Journal* 45.1 (1995), 204–214. Part of the humor of Ovid's depiction of Pythagoreanism in his last book comes from the poet's exploration of the sect's vegetarian practices; in the context of the *Metamorphoses*, vegetarianism becomes a moral imperative so as to avoid eating something that had recently been one's son or lover.

Orphic eschatology of rebirth. Elsewhere in Virgil this failure is evoked, too, in Aeneas' own inability to save his wife Creusa during the fall of Troy (and her name, too, was Eurydice in some traditions); in Ovid, the end of *Metamorphoses* 11 will return to the theme in the snake bite that fells not Eurydice but *Hesperia*, the "Italian" nymph whose name evokes the promised new western home of the Trojan exiles.

As we shall see in the commentary notes on the opening of this book, there is—more or less surprisingly—no extant account of the attempted ransom of Eurydice before Virgil. This is no proof that Virgil *invented* the story of course—and what evidence we have, both in the literary and the visual arts, does not allow for definitive resolution of the question—but Virgil certainly chose to highlight the story at the climax of his own reflections on rebirth and renewal in the *Georgics*. It is possible that both Virgil and Ovid—the two most extensive accounts of Orpheus and Eurydice that survive from classical antiquity—represent an original twist on the story of the famous singer, whereby he *fails* and does not succeed in his attempt to save his newlywed bride.[11] The singer whose name is associated with an extensive lore about the chance for resurrection is presented as unable to bring lasting life to his beloved wife; he *did* save Eurydice, only to lose her almost at once.

All of these aforementioned doctrines of renewal and the hope of resurrection—whether through the Eleusinian mystery rites, or what we might label more or less accurately as Orphic or Pythagorean—were ultimately utterly at variance with the tenets of Epicureanism that one finds explicated in another great Latin epic, the didactic *De Rerum Natura*. Ovid bookends his own epic with two hinge points that provide an important harking back to that earlier poem, that epic

---

[11]   And if the story was not original to Virgil, it is the aspect of the lore that the poet chooses to emphasize, and Ovid follows him in this.

in which the lack of an existence for the soul after death was posited and the notions of either torment in an underworld of hell, or rebirth into some new form, were equally derided as the fantasies of misguided poets and philosophers. At *Metamorphoses* 2.726–729, Ovid describes the passion of Mercury for the mortal girl Herse with a simile about the shot of a leaden bullet from a sling that is inspired by a similar image in Lucretius (*De Rerum Natura* 6.177–179 and 306–308). In the second to last book of his poem, at 14.824–826, Ovid compares the apotheosis of Romulus, the progenitor of the Romans, in similar language—just before the introduction of his wife Hersilie (cf. Herse). It is conceivable that the philosophy that Lucretius describes in his own verses of dactylic hexameter is that to which Ovid would most readily have paid allegiance; a Lucretian seal is placed relatively near the beginning and end of the poet's epic, and the final lines of the work raise questions about the *praesagia vatum* that may point to an expression of doubt and uncertainty about any eschatological system that purports to explain how a soul can live again in some form or other. Poets do not usually come forth with direct, incontrovertible attestations and assertions of their philosophical beliefs; epic poems in particular, with their great length and variety of tenor and tone, resist easy or even consistent philosophical analysis. But the fact that an epic does not present easily digested judgments on matters such as the *post mortem* fate of the soul does not detract from the rich interplay of the work with a wide range of currents of thought and belief.

Philosophical concerns are at the heart of Ovid's poem, but so are interrelated matters that pertain to the historical and temporal context of the author: Augustan Rome and the ethnographic nature of the city, republic and empire that serves as the social laboratory from which the poet's work emerges. Swirling about, too, are the concerns of the poet with his response to literary predecessors, especially Virgil and Homer, the principal epic rivals with whom he might be expected to contend. Book 10 is especially rich in exploration of Ovid's views on Roman ethnography and the relationship of his epic with the *Aeneid* in particular. All of these diverse matters interrelate and combine in one integral poetic composition that works on multiple levels of interpretation and reflection simultaneously. Throughout, too, Ovid is a playful poet; he may have quite serious concerns and sober reflections to make on the fate of the soul, the nature of Rome and the destiny of the Augustan regime—but throughout he is also capable of lighthearted narrative that creates a playful mood that draws the reader towards a deeper appreciation of his points: sometimes, when it is least expected, the poet displays a humorous touch that makes the reader pause and thereby think more deeply about the action being described.

Ovid's tenth book offers the second of two appearances in the epic of the mysterious huntress Atalanta. She is first introduced in Book 8, during the narrative of the Calydonian boar hunt—and the midpoint of the entire epic comes during the account of that ill-fated expedition and its aftermath. She is a key figure in the complicated intertextual relationship between Ovid's poem and its Virgilian epic predecessor, where the swift huntress Camilla plays a significant role in the unfolding of the poet's reflections on the ethnography of the future Rome, the city founded by Trojan exiles that was reborn, as it were, in the splendor of the Augustan achievement.[12]

One of the paramount concerns of Ovid's epic (as also of Virgil's) is the question of the Trojan origins of Rome and the sometimes quite seemingly conflicted influences of Trojan (i.e., eastern) customs and social mores with native Italian practices. The end of Virgil's *Aeneid*

---

[12]   Like Ovid's Atalanta, Virgil's Camilla is in some sense doomed; her death, however, like that of her commander Turnus, is rather mitigated by the fact that in the end, the future Rome will be Italian and not Trojan. In Virgil's *Aeneid*, Camilla can be considered as part of a complex of conflicts: on the divine level, Venus *vs.* Diana; on the mortal, Camilla *vs.* Dido; on the urban, the future Rome *vs.* the dead Troy.

offers a climactic revelation in the final meeting of Jupiter and Juno, the announcement and solemn, Jovian declaration of the destiny that Rome will be Italian, not Trojan. And similar reflections pepper the pages of Ovid's epic, together with related concerns about the nature of Rome in light of the transformations wrought by the Augustan regime and the question of Rome's future *after* the inevitable death of the *princeps* who had done so much to quell the history of internecine strife and civil war at Rome and to bring peace to a republic/empire that was so weary of violence.[13]

The songs of Orpheus that dominate the last book of the second third of the poet's epic have as a recurring theme the untimely death of the young and beautiful. For if death is a tragedy to be averted, or at least to be mitigated in its grim effects via the idea of the possibility of resurrection, then nothing is more tragic than premature death— and herein the poets of Augustan Rome find a powerful metaphor for the problem of the Augustan succession, the vexing question of who might succeed to the work of the *princeps* Augustus, work that has done so much to preserve the social order from a new descent into civil chaos. Intertwined inextricably with the problem of Roman identity is the question of the nature of the imperial principate and the succession motif; in the untimely deaths of the young the poets find an endlessly rich source of material for reflections on Rome and its imperial destiny.

Metamorphoses 10 opens with the sudden introduction of Orpheus and Eurydice, who are depicted in brief and swift compass on the grim day of their nuptial union. What follows the narrative of the loss of Orpheus' wife and his failure to save her from the underworld is essentially a series of Orphic songs, stories that are supposed to be

---

[13] An excellent starting point to a vast topic is Alessandro Barchiesi's *The Poet and the Prince: Ovid and Augustan Discourse* (Berkeley-Los Angeles: The University of California Press, 1997—a translation of the author's original *Il poeta e il principe: Ovidio e il discorso augusteo*, Roma-Bari, 1994).

devoted to the twinned themes of boys loved by the immortals and girls who were enamored of illicit loves. In point of fact, not all of the stories that are told will actually accord with these announced subjects; the distinction, too, between Orpheus' topics and those of the Muses in the songs of Book 5 is glaring. Orpheus' audience is composed of trees that by their very existence embody so many of the metamorphoses of the rest of the epic; the songs of Orpheus are almost an address, as it were, to the rest of the epic—as befits what amounts to the song of the purveyor of a philosophical system that may prove untenable in the light of other (perhaps Lucretian) truths.

The story of Cyparissus is told as part of the unfolding of the arboreal queue; the death of his pet deer is directly evocative of the loss of Sylvia's stag in *Aeneid* 7 that helped to instigate the war in Latium between the Trojans and Italians: Ovid thereby brings to the fore the issues of ethnographic conflict that coexist with philosophical and eschatological concerns, and contemporary (i.e., Augustan) political realities in so many of the works of the poets of the Augustan Age. But Cyparissus is also beloved by Apollo; the story directly presages part of the announced subject matter of Orpheus' song, of boys loved by the immortals.

The story of Ganymede is the first of Orpheus' songs as his hymn commences *ab Iove*, "from Jove"; the *Trojan* Ganymede was beloved by Jupiter, and, further, had been named by Virgil as a source of Juno's irritation with the Trojans. Following the story of Ganymede we once again encounter Apollo, a patron deity of the Augustan regime, in the context of his own love affair, the doomed story of Hyacinthus; the scene (like that with Cyparissus) is very different from that of *Metamorphoses* 1, so soon after the flood, when Ovid had depicted Apollo in love with Daphne, the source of the laurel that is connected by Virgil with the palace of Latinus in *Aeneid* 7 and the origins of the future Rome in central *Italy:* a world very far removed from that of the Trojan boy lover of Jupiter. The story of Cyparissus and his deer was very different from that of Sylvia and hers in Virgil (and the gender issues are relevant, here, too, especially in light of how Ovid's Orpheus shuns the company of women in the wake of the loss of his Eurydice and teaches the people of Thrace the arts of pederasty); the Orphic world that Ovid presents in *Metamorphoses* 10 represents the threat of what some would see as a perversion of traditional Roman ideals.

And the conflict that it embodies exists on several interrelated levels: philosophical, social, political and religious, as the master poet exercises control over a narrative that tries (and succeeds) in maintaining multiple avenues of inquiry in one and the same stream of stories.

A sharp transition marks what could be called the division of the Orphic song before its second main theme, the loves of girls that are not sanctioned by law.[14] Brief tales of the Cerastae and Propoetides do not seem to fit this or the first theme, however, anymore than does the lengthy rendition of Pygmalion's love for his statue.[15] But that story leads directly to the tales of Myrrha and her son Adonis—and here, in the matter of the incestuous union of the daughter of Cinyras with her father, we have what could be considered a textbook case of a girl struck by a passion that no social custom would concede to her. In part, once again the poet is reflecting on seemingly conflicting mores and practices; the ethnographic theme is omnipresent. Myrrha is descended from Pygmalion, who was himself possessed of something of an incestuous love for that which he had created; the story of Pygmalion is but *prolegomenon* to that of his troubled descendant.

---

[14] The movement, too, is geographical, as the focus shifts to the sacred island of Cyprus, the isle of Venus—a patron goddess for both Troy and, by extension, Rome.

[15] The briefly alluded to story of the Cerastae does focus on the question of hospitality and the violation thereof; the theme of mistreatment of guests is one that Ovid returns to time and again; cf. the story of Lycaon in Book 1, which set the stage for the flood narrative.

Pygmalion falls in love with his statue, in something of a turning inward toward himself in revulsion and disgust at the feminine world around him; he is like Orpheus, who eschews the company of women after the loss of Eurydice. The story of Myrrha—the lengthiest single tale in the book—looks both backward to Pygmalion and forward to Adonis; Myrrha is the lynchpin that maintains the integrity and unity of the Cypriot tales.

Pygmalion's descendant Myrrha is the mother of Adonis, who will be loved by Venus—a full circle return, one might think, to the start of the book, though with a gender shift back to a heterosexual relationship. But Adonis has affinities with Attis, the devotee of the Trojan mother goddess Cybele and emasculated servant of the patron deity of the Trojans—the return of the ethnographic theme. Like Adonis, in some versions of the lore Attis was killed by a *boar*—we might compare the Calydonian boar hunt narrative that introduced Atalanta in Book 8, and how Atalanta will soon enough return to the epic in rather different guise.[16] Adonis is loved by Venus, and thus he is like another Ganymede, and the song of Orpheus has come full circle indeed to the loves of deities—in this case the apparently heterosexual union is actually evocative of the castrated boy servant of the Trojan goddess (who could be conveniently associated with both Venus, one of the great patronesses of Troy, and Jupiter her father).[17]

Venus cautions her young lover about the hazards of hunting big game. The tale she uses to warn her young lover is that of Atalanta and Hippomenes, who were transformed into lions because Hippomenes

[16] Cf., too, Atys, the son of Croesus, killed in a hunting accident at Herodotus 1.34–45.
[17] Atys (cf. Attis) is the name of one of the Trojan Ascanius' compatriots in the glorious equestrian *lusus Troiae* of *Aeneid* 5, where he is described (5.569) as *parvus Atys pueroque puer dilectus Iulo*, a passage that was a likely influence on Ovid, *Metamorphoses* 10.107, of Cyparissus, and more generally of the theme of boys loved by the immortals. The connection of the family of Octavian's mother Atia lends further interesting associations and analysis to the matter of the complex intertextual nomenclatures, in particular with respect to the reinvention of the image of the old Troy in the birth of a new (Italian) Rome.

failed to thank the goddess for her help in orchestrating his successful union with the swift and beautiful runner (in striking contrast to the more devout Pygmalion, who was, after all, an ancestor of her beloved Adonis). Atalanta and Hippomenes are transformed into lions that are employed in the service of *Cybele*'s chariot—but they are hateful to Venus because they represent the insult and affront to her deity (cf. Juno's anger at the Trojans over perceived slights), and, too, because they represent a threat to her beloved. Venus will have her vengeance on Atalanta and Hippomenes, but her beloved Adonis will be slain by a wild boar; he will be transformed into a flower, but the crimson anemone will forever memorialize the blood shed by the beast on that fateful forest day, and his memorial flower will be eminently susceptible to the slightest breeze of the wind.

Ovid's Atalanta is herself inspired by the depiction in Virgil's *Aeneid* of Camilla, the Volscian huntress heroine who is associated with the goddess Diana, whose mortal avatar she is. Camilla represents in Virgil so much of the traditional Italy that is at variance with the Trojan culture that clashes with it so uncomfortably throughout the second, Iliadic half of his epic. Indeed, *Metamorphoses* 11 will largely unfold a retelling of key aspects of both Book 11 of Virgil's *Aeneid* (the book of Camilla), and the related, sister Book 5 (together the two books constitute the "penultimate" books of the first and second halves of Virgil's poem); at the end of Book 11, Ovid will tell of how Aesacus, another Trojan scion, fails to secure the love of the nymph Hesperia—the climax of the ethnographic theme of how Troy will never capture Italy.[18] As in Virgil,

---

[18] "The eleventh book of Ovid's *Metamorphoses* is one of his most extraordinary, with echoes both loud and faint of Books 5 and 11 of Virgil's *Aeneid*, and, like Virgil's poem, a 'surprise' ending that parallels the divine conversation between Jupiter and Juno that comes near the end of *Aeneid* 12. This '*Aeneid*' in miniature becomes a deliberate trick of the poet before he launches into his own examination of Homeric and Virgilian lore proper in Books 12–14 of his epic. Book 11 of the *Metamorphoses* is a stunning opening to the last third of Ovid's epic, a grand introduction to the great themes that will dominate the final major movement of the poet's perpetual song." (Fratantuono 2011: 307). The perpetual nature of a song with an end is part of the enigma of the last lines of Ovid's work.

so in Ovid the Diana-like figure will meet death, but so will that which she inherently opposes; Venus will succeed in conquering Atalanta (after a fashion), but the last image of the book is one redolent with the sorrow of the goddess who has lost her darling.

Book 10 of the *Metamorphoses* thus contains much material of significance in the scholarly debates over the richly complicated issues raised in this introduction and throughout the commentary. But whatever the conclusions of individual readers of Ovid's epic on the various problems of philosophy; ethnography; intertextuality; political and social thought; religious and mythological lore; narrative technique and poetic form; gender and sexuality; and so much more that is contained in the pages of Ovid's *magnum opus*, the tenth book offers something of the quintessential Ovid in his capacity as master *raconteur*.

Metamorphoses 10, then, neatly encapsulates many of the problems of greatest interest to the Augustan poets; for lovers of both Ovid as gifted storyteller and Ovid as poet philosopher and political critic of Augustan Rome, Book 10 is rich in meditative material. And, in a manner not unlike that of the aforementioned imitations of the Lucretian simile imagery that mark Books 2 and 14 of the poem, Book 10 has two appearances of a relatively uncommon Latin word that relate to many of these larger issues, in its citations of the *bulla* of both Cyparissus' deer (114, of a *bulla argentea* of "silvery ornament" for the pet animal), and that which appears in the mysterious simile that describes the rising of the Adonis anemone at 733–734, near the end of the book. The *bulla* was worn by young Roman aristocrats until they reached manhood; it was something of a symbol of their age and status.[19]

---

[19]   Much of Book 10 is concerned with the question of what we might call "liminality," the line between one state of life or being and another; this matter may well have been of special consideration for the poets of the Augustan Age in light of the obvious transition politically that they were witnessing in Rome. In the case of the premature death of the young, there is something of a case of arrested development; the dead youth is, as it were, frozen in a moment of time—and/or reimagined through the prism of the metamorphosis the poet describes.

In a Roman context, neither *bulla* of Book 10 is appropriate; the deer of Cyparissus, moreover, is a poetic, intertextual response to the pet that Sylvia lost in *Aeneid* 7. The patron deity of the victory of Octavian at Actium is reduced in *Metamorphoses* 10 to the lover of first Cyparissus and then Hyacinthus; the *bulla* of Roman youths is associated with the pet of his *eromenos*, and with the metamorphosis of a virtual doublet of Phrygian Attis in the person of the lover of the goddess who in Virgil is the devoted patroness of her son Aeneas and his fellow Phrygians. The world presented by the songs of Orpheus is one strikingly at variance with the image of an Italian, not Trojan Rome; it is a world that also evokes philosophical and eschatological doctrines that might arouse question and comment from a Virgil or an Ovid (especially in light of their Epicurean poetic predecessor Lucretius). It is a world that in the end will prove as fleeting as the Adonis-anemone whose fragile character and delicate state provide the closing image of the book, a flower ready to be blown off by the wind.[20]

---

[20] Book 11 will commence at once with the death scene of Orpheus; more pointedly for the ethnographic question, it will end with the story of Aeasacus' failure to secure the nymph Hesperia, whose name so evokes the western land (i.e., Italy) that is the geographic destination and hopeful dream of the Trojans in Virgil's *Aeneid*—and Hesperia, like Orpheus' wife Eurydice, will trample on a serpent and be killed by its venomous bite in a new version of the story from the opening verses of Book 10. On the very cusp of Ovid's version of the lore of Troy and Rome, then, he will depict how Troy can never capture Rome, even if the alternative spells the death of Rome and the wasting away of Troy (as symbolized by the metamorphosis of Aesacus into an eternally grieving, emaciated bird). See further Fratantuono 2011: 328–331.

Latin Text

Inde per immensum croceo velatus amictu
aethera digreditur Ciconumque Hymenaeus ad oras
tendit et Orphea nequiquam voce vocatur.
adfuit ille quidem, sed nec sollemnia verba
nec laetos vultus nec felix attulit omen;   5
fax quoque quam tenuit lacrimoso stridula fumo
usque fuit nullosque invenit motibus ignes.
exitus auspicio gravior; nam nupta per herbas
dum nova Naiadum turba comitata vagatur,
occidit in talum serpentis dente recepto.   10
quam satis ad superas postquam Rhodopeius auras
deflevit vates, ne non temptaret et umbras,
ad Styga Taenaria est ausus descendere porta,
perque leves populos simulacraque functa sepulcro
Persephonen adiit inamoenaque regna tenentem   15
umbrarum dominum, pulsisque ad carmina nervis
sic ait: 'o positi sub terra numina mundi,
in quem reccidimus quidquid mortale creamur,
si licet et falsi positis ambagibus oris
vera loqui sinitis, non huc ut opaca viderem   20
Tartara descendi, nec uti villosa colubris
terna Medusaei vincirem guttura monstri;
causa viae est coniunx, in quam calcata venenum

[handwritten note: orpheus talking to persephone]

vipera diffudit crescentesque abstulit annos.
posse pati volui nec me temptasse negabo;   25
vicit Amor. supera deus hic bene notus in ora est;
an sit et hic dubito. sed et hic tamen auguror esse,
famaque si veteris non est mentita rapinae,
vos quoque iunxit Amor. per ego haec loca plena timoris,
per Chaos hoc ingens vastique silentia regni,   30
Eurydices, oro, properata retexite fata.
omnia debemur vobis, paulumque morati
serius aut citius sedem properamus ad unam;
tendimus huc omnes, haec est domus ultima, vosque
humani generis longissima regna tenetis.   35
haec quoque, cum iustos matura peregerit annos,
iuris erit vestri; pro munere poscimus usum.
quod si fata negant veniam pro coniuge, certum est
nolle redire mihi; leto gaudete duorum.
talia dicentem nervosque ad verba moventem   40
exsangues flebant animae; nec Tantalus undam
captavit refugam, stupuitque Ixionis orbis,
nec carpsere iecur volucres, urnisque vacarunt
Belides, inque tuo sedisti, Sisyphe, saxo.
tum primum lacrimis victarum carmine fama est   45
Eumenidum maduisse genas, nec regia coniunx
sustinet oranti nec qui regit ima negare,
Eurydicenque vocant. umbras erat illa recentes
inter et incessit passu de vulnere tardo.
hanc simul et legem Rhodopeius accipit heros,   50
ne flectat retro sua lumina, donec Avernas
exierit valles; aut inrita dona futura.
carpitur acclivis per muta silentia trames,
arduus, obscurus, caligine densus opaca.
nec procul abfuerunt telluris margine summae;   55

hic ne deficeret metuens avidusque videndi
flexit amans oculos, et protinus illa relapsa est,
bracchiaque intendens prendique et prendere certans
nil nisi cedentes infelix adripit auras.   60
iamque iterum moriens non est de coniuge quidquam
questa suo (quid enim nisi se quereretur amatam?)
supremumque vale, quod iam vix auribus ille
acciperet, dixit revolutaque rursus eodem est.
non aliter stupuit gemina nece coniugis Orpheus   65
quam tria qui Stygii, medio portante catenas,
colla canis vidit; quem non pavor ante reliquit
quam natura prior, saxo per corpus oborto;
quique in se crimen traxit voluitque videri
Olenos esse nocens, tuque, o confisa figurae,
infelix Lethaea, tuae, iunctissima quondam   70
pectora, nunc lapides, quos umida sustinet Ide.
orantem frustraque iterum transire volentem
portitor arcuerat. septem tamen ille diebus
squalidus in ripa Cereris sine munere sedit;
cura dolorque animi lacrimaeque alimenta fuere.   75
esse deos Erebi crudeles questus in altam
se recipit Rhodopen pulsumque aquilonibus Haemum.
tertius aequoreis inclusum Piscibus annum
finierat Titan, omnemque refugerat Orpheus
femineam Venerem, seu quod male cesserat illi,   80
sive fidem dederat. multas tamen ardor habebat
iungere se vati; multae dolore repulsae.
ille etiam Thracum populis fuit auctor amorem
in teneros transferre mares citraque iuventam
aetatis breve ver et primos carpere flores.   85
collis erat collemque super planissima campi
area, quam viridem faciebant graminis herbae

umbra loco deerat; qua postquam parte resedit
dis genitus vates et fila sonantia movit,
umbra loco venit. non Chaonis abfuit arbor,   90
non nemus Heliadum, non frondibus aesculus altis,
nec tiliae molles, nec fagus et innuba laurus,
et coryli fragiles et fraxinus utilis hastis
enodisque abies curvataque glandibus ilex
et platanus genialis acerque coloribus impar   95
amnicolaeque simul salices et aquatica lotos
perpetuoque virens buxum tenuesque myricae
et bicolor myrtus et bacis caerula tinus.
vos quoque, flexipedes hederae, venistis et una
pampineae vites et amictae vitibus ulmi   100
ornique et piceae pomoque onerata rubenti
arbutus et lentae, victoris praemia, palmae
et succincta comas hirsutaque vertice pinus
grata deum Matri; siquidem Cybeleius Attis
exuit hac hominem truncoque induruit alto.   105
adfuit huic turbae metas imitata cupressus,
nunc arbor, puer ante deo dilectus ab illo
qui citharam nervis et nervis temperat arcum
namque sacer nymphis Carthaea tenentibus arva
ingens cervus erat lateque patentibus altas   110
ipse suo capiti praebebat cornibus umbras.
cornua fulgebant auro, demissaque in armos
pendebant tereti gemmata monilia collo;
bulla super frontem parvis argentea loris
vincta movebatur, parilesque ex aere nitebant   115
auribus e geminis circum cava tempora bacae.
isque metu vacuus naturalique pavore
deposito celebrare domos mulcendaque colla
quamlibet ignotis manibus praebere solebat.

sed tamen ante alios, Ceae pulcherrime gentis, 120
gratus erat, Cyparisse, tibi; tu pabula cervum
ad nova, liquidi ducebas fontis ad undam
tu modo texebas varios per cornua flores,
nunc eques in tergo residens huc laetus et illuc
mollia purpureis frenebas ora capistris. 125
aestus erat mediusque dies, solisque vapore
concava litorei fervebant bracchia Cancri;
fessus in herbosa posuit sua corpora terra
cervus et arborea frigus ducebat ab umbra.
hunc puer imprudens iaculo Cyparissus acuto 130
fixit et, ut saevo morientem vulnere vidit,
velle mori statuit. quae nec solacia Phoebus
dixit et ut leniter pro materiaque doleret
admonuit! gemit ille tamen munusque supremum
hoc petit a superis, ut tempore lugeat omni. 135
iamque per immensos egesto sanguine fletus
in viridem verti coeperunt membra colorem,
et modo qui nivea pendebant fronte capilli
horrida caesaries fieri, sumptoque rigore
sidereum gracili spectare cacumine caelum. 140
ingemuit tristisque deus lugebere nobis
lugebisque alios aderis dolentibus inquit.
tale nemus vates attraxerat inque ferarum
concilio medius turba volucrumque sedebat.
ut satis impulsas temptavit pollice chordas 145
et sensit varios, quamvis diversa sonarent,
concordare modos, hoc vocem carmine movit:
Ab Iove, Musa parens (cedunt Iovis omnia regno),
carmina nostra move. Iovis est mihi saepe potestas
dicta prius; cecini plectro graviore Gigantas 150
sparsaque Phlegraeis victricia fulmina campis

nunc opus est leviore lyra; puerosque canamus
dilectos superis inconcessisque puellas
ignibus attonitas meruisse libidine poenam.
Rex superum Phrygii quondam Ganymedis amore   155
arsit, et inventum est aliquid quod Iuppiter esse
quam quod erat mallet. nulla tamen alite verti
dignatur, nisi quae posset sua fulmina ferre.
nec mora, percusso mendacibus aere pennis
abripit Iliaden, qui nunc quoque pocula miscet   160
invitaque Iovi nectar Iunone ministrat.
Te quoque, Amyclide, posuisset in aethere Phoebus,
tristia si spatium ponendi fata dedissent.
qua licet, aeternus tamen es, quotiensque repellit
ver hiemem Piscique Aries succedit aquoso,   165
tu totiens oreris viridique in caespite flores.
te meus ante omnes genitor dilexit, et orbe
in medio positi caruerunt praeside Delphi
dum deus Eurotan immunitamque frequentat
Sparten. nec citharae nec sunt in honore sagittae;   170
immemor ipse sui non retia ferre recusat,
non tenuisse canes, non per iuga montis iniqui
ire comes, longaque alit adsuetudine flammas.
iamque fere medius Titan venientis et actae
noctis erat spatioque pari distabat utrimque;   175
corpora veste levant et suco pinguis olivi
splendescunt latique ineunt certamina disci.
quem prius aerias libratum Phoebus in auras
misit et oppositas disiecit pondere nubes;
reccidit in solidam longo post tempore terram   180
pondus et exhibuit iunctam cum viribus artem.
protinus imprudens actusque cupidine lusus
tollere Taenarides orbem properabat; at illum

dura repercusso subiecit pondere tellus
in vultus, Hyacinthe, tuos, expalluit aeque   185
quam puer ipse deus conlapsosque excipit artus;
et modo te refovet, modo tristia vulnera siccat,
nunc animam admotis fugientem sustinet herbis.
nil prosunt artes; erat immedicable vulnus.
ut, si quis violas riguoque papavera in horto   190
liliaque infringat fulvis horrentia linguis,
marcida demittant subito caput illa gravatum
nec se sustineant spectentque cacumine terram,
sic vultus moriens iacet, et defecta vigore
ipsa sibi est oneri cervix umeroque recumbit.   195
laberis, Oebalide, prima fraudate iuventa
Phoebus ait, videoque tuum, mea crimina, vulnus.
tu dolor es facinusque meum; mea dextera leto
inscribenda tuo est; ego sum tibi funeris auctor.
quae mea culpa tamen? nisi si lusisse vocari   200
culpa potest, nisi culpa potest et amasse vocari.
atque utinam pro te vitam tecumve liceret
reddere! quod quoniam fatali lege tenemur,
semper eris mecum memorique haerebis in ore.
te lyra pulsa manu, te carmina nostra sonabunt,   205
flosque novus scripto gemitus imitabere nostros.
tempus et illud erit, quo se fortissimus heros
addat in hunc florem folioque legatur eodem.
talia dum vero memorantur Apollinis ore,
ecce cruor, qui fusus humo signaverat herbas,   210
desinit esse cruor, Tyrioque nitentior ostro
flos oritur formamque capit quam lilia, si non
purpureus color his, argenteus esset in illis.
non satis hoc Phoebo est (is enim fuit auctor honoris)
ipse suos gemitus foliis inscribitur et AI AI   215

flos habet inscriptum funestaque littera ducta est.
nec genuisse pudet Sparten Hyacinthon honorque
durat in hoc aevi celebrandaque more priorum
annua praelata redeunt Hyacinthia pompa.
At si forte roges fecundam Amathunta metallis   220
an genuisse velit Propoetidas, abnuat aeque
atque illos, gemino quondam quibus aspera cornu
frons erat; unde etiam nomen traxere Cerastae.
ante fores horum stabat Iovis Hospitis ara,
ignarus sceleris quam si quis sanguine tinctam   225
advena vidisset, mactatos crederet illic
lactentes vitulos Amathusiacasque bidentes;
hospes erat caesus! sacris offensa nefandis
ipsa suas urbes Ophiusiaque arva parabat
deserere alma Venus, sed quid loca grata, quid urbes   230
peccavere meae? quod dixit crimen in illis?
exilio poenam potius gens impia pendat
vel nece vel si quid medium est mortisque fugaeque.
idque quid esse potest, nisi versae poena figurae?
dum dubitat quo mutet eos, ad cornua vultum   235
flexit et admonita est haec illis posse relinqui;
grandiaque in torvos transformat membra iuvencos.
sunt tamen obscenae Venerem Propoetides ausae
esse negare deam; pro quo sua numinis ira
corpora cum forma primae vulgasse feruntur;   240
utque pudor cessit sanguisque induruit oris,
in rigidum parvo silicem discrimine versae.
quas quia Pygmalion aevum per crimen agentes
viderat, offensus vitiis quae plurima menti
femineae natura dedit, sine coniuge caelebs   245
vivebat thalamique diu consorte carebat.
interea niveum mira feliciter arte

sculpsit ebur formamque dedit, qua femina nasci
nulla potest, operisque sui concepit amorem.
virginis est verae facies, quam vivere credas   250
et, si non obstet reverentia, velle moveri;
ars adeo latet arte sua. miratur et haurit
pectore Pygmalion simulati corporis ignes.
saepe manus operi temptantes admovet, an sit
corpus an illud ebur, nec adhuc ebur esse fatetur,   255
oscula dat reddique putat loquiturque tenetque
sed credit tactis digitos insidere membris
et metuit pressos veniat ne livor in artus.
et modo blanditias adhibet, modo grata puellis
munera fert illi, conchas teretesque lapillos   260
et parvas volucres et flores mille colorum
liliaque pictasque pilas et ab arbore lapsas
Heliadum lacrimas. ornat quoque vestibus artus;
dat digitis gemmas, dat longa monilia collo,
aure leves bacae, redimicula pectore pendent.   265
cuncta decent; nec nuda minus formosa videtur.
conlocat hanc stratis concha Sidonide tinctis
appellatque tori sociam acclinataque colla
mollibus in plumis tamquam sensura reponit.
festa dies Veneris tota celeberrima Cypro   270
venerat, et pandis inductae cornibus aurum
conciderant ictae nivea cervice iuvencae.
turaque fumabant, cum munere functus ad aras
constitit et timide si, di, dare cuncta potestis,
sit coniunx, opto, non ausus eburnea virgo   275
dicere Pygmalion similis mea dixit eburnae.
sensit, ut ipsa suis aderat Venus aurea festis
vota quid illa velint et, amici numinis omen,
flamma ter accensa est apicemque per aera duxit.

ut rediit, simulacra suae petit ille puellae   280
incumbensque toro dedit oscula; visa tepere est.
admovet os iterum, manibus quoque pectora temptat;
temptatum mollescit ebur positoque rigore
subsedit digitis ceditque, ut Hymettia sole
cera remollescit tractataque pollice multas   285
flectitur in facies ipsoque fit utilis usu.
dum stupet et dubie gaudet fallique veretur,
rursus amans rursusque manu sua vota retractat.
corpus erat; saliunt temptatae pollice venae.
tum vero Paphius plenissima concipit heros   290
verba quibus Veneri grates agit, oraque tandem
ore suo non falsa premit; dataque oscula virgo
sensit et erubuit, timidumque ad lumina lumen
attollens pariter cum caelo vidit amantem.
coniugio, quod fecit, adest dea, iamque coactis   295
cornibus in plenum noviens lunaribus orbem
illa Paphon genuit, de qua tenet insula nomen.
Editus hac ille, qui si sine prole fuisset,
inter felices Cinyras potuisset haberi.
dira canam; procul hinc, natae, procul este, parentes!   300
aut, mea si vestras mulcebunt carmina mentes,
desit in hac parte mihi fides, nec credite factum,
vel, si credetis, facti quoque credite poenam.
si tamen admissum sinit hoc natura videri
⌈gentibus Ismariis et nostro gratulor orbi,⌉   305
gratulor huic terrae, quod abest regionibus illis
quae tantum genuere nefas. sit dives amomo,
cinnamaque costumque suum sudataque ligno
tura ferat floresque alios Panchaia tellus,
dum ferat et murram; tanti nova non fuit arbor.   310
ipse negat nocuisse tibi sua tela Cupido,

Myrrha, facesque suas a crimine vindicat isto;
stipite te Stygio tumidisque adflavit echidnis
e tribus una soror. scelus est odisse parentem,
hic amor est odio maius scelus. undique lecti 315
te cupiunt proceres, totoque oriente iuventus
ad thalami certamen adest. ex omnibus unum
elige, Myrrha, virum—dum ne sit in omnibus unus.
illa quidem sentit foedoque repugnat amori,
et secum quo mente feror? quid molior? inquit 320
di precor, et pietas sacrataque iura parentum,
hoc prohibete nefas scelerique resistite nostro,
si tamen hoc scelus est. sed enim damnare negatur
hanc Venerem pietas, coeuntque animalia nullo
cetera dilectu, nec habetur turpe iuvencae 325
ferre patrem tergo; fit equo sua filia coniunx,
quasque creavit init pecudes caper, ipsaque, cuius
semine concepta est, ex illo concipit ales.
felices quibus ista licent! humana malignas
cura dedit leges, et quod natura remittit 330
invida iura negant. gentes tamen esse feruntur
in quibus et nato genetrix et nata parenti
iungitur, ut pietas geminato crescat amore.
me miseram, quod non nasci mihi contigit illic
fortunaque loci laedor! quid in ista resolvor? 335
spes interdictae, discedite! dignus amari
ille, sed ut pater, est. ergo si filia magni
non essem Cinyrae, Cinyrae concumbere possem.
nunc, quia iam meus est, non est meus, ipsaque damno
est mihi proximitas; aliena potentior essem. 340
ire libet procul hinc patriaeque relinquere fines,
dum scelus effugiam; retinet malus ardor amantem,
ut praesens spectem Cinyran tangamque loquarque

osculaque admoveam, si nil conceditur ultra.
ultra autem sperare aliquid potes, impia virgo,   345
nec quot confundas et iura et nomina sentis?
tune eris et matris paelex et adultera patris?
tune soror nati genetrixque vocabere fratris?
nec metues atro crinitas angue sorores,
quas facibus saevis oculos atque ora petentes   350
noxia corda vident? at tu, dum corpore non es
passa nefas, animo ne concipe, neve potentis
concubitu vetito naturae pollue foedus.
velle puta; res ipsa vetat. pius ille memorque est
moris—et o vellem similis furor esset in illo!   355
dixerat, at Cinyras, quem copia digna procorum
quid faciat dubitare facit, scitatur ab ipsa
nominibus dictis, cuius velit esse mariti.
illa silet primo patriisque in vultibus haerens
aestuat et tepido suffundit lumina rore.   360
virginei Cinyras haec credens esse timoris
flere vetat siccatque genas atque oscula iungit.
Myrrha datis nimium gaudet consultaque, qualem
optet habere virum, similem tibi dixit; at ille
non intellectam vocem conlaudat et esto   365
tam pia semper ait, pietatis nomine dicto
demisit vultus sceleris sibi conscia virgo.
noctis erat medium, curasque et corpora somnus
solverat; at virgo Cinyreia pervigil igni
carpitur indomito furiosaque vota retractat.   370
et modo desperat, modo vult temptare, pudetque
et cupit, et quid agat non invenit; utque securi
saucia trabs ingens, ubi plaga novissima restat,
quo cadat in dubio est omnique a parte timetur,
sic animus vario labefactus vulnere nutat   375

huc levis atque illuc momentaque sumit utroque.
nec modus aut requies, nisi mors, reperitur amoris;
mors placet. erigitur laqueoque innectere fauces
destinat, et zona summo de poste revincta
care vale Cinyra; causam te intellige mortis.   380
dixit et aptabat pallenti vincula collo.
murmura verborum fidas nutricis ad aures
pervenisse ferunt limen servantis alumnae;
surgit anus reseratque fores mortisque paratae
instrumenta videns spatio conclamat eodem   385
seque ferit scinditque sinus ereptaque collo
vincula dilaniat. tum denique flere vacavit,
tum dare complexus laqueique requirere causam.
muta silet virgo terramque immota tuetur
et deprensa dolet tardae conamina mortis.   390
instat anus canosque suos et inania nudans
ubera per cunas alimentaque prima precatur
ut sibi committat quidquid dolet. illa rogantem
aversata gemit; certa est exquirere nutrix
nec solam spondere fidem. dic inquit opemque   395
me sine ferre tibi; non est mea pigra senectus.
seu furor est, habeo quae carmine sanet et herbis;
sive aliquis nocuit, magico lustrabere ritu;
ira deum sive est, sacris placabilis ira.
quid rear ulterius? certe fortuna domusque   400
sospes et in cursu est; vivit genetrixque paterque.
Myrrha patre audito suspiria duxit ab imo
pectore. nec nutrix etiamnum concipit ullum
mente nefas, aliquemque tamen praesentit amorem.
propositique tenax quodcumquest orat ut ipsi   405
indicet, et gremio lacrimantem tollit anili
atque ita complectens infirmis membra lacertis

sensimus inquit; amas. sed et hic mea (pone timorem)
sedulitas erit apta tibi. nec sentiet umquam
hoc pater. exsiluit gremio furibunda torumque   410
ore premens discede, precor, miseroque pudori
parce ait; instanti discede, aut desine dixit
quaerere quid doleam; scelus est quod scire laboras.
horret anus tremulasque manus annisque metuque
tendit et ante pedes supplex procumbit alumnae;   415
et modo blanditur, modo, si non conscia fiat,
terret et indicium laquei coeptaque minatur
mortis, et officium commisso spondet amori.
extulit illa caput lacrimisque implevit obortis
pectora nutricis conataque saepe fateri   420
saepe tenet vocem pudibundaque vestibus ora
texit et o dixit felicem coniuge matrem!
hactenus, et gemuit. gelidus nutricis in artus
ossaque (sensit enim) penetrat tremor, albaque toto
vertice canities rigidis stetit hirta capillis.   425
multaque ut excuteret diros, si posset, amores
addidit; at virgo scit se non falsa moneri,
certa mori tamen est, si non potiatur amore.
vive ait haec, potiere tuo—et non est ausa parente
dicere conticuit promissaque numine firmat.   430
festa piae Cereris celebrabant annua matres
illa, quibus nivea velatae corpora veste
primitias frugum dant spicea serta suarum
perque novem noctes Venerem tactusque viriles
in vetitis numerant. turba Cenchreis in illa   435
regis adest coniunx arcanaque sacra frequentat.
ergo legitima vacuus dum coniuge lectus,
nacta gravem vino Cinyran male sedula nutrix
nomine mentito veros exponit amores

et faciem laudat; quaesitis virginis annis   440
par ait est Myrrhae. quam postquam adducere iussa est
utque domum rediit, gaude, mea dixit alumna;
vicimus! infelix non toto pectore sentit
laetitiam virgo, praesagaque pectora maerent,
sed tamen et gaudet; tanta est discordia mentis.   445
tempus erat quo cuncta silent, interque Triones
flexerat obliquo plaustrum temone Bootes;
ad facinus venit illa suum. fugit aurea caelo
luna, tegunt nigrae latitantia sidera nubes,
nox caret igne suo; primus tegis, Icare, vultus   450
Erigoneque pio sacrata parentis amore.
ter pedis offensi signo est revocata, ter omen
funereus bubo letali carmine fecit;
it tamen, et tenebrae minuunt noxque atra pudorem,
nutricisque manum laeva tenet, altera motu   455
caecum iter explorat. thalami iam limina tangit,
iamque fores aperit, iam ducitur intus; at illi
poplite succiduo genua intremuere fugitque
et color et sanguis animusque relinquit euntem.
quoque suo propior sceleri est, magis horret et ausi   460
paenitet et vellet non cognita posse reverti.
cunctantem longaeva manu deducit et alto
admotam lecto cum traderet accipe dixit
ista tua est, Cinyre devotaque corpora iunxit.
accipit obsceno genitor sua viscera lecto   465
virgineosque metus levat hortaturque timentem.
forsitan aetatis quoque nomine filia dixit,
dixit et illa pater, sceleri ne nomina desint.
plena patris thalamis excedit et impia diro
semina fert utero conceptaque crimina portat.   470
postera nox facinus geminat, nec finis in illa est,

cum tandem Cinyras, avidus cognoscere amantem
post tot concubitus, inlato lumine vidit
et scelus et natam; verbisque dolore retentis
pendenti nitidum vagina deripit ensem.   475
Myrrha fugit tenebrisque et caecae munere noctis
intercepta neci est, latosque vagata per agros
palmiferos Arabas Panchaeaque rura relinquit.
perque novem erravit redeuntis cornua lunae,
cum tandem terra requievit fessa Sabaea;   480
vixque uteri portabat onus. tum nescia voti
atque inter mortisque metus et taedia vitae
est tales complexa preces: o si qua patetis
numina confessis, merui nec triste recuso
supplicium. sed ne violem vivosque superstes   485
mortuaque exstinctos, ambobus pellite regnis
mutataeque mihi vitamque necemque negate.
numen confessis aliquod patet; ultima certe
vota suos habuere deos. nam crura loquentis
terra supervenit, ruptosque obliqua per ungues   490
porrigitur radix, longi firmamina trunci,
ossaque robur agunt, mediaque manente medulla
sanguis it in sucos, in magnos bracchia ramos,
in parvos digiti, duratur cortice pellis.
iamque gravem crescens uterum praestrinxerat arbor   495
pectoraque obruerat collum operire parabat;
non tulit illa moram venientique obvia ligno
subsedit mersitque suos in cortice vultus.
quae quamquam amisit veteres cum corpore sensus,
flet tamen, et tepidae manant ex arbore guttae.   500
est honor et lacrimis, stillataque robora murra
nomen erile tenet nulloque tacebitur aevo.
At male conceptus sub robore creverat infans

quaerebatque viam qua se genetrice relicta
exsereret; media gravidus tumet arbore venter. 505
tendit onus matrem, neque habent sua verba dolores,
nec Lucina potest parientis voce vocari.
nitenti tamen est similis curvataque crebros
dat gemitus arbor lacrimisque cadentibus umet.
constitit ad ramos mitis Lucina dolentes 510
admovitque manus et verba puerpera dixit;
arbor agit rimas et fissa cortice vivum
reddit onus, vagitque puer, quem mollibus herbis
Naides impositum lacrimis unxere parentis.
laudaret faciem Livor quoque: qualia namque 515
corpora nudorum tabula pinguntur Amorum,
talis erat; sed, ne faciat discrimina cultus,
aut huic adde leves aut illis deme pharetras.
labitur occulte fallitque volatilis aetas,
et nihil est annis velocius. ille sorore 520
natus avoque suo, qui conditus arbore nuper,
nuper erat genitus, modo formosissimus infans,
iam iuvenis, iam vir, iam se formosior ipse est;
iam placet et Veneri matrisque ulciscitur ignes.
iamque pharetratus dum dat puer oscula matri, 525
inscius exstanti destrinxit harundine pectus.
laesa manu natum dea reppulit; altius actum
vulnus erat specie primoque fefellerat ipsam.
capta viri forma non iam Cythereia curat
litora, non alto repetit Paphon aequore cinctam 530
piscosamque Cnidon gravidamque Amathunta
abstinet et caelo; caelo praefertur Adonis.
hunc tenet, huic comes est, adsuetaque semper in umbra
indulgere sibi formamque augere colendo
per iuga per silvas dumosaque saxa vagatur 535

fine genus vestem ritu succincta Dianae.
hortaturque canes tutaeque animalia praedae,
aut pronos lepores aut celsum in cornua cervum
aut agitat dammas; a fortibus abstinet apris
raptoresque lupos armatosque unguibus ursos   540
vitat et armenti saturatos caede leones
te quoque ut hos timeas, si quid prodesse monendo
possit, Adoni, monet fortisque fugacibus esto
inquit, in audaces non est audacia tuta.
parce meo, iuvenis, temerarius esse periclo,   545
neve feras quibus arma dedit natura lacesse,
stet mihi ne magno tua gloria. non movet aetas
nec facies nec quae Venerem movere leones.
saetigerosque sues oculosque animisoque ferarum.
fulmen habent acres in aduncis dentibus apri,   550
impetus est fulvis et vasta leonibus ira,
invisumque mihi genus est. quae causa roganti
dicam ait et veteris monstrum mirabere culpae.
sed labor insolitus iam me lassavit, et ecce
opportuna sua blanditur populus umbra   555
datque torum caespes; libet hac requiescere tecum
—et requievit—humo pressitque et gramen et ipsum,
inque sinu iuvenis posita cervice reclinis
sic ait ac mediis interserit oscula verbis:
Forsitan audieris aliquam certamine cursus   560
veloces superasse viros: non fabula rumor
ille fuit—superabat enim—, nec dicere posses,
laude pedum, formaene bono praestantior esset.
scitanti deus huic de coniuge coniuge dixit
nil opus est, Atalanta, tibi. fuge coniugis usum!   565
nec tamen effugies teque ipsa viva carebis.
territa sorte dei per opacas innuba silvas

vivit et instantem turbam violenta procorum
condicione fugat, nec sum potienda, nisi inquit
victa prius cursu. pedibus contendite mecum. 570
praemia veloci coniunx thalamique dabuntur:
mors pretium tardis: ea lex certaminis esto!
illa quidem immitis; sed (tanta potentia formae est)
venit ad hanc legem temeraria turba procorum.
sederat Hippomenes cursus spectator iniqui 575
et petitur cuiquam per tanta pericula coniunx?
dixerat ac nimios iuvenum damnarat amores;
ut faciem et posito corpus velamine vidit
(quale meum, vel quale tuum, si femina fias),
obstipuit tollensque manus ignoscite dixit, 580
quos modo culpavi; nondum mihi praemia nota,
quae peteretis, erant. laudando concipit ignes
et ne quis iuvenum currat velocius optat
insidiasque timet. sed cur certaminis huius
intemptata mihi fortuna relinquitur? inquit 585
audentes deus ipse iuvat. dum talia secum
exigit Hippomenes, passu volat alite virgo.
quae quamquam Scythica non setius ire sagitta
Aonio visa est iuveni, tamen ille decorem
miratur magis; et cursus facit ipse decorem. 590
aura refert ablata citis talaria plantis,
tergaque iactantur crines per eburnea, quaeque
poplitibus suberant picto genualia limbo;
inque puellari corpus candore ruborem
traxerat, haud aliter quam cum super atria velum 595
candida purpureum simulatas inficit umbras.
dum notat haec hospes, decursa novissima meta est
et tegitur festa victrix Atalanta corona;
dant gemitum victi penduntque ex foedere poenas.

non tamen eventu iuvenis deterritus horum   600
constitit in medio vultuque in virgine fixo
quid facilem titulum superando quaeris inertes?
mecum confer ait. seu me fortuna potentem
fecerit, a tanto non indignabere vinci;
namque mihi genitor Megareus Onchestius, illi   605
est Neptunus avus, pronepos ego regis aquarum,
nec virtus citra genus est. seu vincar, habebis
Hippomene victo magnum et memorabile nomen.
talia dicentem molli Schoeneia vultu
aspicit et dubitat, superari an vincere malit.   610
atque ita quis deus hunc formosis inquit iniquus
perdere vult caraeque iubet discrimine vitae
coniugium petere hoc? non sum, me iudice, tanti!
nec forma tangor (poteram tamen hac quoque tangi),
sed quod adhuc puer est: non me movet ipse, sed aetas.   615
quid quod inest virtus et mens interrita leti?
quid quod ab aequorea numeratur origine quartus?
quid quod amat tantique putat conubia nostra
ut pereat, si me fors illi dura negarit?
dum licet, hospes, abi thalamosque relinque cruentos.   620
coniugium crudele meum est; tibi nubere nulla
nolet, et optari potes a sapiente puella.
cur tamen est mihi cura tui tot iam peremptis?
viderit! intereat, quoniam tot caede procorum
admonitus non est agiturque in taedia vitae.   625
occidet hic igitur, voluit quia vivere mecum
indignamque necem pretium patietur amoris?
non erit invidiae victoria nostra ferendae.
sed non culpa mea est. utinam desistere velles,
aut, quoniam es demens, utinam velocior esses!   630
at quam virgineus puerili vultus in ore est!

a, miser Hippomene, nollem tibi visa fuissem!
vivere dignus eras. quod si felicior essem
nec mihi coniugium fata importuna negarent,
unus eras cum quo sociare cubilia vellem. 635
dixerat, utque rudis primoque cupidine tacta,
quod facit ignorans amat et non sentit amorem.
iam solitos poscunt cursus populusque paterque,
cum me sollicita proles Neptunia voce
invocat Hippomenes Cythereaque comprecor ausis 640
adsit ait nostris et quos dedit adiuvet ignes.
detulit aura preces ad me non invida blandas;
motaque sum, fateor, nec opis mora longa dabatur.
est ager, indigenae Tamasenum nomine dicunt,
telluris Cypriae pars optima, quem mihi prisci 645
sacravere senes templisque accedere dotem
hanc iussere meis; medio nitet arbor in arvo,
fulva comas, fulvo ramis crepitantibus auro.
hinc tria forte mea veniens decerpta ferebam
aurea poma manu; nullique videnda nisi ipsi 650
Hippomenen adii docuique quis usus in illis.
signa tubae dederant, cum carcere pronus uterque
emicat et summam celeri pede libat harenam;
posse putes illos sicco freta radere passu
et segetis canae stantis percurrere aristas. 655
adiciunt animos iuveni clamorque favorque
verbaque dicentum nunc, nunc incumbere tempus;
Hippomene, propera! nunc viribus utere totis;
pelle moram, vinces! dubium, Megareius heros
gaudeat an virgo magis his Schoeneia dictis. 660
o quotiens, cum iam posset transire, morata est
spectatosque diu vultus invita reliquit!
aridus e lasso veniebat anhelitus ore,

metaque erat longe; tum denique de tribus unum
fetibus arboreis proles Neptunia misit.   665
obstipuit virgo nitidique cupidine pomi
declinat corpus aurumque volubile tollit.
praeterit Hippomenes; resonant spectacula plausu.
illa moram celeri cessataque tempora cursu
corrigit atque iterum iuvenem post terga relinquit;   670
et rursus pomi iactu remorata secundi
consequitur transitque virum. pars ultima cursus
restabat. nunc inquit ades, dea muneris auctor
inque latus campi, quo tardius illa rediret,
iecit ab obliquo nitidum iuvenaliter aurum.   675
an peteret, virgo visa est dubitare; coegi
tollere et adieci sublato pondere malo
impediique oneris pariter gravitate moraque.
neve meus sermo cursu sit tardior ipso,
praeterita est virgo, duxit sua praemia victor.   680
dignaque cui grates ageret, cui turis honorem
ferret, Adoni, fui? nec grates immemor egit
nec mihi tura dedit. subitam convertor in iram
contemptuque dolens ne sim spernenda futuris
exemplo caveo meque ipsa exhortor in ambos.   685
templa, deum Matri quae quondam clarus Echion
fecerat ex voto, nemorosis abdita silvis,
transibant, et iter longum requiescere suasit.
illic concubitus intempestiva cupido
occupat Hippomenen, a numine concita nostro.   690
luminis exigui fuerat prope templa recessus,
speluncae similis, nativo pumice tectus,
religione sacer prisca, quo multa sacerdos
lignea contulerat veterum simulacra deorum;
hunc init et vetito temerat sacraria probro.   695

sacra retorserunt oculos, turritaque Mater
an Stygia sontes dubitavit mergeret unda;
poena levis visa est. ergo modo levia fulvae
colla iubae velant, digiti curvantur in ungues,
ex umeris armi fiunt, in pectora totum   700
pondus abit, summae cauda verruntur harenae;
iram vultus habet, pro verbis murmura reddunt,
pro thalamis celebrant silvas aliisque timendi
dente premunt domito Cybeleia frena leones.
hos tu, care mihi, cumque his genus omne ferarum   705
quod non terga fugae, sed pugna pectora praebet
effuge, ne virtus tua sit damnosa duobus.
illa quidem monuit iunctisque per aera cycnis
carpit iter; sed stat monitis contraria virtus.
forte suem latebris vestigia certa secuti   710
excivere canes, silvisque exire parantem
fixerat obliquo iuvenis Cinyreius ictu;
protinus excussit pando venabula rostro
sanguine tincta suo trepidumque et tuta petentem
trux aper insequitur totosque sub inguine dentes   715
abdidit et fulva moribundum stravit harena.
vecta levi curru medias Cytherea per auras
Cypron olorinis nondum pervenerat alis;
agnovit longe gemitum morientis et albas
flexit aves illuc, utque aethere vidit ab alto   720
exanimem inque suo iactantem sanguine corpus,
desiluit pariterque sinum pariterque capillos
rupit et indignis percussit pectora palmis.
questaque cum fatis at non tamen omnia vestri
iuris erunt, dixit; luctus monimenta manebunt   725
semper, Adoni, mei, repetitaque mortis imago
annua plangoris peraget simulamina nostri.

at cruor in florem mutabitur. an tibi quondam
femineos artus in olentes vertere mentas,
Persephone, licuit, nobis Cinyreius heros   730
invidiae mutatus erit? sic fata cruorem
nectare odorato sparsit, qui tactus ab illo
intumuit sic, ut fulvo perlucida caelo
surgere bulla solet; nec plena longior hora
facta mora est, cum flos de sanguine concolor ortus,   735
qualem quae lento celant sub cortice granum
punica ferre solent. brevis est tamen usus in illo;
namque male haerentem et nimia levitate caducum
excutiunt idem, qui praestant nomina, venti.   739

Commentary

1–85. *Orpheus and Eurydice.* The tenth book of Ovid's epic opens with the story that is the most famous of those associated with Orpheus: the loss of his wife Eurydice and his attempt to rescue her from the nether world. Perhaps somewhat surprisingly, there is no surviving version of the celebrated tale before Virgil, *Georgic* 4.453–527; the name of Orpheus occurs nowhere in Homer, in Hesiod, in the so-called *Homeric Hymns*, or in any of the poems associated with Hesiod (see here Gantz, 1993: 721). Euripides' Admetus says that he would be able to descend to the underworld to reclaim his wife, if he had a voice like Orpheus' (*Alcestis* 357–362), a passage that may well allude to the attempted recovery of Eurydice—though in the original story, the attempt may have been successful. Ovid makes no mention of the beekeeper Aristaeus and his part in the Virgilian Eurydice story (indeed, Virgil may have invented the connection); Orpheus and his impending marriage are introduced briskly, and the story is told with economy and in swift compass. Similarly, the death of the master musician will be the subject of a succinct rendition at the start of Book 11; the transition to the final third of the epic will be presided over, in an important sense, by the doomed Orpheus, whose sad image broods over the close of the second movement of Ovid's poem of transformation—a poem that in no small way is a meditation on the quest for immortality, a quest in which Ovid's Orpheus, like Virgil's before him, will meet with mixed results. Lucan composed an *Orpheus*, of which but two fragments survive; Servius' note on Virgil, *Georgic* 4.492 preserves the intriguing *gaudent a luce relictam / Eurydicen iterum sperantes Orphea manes*, where there seems to be rejoicing in the underworld over the return of Eurydice to the realm of the dead; Lucan's work may have been an impromptu composition for the Neronia festival of A.D. 60. There are also brief allusions to the story in Seneca's tragedies (cf. *Hercules Furens* 569–591; *Hercules Oetaeus* 1061–1089); also in the Pseudo-Virgilian *Culex* (268–295). On these other witnesses to the traditions see especially C. Bowra, "Orpheus and Eurydice," in *The Classical Quarterly* N.S. 2.3–4 (1952), 113–126. On the vexed problem of what the "original" ending of the story may have been (i.e., the question of Orpheus' success), see J. Heath, "The Failure of Orpheus," in *Transactions of the American Philological Association* 124 (1994), 163–196.

And too, the Virgilian story is told by Proteus, a celebrated shape-shifter; the intertext is thus especially appropriate for an epic of metamorphosis.

On this passage much has been written, of which see especially C. Segal, "Ovid's Orpheus and Augustan Ideology," in *Transactions of the American Philological Association* 103 (1972), 473–494; "Ovid's Orpheus: Immoral Lovers, Immortal Poets," in *Materiali e discussioni per l'analisi dei testi classici* 40 (1998), 99–109; and E. Young, "Inscribing Orpheus: Ovid and the Invention of a Greco-Roman Corpus," in *Representations* 101.1 (2008), 1–31, all with helpful general remarks. Useful on the vast afterlife of the myth and its reception in music is F. Sternfeld, "Orpheus, Ovid, and Opera," in *Journal of the Royal Musical Association* 113.2 (1988), 162–202; J. Buller, "Looking Backwards: Baroque Opera and the Ending of the Orpheus Myth," in *International Journal of the Classical Tradition* 1.3 (1995), 57–79. Certain aspects of the potential pedagogical value of the story for appreciation of Ovid's artistry are the concern of S. Mack, "Teaching Ovid's Orpheus to Beginners," in *The Classical Journal* 90.3 (1995), 279–285. Gantz (1993:

724) offers a brief survey of the scanty evidence for the story in the early visual art record. Reed draws attention to the fact that Ovid does not include Orpheus in his version of the *Argonautica* lore of Book 7; the celebrated singer was traditionally associated with the voyage in quest of the Golden Fleece. Rather, the poet reserves his introduction of Orpheus to the eschatologically significant tenth book, and his presence will straddle the last book of the epic's first third and the first of its last.

1   Inde per immensum croceo velatus amictu

Inde: The book continues at once from the nuptials of Iphis and Ianthe that marked the close of its predecessor. *Metamorphoses* 10 will open with a failed union (Orpheus and Eurydice); it will close with another severed relationship (Venus and Adonis). Reed comments here in his Italian edition of the book on this contrast between the night that witnessed the happy union of Iphis and Ianthe and the present experience of the nuptial god; the wedding night of Orpheus and Eurydice will have a far different outcome.

immensum: To be taken with 2 *aethera*. The airy realm of the immortals is vast; the effect of the Ovidian narrative is to convey the sense that action is going on all over the world, with the gods traversing vast tracts of territory, as well as the sense of scale of this particular action, that is, both the general and the specific. The spondaic second foot of the verse, with its slow rhythm, conveys metrically the great space the god traverses to reach the doomed couple.

croceo ... amictu: "Yellow is a traditionally seductive color" (Gibson's commentary on Ovid, *Ars Amatoria* 3.179). In the earlier Ovidian passage, it is the dawn goddess Aurora who wears a yellow robe; the reference here to the vesture of the wedding god thus takes on something of the flavor of the traditional dawn formula, as the poet commences a new book. The precise color is not possible to determine definitively; *croceus* could embrace both English "saffron" and "red" (as Bömer's commentary note observes).

2   aethera digreditur Ciconumque Hymenaeus ad oras

aethera: Greek accusative. The *aether* is the heavenly air, in contrast to the terrestrial *aer*.

digreditur: The god "departs" from the upper air; there may be a hint that he separates (*di-*) the mists as he descends to earth; Reed comments on the force of the prefix in expressing several different aspects and qualities of the god's action here, as the nuptial god both leaves the upper air and separates the clouds.

Ciconum: Genitive plural. The Ciconians were a people of western Thrace, and the place is associated with the eventual violent death of Orpheus; Virgil names them at *Georgic* 4.520 in his own version of the Orpheus story. Geographical markers recur throughout the present book, which invest its content with an ethnographic flavor; the action also acquires something of a more immediate reality by the frequent use of place names. The Iphis and Ianthe tale at the end of Book 9 had a prominent place for the goddess Isis; part of the concern of ethnography is the question of the transportation of foreign cults and the acceptance of alien religious rites and divinities at Rome. The Ciconians will be mentioned again, at the beginning of Book 11—as Ovid shifts his narrative to the violent death of Orpheus at the hands of maddened women; Ovid enjoys connecting the disparate parts of his narrative by parallelisms that effect a tighter, more cohesive narrative.

Hymenaeus: The book opens with the wedding god coming to preside (however balefully) over the marriage of Orpheus and Eurydice; it will draw to a close with Venus rushing to the scene of her own lover's demise.

3   tendit et Orphea nequiquam voce vocatur.

tendit: Bömer notes this "simple" use of the verb here and at, for example, 34 *tendimus*, as opposed to the compound *contendit*; the effect is to give a rapid flavor to the narrative, as Ovid proceeds to his next story and theme (and below to highlight the inexorable advance of mortals toward the grave).

Orphea: Orpheus is the first figure encountered by Aeneas in Virgil's Elysium in the underworld (*Aeneid* 6.645); the appearance of Orpheus comes just before the great account of Anchises of the rebirth of souls (*Aeneid* 6.679 ff.). Reed's commentary note compares Euripides, *Alcestis* 969–970 for the use of the adjective in place of a possessive genitive; Ovid may be deliberately imparting a Greek tragic sense to the verse, which would be fitting given the dark sentiments implied here so early in the book.

nequiquam: The marriage god is summoned by the musician's melodic voice, and he does arrive (cf. 4 *adfuit ille quidem*)—but the outcome of this particular nuptial union will not be celebratory. The placement of the adverb is significant; it comes not before the verb, but closely with *voce,* to underscore the inadequacy of the voice's utterance.

voce vocatur: The tautology (repetition) and alliteration serve to recreate something of the musician's melodic summons of the god to his nuptials. Reed offers comparisons for the so-called *figura etymologica,* including the ritual passage of Virgil, *Aeneid* 6.506; the summons of the deity may here be invested in appropriately sacral language.

4   adfuit ille quidem, sed nec sollemnia verba

adfuit ille: The epiphany of the god Hymenaeus is announced; see Reed ad loc. for the use of the verb in divine manifestations.

quidem: "To be sure."

sollemnia verba: A hint of legalism: the god was present, but he did not bring the solemn words that would ratify the union. See here especially R. VerSteeg and N. Barclay, "Rhetoric and Law in Ovid's Orpheus," in *Law and Literature* 15.3 (2003), 395–420, with discussion of how Ovid uses the language of litigation and the Roman law courts to express Orpheus' appeal to the underworld deities about his wife.

5   nec laetos vultus nec felix attulit omen;

laetos vultus: Poetic plural. Much of the drama of the present book will depend on the contrast between what should be a source of immense joy (love and romance) and the all too deadly results of erotic passion and union. Bömer notes in his commentary that a deity should bring a happy countenance, so as to portend luck. Reed comments on the use of the adjective in contexts proper to divine aspects and appearances. The plural also allows the noun to apply not only to the god, but to more people (i.e., the attendees at the wedding ceremony)—though this type of plural for singular occurs frequently in poetry; cf. 450, where the plural *vultus* must refer solely to Icarus; 662, where it must be Hippomenes alone, and elsewhere.

felix … omen: cf. *OLD s.v.* 1c, of the *prima omina* of the nuptial ceremony; Austin's commentary note on Virgil, *Aeneid* 1.346; the commentary of Heyworth and Morwood on Propertius, c. 3.20.24. Weddings, like all great private and public events in Roman life, began with a certain omen or tenor that gave some indication of what one could expect from the new state of life or occurrence; here there is no happy harbinger of a blissful union.

6   fax quoque quam tenuit lacrimoso stridula fumo

fax: Reed provides a convenient summary of the evidence in both the Greek and the Roman traditions of the torch of the wedding god

(Roman weddings were, after all, held at night), as well as the transformed symbolism of the nuptial light into what amounts to a torch to illumine Eurydice's requiem.

lacrimoso: Tears will be a recurring theme of this sad book; there may be a hint of black humor here, but the mood is decidedly somber.

stridula: cf. the *stridula cornus* that announces renewed warfare at Virgil, *Aeneid* 12.267. Ovid has this adjective elsewhere only at *Tristia* 3.12.30 (of the sound of the wagons of the Sauromates); the almost hissing sound of the torch is what the god brings, and the eerie sound heralds a baleful outcome for the marriage. The torch hisses (or sputters) in token of the disaster that is soon to befall the young couple.

7   usque fuit nullosque invenit motibus ignes.

usque: cf. *OLD s.v.* 5: The point is that the god's effort to kindle his torch continued indefinitely, as it were, and with no success; this use of *usque* with a verb is mostly poetic.

nullos … ignes: The passion of Orpheus for Eurydice will come to naught; the loss of his wife will lead directly to the musician's decision to eschew the company of women and to announce his intention to sing of rather different unions. *Ignes* could be used of the metaphorical fire of passion; this love affair will end in doom.

invenit: An interesting use of the verb, for which Reed's commentary note compares *Ars Amatoria* 2.441–442 *sed tamen extinctas admoto sulphure flammas / invenit* (sc. *ignis*).

motibus: Ablative of means; the god found no fires/kindles no flames with the motion of the torch.

8   exitus auspicio gravior; nam nupta per herbas

exitus: The outcome or event; here the word also foreshadows the death or "exit" of Orpheus' young bride. Bömer compares Virgil, *Aeneid* 10.630 *manet ... gravis exitus* (of the doomed hero Turnus).

auspicio: Ablative of comparison. The ill omens were not sufficiently baleful.

gravior: "More serious" or "grave," indeed to the point of death.

nam: Explanatory. The light rhythm here and the alliteration of *nam nupta* expresses subtly and with fitting brevity the all too fleeting carefree progression of the doomed girl through the meadow before her death (and cf. 9 *nova Naiadum*).

9   dum nova Naiadum turba comitata vagatur,

nova: The final syllable is long; the scansion helps the reader to ascertain that this is ablative with *turba*. The ablative singular of the first declension ended in -*ad* originally, not -*a*; the loss of the letter "d" is what caused the final vowel to lengthen—a phenomenon sometimes thus called "compensatory lengthening."

Naiadum: Properly the Naiads were river nymphs, though the name could be applied to any sort of nymph. Ovid's Eurydice is not unlike his Persephone from *Metamorphoses* 5; she is accompanied by female companions just before she enters the lower world. At Virgil, *Georgic* 4.460, Eurydice is one of the dryads or tree nymphs.

turba comitata: The phrase may be borrowed from Virgil, *Aeneid* 2.580.

10   occidit in talum serpentis dente recepto.

The image is reminiscent of Virgil, *Eclogue* 3.93 *latet anguis in herba.* Hesperia will die similarly at the close of Book 11, as she flees from the Trojan prince Aesacus in an overtly ethnographic retelling of the present scene that neatly links the two books together.

occidit: Anderson (1972) comments here in his edition of Books 6–10 of the poem on the absence of pathos from Ovid's crisp description; of course one could also argue that the pathos is increased by the very fact of the unadorned narrative.

in talum: The serpent bit Eurydice in the ankle (it could be argued, though likely overly subtly, that she also fell dead on her ankle); in any case the prepositional phrase coordinates with both the main verb and the ablative *dente recepto*.

11   quam satis ad superas postquam Rhodopeius auras

Reed comments on the contrasts inherent to the language of 11–12; in some ways the dichotomy between the realm of the living and the dead, the mourning coupled with the heroic action of the descent of the singer to the underworld in quest for his lost wife, all of it reflects the manner in which Orphic tenets of rebirth and renewal after death straddle the divide between life and the grave, between shadow and substance.

quam: Latin often commences a sentence or clause with a relative pronoun, which creates an effect that is often difficult to translate into English; here the placement of the accusative, however compulsory, prominently highlights Eurydice.

superas … auras: The phrase is borrowed from Virgil's description of Eurydice's return to the upper world at *Georgic* 4.486 *redditaque Eurydice superas veniebat ad auras*. The immortals on high do nothing to respond to Orpheus' lament for his lost wife.

Rhodopeius: cf. 50; the appellation comes from Mount Rhodope in Thrace. The "Rhodopeian bard" = Orpheus.

12   deflevit vates, ne non temptaret et umbras,

deflevit: Orpheus shed copious tears for his lost wife (the object is 11 *quam*); in its intransitive uses the verb can convey the sense that the tears were especially bitter (*OLD s.v.* 3).

vates: cf. 82 *vati.* The word is rich with complex meanings and associations; at the very end of the poem, Ovid will announce his own (poetic) immortality, if the *praesaga vatum* have something of truth in them: the great theme of lies, especially lies mingled with truths, will close the epic. Orpheus is one of the *vates* in Ovid's mind at the end of Book 15.

ne non: The double negative conveys something of the pathos of the seemingly hopeless situation of the grieved husband.

et: "Also" or "even" (adverbial).

temptaret: For the use of the verb with a personal object (*umbras*), Bömer compares 11.239.

13   ad Styga Taenaria est ausus descendere porta,

Styga: Greek accusative. Bömer's commentary notes the importance of the Styx as the source of the oaths of the immortals; the point here may be that what is determined by Pluto and Proserpina is especially binding (and that no tricks were afoot in the injunction by which Orpheus was to return his wife to the upper world). Reed gathers useful attestations of its mention in other sources.

Taenaria: Ablative of route with *porta*. Taenarum was at the southernmost point of the Peloponnese, where there was said to be a cave that led to the underworld; the modern Cape Tenaro or Matapan. cf. 183 *Taenarides*; Virgil has *Taenarias ... fauces* at *Georgic* 4.467. The whole area was renowned for black marble quarries (so Pliny's *Natural History* 36.135), a geological reality that likely gave rise to the chthonic, underworld associations of the locale.

ausus: The book opens with the daring of Orpheus, who is willing to brave the lower regions to rescue his wife; it will close with Venus' urging of Adonis not to display *audacia* against ferocious prey in hunting, and his cowardly attempt to flee the wild boar that will be his undoing. Reed discusses Orphic boldness in his descent; the point is to underscore his heroic status, at least insofar as he makes his entrance to Avernus (though the results of the successful visit will provide rather a different tale).

descendere: The tenth *Metamorphoses* moves quickly to an underworld descent, a *katabasis*; the Orpheus/Eurydice narrative presents what we might identify as a "traditional" underworld presided over by Pluto and Proserpina. The abduction of the latter had been told by Ovid in the final book of the first third of his epic; now, in the final book of his second third, we are introduced to a figure who will represent a different sort of understanding of the afterlife. See here especially W. Stephens, "Descent to the Underworld in Ovid's *Metamorphoses*," in *The Classical Journal* 53.4 (1958), 177–183, with consideration in particular of the philosophical aspects of Ovid's portrayal of the underworld.

porta: Ablative of route.

14   perque leves populos simulacraque functa sepulcro

leves: "Insubstantial."

simulacra: "Images," that is, of the once living beings. cf. 280, where the word will recur in the rather different context of the Pygmalion episode, a story that is not unlike the Orpheus/Eurydice narrative in that a hero will pray that his "wife" may know life.

functa: The verb *fungi* regularly takes an ablative object and not an accusative; the ablative is conceived of as a sort of ablative of means. *Uti* is a common example of another verb that takes such an ablative object.

15   Persephonen adiit inamoenaque regna tenentem

Persephonen: Both this Greek (here in the accusative) name and the Latin *Proserpina* occur in Augustan poetry. It is unclear whether or not Ovid has in mind here the Orphic tradition that Zeus and Persephone had an illicit relationship that resulted in the birth of Dionysus, complete with the eventual story of the rebirth of the god after he was killed by the Titans at the behest of Hera.

inamoena: A rare adjective that may have been coined by Ovid; this is its first appearance in surviving literature. For the connection between the goddess and her mortal avatar, as it were (both Eurydice and Proserpina fail to return to the upper world), see P. Johnston, "Eurydice and Proserpina in the *Georgics*," in *Transactions of the American Philological Association* 107 (1977), 161–172, with consideration of Virgil's possible reworking of the traditions about Orpheus and his lost wife. In Virgil's account it is Persephone who requires Eurydice to exit the underworld by following her husband; no explanation is given for the injunction.

16   umbrarum dominum, pulsisque ad carmina nervis

umbrarum dominum: that is, Pluto.

carmina: Orpheus will sing to the underworld deities to achieve the would-be salvation of his dead wife; soon enough he will perform rather different songs.

nervis: Opening a ring that will close at 40 *nervos*; cf. 108. Bömer notes in his commentary here that the expression *pulsis ... nervis* is a variation of *nervos percutere* (11.5) and *nervos movere* (40 below); the verb here vividly describes how the strings of the instrument are driven toward music and song.

17   sic ait: o positi sub terra numina mundi,

Reed discusses the *suasoria* elements of Orpheus' address to the underworld divinities, as he seeks to persuade them to agree to the release of Eurydice; a *suasoria* was meant to appeal via rhetoric to an interlocutor or judge, and so the person making a case would assemble evidence to defend a given position/effect a desired outcome.

ait: The verb is defective; both *aio* and *aiio* are found (and both are words of two syllables).

numina: "Divine powers"; the root of the word is the verb "to nod," from the idea of the supreme, Jovian nod that seems to exercise control over affairs both human and divine. The underworld's *numina* = Pluto and Proserpina.

mundi: A more general term than *terra*; the *mundus* could be the universe, the heavens and the firmament, the "world" in an encompassing sense. Orpheus sings of the *regnum tertium*, as Bömer notes; the underworld is regularly depicted as the rich realm that will one day receive everything that is mortal and thus doomed to die.

18   in quem reccidimus quidquid mortale creamur,

reccidimus: cf. 180 *reccidit*, of the fateful discus that will kill Hyacinthus.

quidquid mortale: In apposition to the understood "we" in *creamur*; the neuter singular is in apposition to a plural subject. Ovid also uses the phrase at 14.603 *quidquid in Aenea fuerat mortale*, of the purification and expurgation of Aeneas' mortal part before his apotheosis. In this detail of purgatorial cleansing we see a revelation of Orphic eschatology or beliefs in the afterlife and the potential for the rebirth of souls after a process of purification; there is something mortal that must be purged before the eternal can live again in a new body; "eschatology" refers to the study of the "last things" or the fate of the soul/the afterlife.

19   si licet et falsi positis ambagibus oris

positis: Bömer notes the simple verb (as opposed to the compound *depositis*); once again the emphasis is on rapid narrative, in this case to move quickly to the rescue of the singer's lost wife. With the *falsi . . . oris* cf. 2.631, during the story of Apollo and the raven; Reed compares 302 below and discusses the connection of this remark with the broader issue of the songs of Orpheus that serve as the prime focus of the book.

ambagibus: The word is typically used in the plural, and refers to a roundabout way of speaking, a labyrinthine manner of discourse (cf. Virgil, *Aeneid* 6.29) that leads in circles. There may be a hint of humor on the poet's part here, if in *ambagibus* the audience is meant to think of some of the afterlife doctrines associated with Orphic and Pythagorean thought. In Virgil's *Aeneid* the mention of *ambages* is associated with the Cretan labyrinth, itself a type of the underworld; ultimately the point in Ovid may be that Orpheus wants to put aside the vain image of a "traditional," Homeric underworld from which there is no ready escape—he wants to introduce the idea that a soul can be reborn, that his Eurydice can escape from the infernal regions and return to earth.

20   vera loqui sinitis, non huc ut opaca viderem

opaca: With 21 *Tartara*; the underworld is characteristically dark and foreboding.

viderem: Imperfect subjunctive in a clause of purpose in secondary or historic sequence where the subordinate verb describes an action that takes place simultaneously with or subsequent to the action of the main verb (21 *descendi*). Orpheus has not come on some heroic journey to visit the underworld and vanquish infernal monsters; love has been his impetus, and in a sense there has been a reversal of the situation in Book 5, when Pluto left the underworld, only to try to bring an object of love back to his dread abode.

21   Tartara descendi, nec uti villosa colubris

Tartara: Not just the underworld, but its darkest and most fearsome region.

villosa colubris: The words serve to fashion a moment's suspense: what monstrous underworld denizen will be described?

colubris: For the tradition that Cerberus had a snake's tail and a serpentine coat, cf. Ovid, *Metamorphoses* 4.449; Euripides, *Hercules* 24; 611; also Virgil, *Aeneid* 6.417. Homer never mentions the hound's name; Gantz (1993: 127) notes that the dog is conveniently missing from the *Odyssey katabasis* or underworld journey because Odysseus technically never enters the underworld proper. Stesichorus may have written an entire poem dedicated to the lore about the abduction of the dog as one of the canonical labors of Heracles. But as Gantz does well to note, "subsequent to Homer there is very little preserved on the geography or the rationale of Hades."

22   terna Medusaei vincirem guttura monstri;

The beast is Cerberus; the three-headed sentinel canine of the underworld, whose conquest had been one of the labors of Hercules; the periphrasis is very much in the high epic style, where the poet delights in using more or less abstruse references to mythological stories to describe his characters.

Medusaei ... monstri: The hound of hell is a "Medusaean monster" because it can petrify its victims; the hazards of sight and the perils of vision will be a recurring theme of the book (cf., *inter al.*, Orpheus' fateful decision to look back at Eurydice). Medusa, like Cerberus, is never mentioned in Homer by name, and there is no evidence in Homer of the tradition of Perseus and his conquest of the Gorgon (see here Gantz, 1993: 304). The adjective *Medusaeus* is likely an Ovidian invention; he uses it also at 5.249, of the Gorgon head Perseus wields in his father-in-law's banquet hall. The poet here closely relates the action of Books 10 and 5, the respective closes of two acts of his epic trilogy.

23   causa viae est coniunx, in quam calcata venenum

calcata: The word is somewhat onomatopoeic, as it describes how the snake was trodden upon by the carefree girl; the action of the girl is imitated in the rhythm of *cal, ca, ta.* The pronounced alliteration of the line (*causa, coniunx, calcata*) helps to underscore the image of the girl as she treads on the fatal serpent.

24   vipera diffudit crescentesque abstulit annos.

diffudit: The prefix expresses the spread of the venom; Eurydice was bitten in the ankle, but the poison was diffused throughout her body.

crescentes … annos: Literally "the growing years"; Ovid may well be imagining the age of a Roman bride and the significant physical development that Eurydice never experienced. Reed compares *Ars Amatoria* 1.61 *primis et adhuc crescentibus annis,* for the division of the life of a woman into three ages.

25   posse pati volui nec me temptasse negabo;

Orpheus paints himself as something of a Stoic hero; he wants to be able to endure the loss of his bride on the very day of the wedding, but he has failed because of Amor (26).

pati: The verb means "to endure," to stand firm in the face of adversity.

temptasse: For *temptavisse*.

26   vicit Amor. supera deus hic bene notus in ora est;

Amor: Properly speaking, Amor = Cupid; the noun, however, need not be capitalized and thus personified.

supera: From the point of view of those in the lower world, the adjective refers to the realm "above," that is, the earth—though it can also convey a sense of how Amor rules in the supernal regions of "heaven" as well.

27   an sit et hic dubito. sed et hic tamen auguror esse,

et ... et: Adverbs, not conjunctions. The striking line-opening of four monosyllables helps to convey something of Orpheus' halting, doubtful speech; see here Bömer on 7.686, and cf. the similar effect of the triple *sed et hic*.

hic: "Here," that is, in the lower world.

auguror: The verb is the proper term for the observation of omens and prognostication based on the interpretation of signs. Perhaps Orpheus has read Book 5 of the epic.

28   famaque si veteris non est mentita rapinae,

The theme of truth *vs.* falsehood continues: *if* the story of Pluto's abduction of Proserpina is true, *then* Love is known in the underworld too. The *fama* of the story, of course, rests on *Metamorphoses* 5, at least in the present Ovidian context.

veteris ... rapinae: Much time has elapsed—not least, as it were, between Books 5 and 10.

mentita: Bömer notes that the verb can have an active or a passive sense, or, as he puts it, *fefellit* or *ficta est*.

29   vos quoque iunxit Amor. per ego haec loca plena timoris,

iunxit Amor: cf. Virgil, *Aeneid* 4.28–29, as Dido ruefully recalls to her sister how Sychaeus joined her in love, only to take it from the union by his untimely death. Once again, *Amor* can be capitalized or not with no appreciable difference in meaning. With *iunxit* cf. Orpheus' mention of his *coniunx* above.

per ego: The phrasing has an archaic flair that is appropriate to the solemn context.

plena timoris: Expressions of want and plenty regularly take the genitive. See further here Rimell (2006: 109 ff.), with full consideration of the present scene.

30   per Chaos hoc ingens vastique silentia regni,

Chaos: The primeval state of the world, characterized by a shapeless lack of order; the noun is neuter in gender.

vasti: Hymenaeus had traveled through immense tracts of sky to reach Orpheus and Eurydice, and the underworld is vast (it must, after all, be sufficiently commodious to welcome all the dead).

silentia: In striking contrast to the effect of Orpheus' melodic voice. cf. 53 *per muta silentia.*

31   Eurydices, oro, properata retexite fata.

Eurydices: The *causa viae* is prominently named at the opening of the verse. Only now is the dead girl identified by name. "Eurydice" was the name applied to several women of classical mythology, including the wife of Aeneas at Troy (so the Cyclic *Cypria* according to Pausanias 10.26.1); a wife of Nestor (Homer, *Odyssey* 3.452); even one of the Danaids (Pseudo-Apollodorus 2.1.5). The form is a Greek genitive; Bömer notes in his commentary that this is the only appearance of the ending in classical poetry.

properata ... fata: "Hastened fates"; the premise behind the adjective is that Eurydice could have expected to have lived a longer life. The metaphor in *retexite* is from weaving; the Fates spun out the destines of mortals. cf. 33 *properamus.* As Reed notes, the language conflates the work of Pluto and Proserpina with that of the Parcae.

32   omnia debemur vobis, paulumque morati

Bömer observes that Orpheus now resorts to traditional arguments and *topoi* from the rhetorical schools; we are all going to die, sooner or later, etc.

omnia debemur: cf. 18 *quidquid mortale creamur.* The sentiment is a commonplace.

33   serius aut citius sedem properamus ad unam;

serius aut citius: "Later or sooner"; the forms are comparative adverbs.

sedem properamus ad unam: With this and the following verse cf. the Pseudo-Ovidian *Epicedion Drusi* 359 *tendimus huc omnes, metam properamus ad unam. Properamus* harks back to 31 *properata.* In the notion of the haste of mortals in their race to the grave there may be a hint of dark humor if one is to imagine the carefree Eurydice frolicking in haste through the meadow when she is felled by the deadly serpent. Bömer provides extensive survey of all the parallel passages of the inevitable advance of humanity to the "Totenhaus" or "House of the Dead."

34   tendimus huc omnes, haec est domus ultima, vosque

tendimus: Very different from 3 *tendit,* as the god traveled to preside over the wedding.

huc: "Hither," "to here," or "to this place."

domus ultima: Silius Italicus uses this label for the Hesperides (*Punica* 3.283). The sentiment is worthy of special consideration given the

tenets of Orphic philosophy and the question of the possibility of
rebirth; for now, Orpheus' point is that eventually everyone must
come under the power of Pluto and Proserpina: rather a problematic
assertion given the eschatology associated with his name. Reed
compares Virgil, *Aeneid* 5.731–732, of the *Ditis / infernas domos*; also
Metamorphoses 14.111 *Elysiasque domos et regna novissima mundi.*

35   humani generis longissima regna tenetis.

longissima: Of temporal extent; the human race spends the longest
amount of time in the underworld. There may be a hint, too, of the idea
that the kingdom is constantly expanding in size/numbers of the dead.

tenetis: The two underworld deities hold or maintain the kingdom of
the broadest expanse of time for poor mortals.

36   haec quoque, cum iustos matura peregerit annos,

haec: that is, Eurydice.

peregerit: The prefix expresses the length of life and the passing years;
Latin uses the future perfect to express a precise temporal relation
between subordinate and main (here 37 *erit*) verbs.

iustos ... annos: "Just years," as in, a normal life span that meets the life
expectancy to which one can reasonably aspire; Orpheus wants an
exemption for Eurydice from the perils of sickness and sudden death
to which all mortals are subject.

37   iuris erit vestri; pro munere poscimus usum.

iuris ... vestri: The so-called predicate genitive, where a relationship
between two nouns is made clear by the genitive phrase that describes
the subject (in this case, *haec* from the preceding line).

munere: A common word of richly textured, varied meanings;
Orpheus is asking for the boon or benefit of enjoying Eurydice for

what will be a relatively short period of time in comparison to her long stay in the underworld.

usum: cf. on 565. The sentiment of having life for our use and not as a permanent and lasting treasure is not unique to Ovid, as the commentators note; there may be something of an undercutting of Orpheus' argument here on behalf of his wife, since what he really wishes is immortality—exactly the sort of thing that Orphic doctrines considered in the formulation of theological tenets: the idea that life could be renewed, and not merely so that one would simply die again and not experience another rebirth.

38   quod si fata negant veniam pro coniuge, certum est

si fata negant: Even Pluto and Proserpina must respect the mysterious power of fate; by implication, it was not a violation of the will of destiny for Eurydice to be given back to Orpheus—though it was of course also fated for her to be lost a second time. Bömer notes that *fata negant* occurs first in Ovid in extant literature; he compares 633 and ff. below, of the dictates of destiny concerning the marriage of Atalanta.

certum est: "It is resolved."

39   nolle redire mihi; leto gaudete duorum.

nolle: The present infinitive of *nolo*; the point is that Orpheus is not willing to return/does not wish to live without his lost wife.

mihi: A sort of dative of reference, or what some prefer to call an ethical dative; in the present instance it amounts almost to a first person, that is, "I am resolved not to be willing to return."

leto: A mostly poetic word for death, here used to end Orpheus' pleading song on an epic note. Gantz (1993: 724) takes it as an Ovidian invention that Orpheus vowed that he would remain in the underworld if he were not given the chance to rescue Eurydice; the point in part may be that he has no real choice in the matter. The form = ablative of cause; the immortals are invited to rejoice because of the death of the pair, when before they could only rejoice at the death of one.

40   talia dicentem nervosque ad verba moventem

First the accusative object, then (41) the subject and verb; the emphasis is thereby placed on Orpheus as he moves the underworld shades to pity.

talia: "Such things"; the neuter substantive allows one to imagine that the actual song was longer than the poet's quick summation of its main sentiments.

nervos: Closing a ring with 16 *nervis,* as Orpheus ends his performance. We do not hear Orpheus' musical accompaniment of his words, of course; the immortals of the underworld—and this is the first time they are mentioned in Ovid's epic since the abduction myth of Book 5—will be moved by the melody that enchants them.

41   exsangues flebant animae; nec Tantalus undam

A miniature catalog of traditional denizens of the underworld now commences; one can imagine that the longer version of Orpheus' song that is implied in the narrative might have had a more extensive description of a *katabasis.* The present scene is most indebted to the similar Virgilian underworld passage at *Aeneid* 6.547–627, which is of course more highly developed and expansive, as befits the solemn context of Aeneas' descent to visit the ghost of his father at the climax of the first half of the epic.

flebant: The imperfect can be used to express the start of an action (the inchoative or inceptive use), or its continuation (the durative). The *animae* are insubstantial, which begs the question of whether they are able to shed tears—and the imperfect can express an attempt or effort (the conative).

Tantalus: The story of his infernal punishment was widely circulated in antiquity (Homer, *Odyssey* 11.582–592; he does not appear in the *Iliad*); there were different accounts of why exactly he was tormented with eternal thirst and hunger in the afterlife. What is less clear in the extant tradition is the exact nature of his offense(s); for the tradition that Tantalus may have been involved in the abduction of Ganymede (who will be the first subject of Orpheus' forthcoming song), see Gantz (1993: 536).

42   captavit refugam, stupuitque Ixionis orbis,

captavit: The verb has frequentative force, that is, what was done was done over and over again in repetitive torment.

refugam: Ovid may have introduced this adjective to poetry.

Ixionis: Ixion is most famously associated with his attempted ravishment of Hera, and the fiery wheel that serves as his object of eternal torment. Ixion is known to Homer (*Iliad* 14.317–318), though the brief mention there is only that Zeus had a son, Pirithous, with Ixion's wife. Pindar's *Pythian* 2 is the earliest surviving account of the underworld punishment; Ixion is depicted by Pindar as a warning against mistreatment of benefactors (i.e., the hospitality theme that recurs in classical literature). At *Georgic* 3.37–39, Virgil alludes to the story of the wheel (which is serpentine); at *Aeneid* 6.601, Ixion is tortured like Tantalus (and see Horsfall's notes here in his commentary; also Gantz (1993: 720)).

43   nec carpsere iecur volucres, urnisque vacarunt

carpsere: Third plural perfect indicative active alternative form for *carpserunt*.

iecur: The "liver." The reference is to the giant Tityus, who is said to have assaulted Leto on her way back from Delphi; he was killed by her divine son Apollo and punished with an eternity of having his liver gnawed by vultures (cf. the traditional punishment of Prometheus for bringing fire to mortals).

urnis: Separative ablative; the original use of the ablative case was to express separation (hence the name *ablatus*, literally = "having been taken away").

44   Belides, inque tuo sedisti, Sisyphe, saxo.

Belides: The "daughters of Belus," or, more precisely, the descendants: Belus was the father of Danaus, the sire of the fifty Danaids, who spend eternity trying to fill sieves with water. For the complex history of these descendants of Inachus see Gantz (1993: 198 ff). There may be a deliberate mention here of the Belides because of the connection of the name of Belus with the father of Dido and his conquest of the island of Cyprus (cf. Virgil, *Aeneid* 1.621–622); Cyprus will be the locus for much of the action of the present book.

Sisyphe: Vocative; the apostrophe varies the miniature catalog of the underword's most notorious sinners. Sisyphus is another of the infamous malefactors Odysseus encounters during his own *katabasis* (*Odyssey* 11.593–600); he was the subject of at least one tragedy of Aeschylus (cf. the Danaids and their Aeschylean treatment).

45   tum primum lacrimis victarum carmine fama est

lacrimis: The tears this time are of the dread Furies; see Reed here for other appearances of this sort of almost magical crying; the point is likely simply that Orpheus' song is so powerful that so much is possible now that would otherwise be unbelievable (cf. the idea of a catalog of so-called *adunata* or things that cannot happen in a "normal" world, from the Greek for "impossible"); there may also be something of the falsehood theme here, consideration of the question of whether or not the stories are true (cf. on *fama est* below).

victarum: With 46 *Eumenidum*; Ovid builds a momentary suspense over the scene, as he describes the conquest of the Furies by the power of Orpheus' song (*carmine*).

fama est: "The rumor (or the report/story) is …" The language once again evokes the idea of truth *vs.* falsehood, of report and retelling.

46   Eumenidum maduisse genas, nec regia coniunx

Eumenidum: The euphemism for the three hellish avengers is dramatically placed at the start of the line. The form is genitive plural, and is to be taken closely with *genas* (= "cheeks"). One can smile at the detail about the Furies and their tears; Ovid is having fun at the expense of his subject.

maduisse: The perfect infinitive indicates that the action of the subordinate verb in indirect discourse took place prior to that of the main verb.

regia coniunx: Persephone. "Antonomasia," as Bömer notes, from the Greek for "instead of the name." In this case the appellation and the descriptor emphasize the royal status of the seemingly helpless girl of the abduction sequence in Book 5. This *coniunx* is very different from that of Orpheus. The Latin poets enjoy using such periphrases to vary the content in a narrative that might otherwise see a frequent repetition of names and pronouns.

47   sustinet oranti nec qui regit ima negare,

oranti: that is, Orpheus.

negare: An "epexegetical" infinitive, or one that "explains" the action of the main verb (*sustinet*); Bömer compares 11.322 for the use of *sustinere* with such a complement, cf. also 188 below.

ima: Neuter plural as substantive = "the lower regions."

48   Eurydicenque vocant. umbras erat illa recentes

Reed compares the present passage's detail about the *umbras ...
recentes* to 4.432–438 (a description of an underworld scene that is a
clear inspiration for the opening of this book), with detailed
consideration of the appearances of *umbrae* and the vocabulary of
shadows and shades in Latin and Greek verse. Poetry does not usually
abide rigorous theological analysis, and dogmatic coherence between
even related passages in the same epic can sometimes be lacking.

Eurydicenque: The rhythm and sound effect echoes 46 *Eumenidum.*
For the tradition that the Eumenides were the daughters of Apollo
and Persephone, see Gantz (1993: 742).

umbras ... recentes: Accusative after 49 *inter.* The key word, *umbras,* is
highlighted by the word order.

49   inter et incessit passu de vulnere tardo.

Though insubstantial, the shade bears the distinguishing characteristic
of its end—in this case, the limp from the ankle bite.

passu ... tardo: "With slow step."

de vulnere: Ablative of cause.

50   hanc simul et legem Rhodopeius accipit heros,

hanc ... legem: Once again the legal theme predominates. In Virgil
(*Georgic* 4.487), it is explicitly Proserpina who gives the order about
how Eurydice must return to the upper world; the goddess of the
underworld has a special interest, of course, in the matter of how one
exits the lower regions given the history of her abduction and the
"rules" surrounding her own release (and it should be noted again
that we seem always to find Proserpina in the underworld after her

kidnapping—as if all heroic *katabaseis* occur in winter—and we never encounter her again in the upper world/Olympus with her mother). Bömer provides extensive notes here on the mysterious and vexed origins of the celebrated injunction.

Rhodopeius: cf. 11–12. There, Orpheus was the Rhodopeian *vates* or bard; here, having sung his song and achieved his wish, he is the Rhodopeian *heros*. The full implication is that now he could win his wife back, were he only to follow the prescribed *lex*.

heros: This is the reading of two eleventh-century manuscripts (U and P, in the Vatican and Paris), vs. *Orpheus* of the other extant witnesses; the effective contrast with 12 *vates* helps to secure the reading, but the matter cannot be resolved definitively (and cf. *Orpheus* at the end of 64 and 79).

51   ne flectat retro sua lumina, donec Avernas

ne: Introducing the prohibition; the verb *flectat* is in the subjunctive since, most fundamentally, it describes an action that has not happened (and, in the present, poignant case, will *never* happen).

lumina: "Eyes." The reflexive possessive adjective *sua* places the full weight of responsibility on Orpheus.

Avernas: With 52 *valles*.

52   exierit valles; aut inrita dona futura.

exierit: The future perfect indicative is used with *donec* in poetry: Orpheus is not to turn back his eyes until he shall have existed the underworld valley/valley of Avernus.

inrita: The legal metaphor (50 *legem*) continues: the boon of receiving back his wife will be rendered null and void if Orpheus looks back before exiting the underworld.

53   carpitur acclivis per muta silentia trames,

carpitur: cf. 85 *carpere.*

acclivis: "Sloping upwards." The adjective agrees with *trames.*

silentia: cf. 30 *vastique silentia regni.* The silence contrasts with the effective melodic splendor of Orpheus' voice. *Muta silentia* is a pleonasm, as Bömer notes (silence is always mute!); the force of the tautology is to underscore the soundless ambience of the lower world.

54   arduus, obscurus, caligine densus opaca.

An ascending tricolon or progression of three details describes the difficult pathway back to the upper world; the verse captures the image of the transitional space between two worlds—a theme that will recur at the climax of the Myrrha story.

caligine: The word derives from a root that means dark or black; it is regularly applied to the darkness that comes from storms, or the darkness of the lower or nether world.

55   nec procul abfuerunt telluris margine summae;

margine: Ablative of separation after the verb *abfuerunt.* They were not far removed from the border of the upper air/the surface of the earth when Orpheus was struck by fear.

56   hic ne deficeret metuens avidusque videndi

deficeret: The primary intransitive sense of the verb is to fall short of something or to fail (*OLD s.v.* B3); it can mean to die or fade away; the subject is most likely Eurydice, though it could be taken of Orpheus— the two lovers almost shade into one.

avidusque videndi: Orpheus is impatient to see his wife. The genitive of a gerund can be used after an adjective as a subjective or objective genitive. *Metuens* and *avidus* work togther to offer a brief yet telling psychological portrait of the lover (57 *amans*).

57   flexit amans oculos, et protinus illa relapsa est,

amans: Orpheus is described by reference to the quality most responsible for his (and Eurydice's) ruin; he was afraid that his ghostly wife would not follow him through to the upper regions, and he was impatient to see his beloved.

illa: that is, Eurydice.

relapsa: From *relabi.* What happened, happened at once; *protinus* has deliberate pathos and high emotional register.

58   bracchiaque intendens prendique et prendere certans

bracchiaque intendens: The elision here and especially et *prendique et prendere* is poignant, as the poet expresses the desire of the lover to grasp the insubstantial shade he was so close to liberating. As Bömer notes here, the topos of the stretching forth of the arms in supplication and longing, etc., dates to Homer.

prendique et prendere: A typically Ovidian antithesis: Orpheus tries to grasp his wife and to be grasped in turn—but Eurydice remains an insubstantial shade, incapable of either experience or action.

certans: The verb gives better sense than *captans,* though the latter has better manuscript support.

59   nil nisi cedentes infelix adripit auras.

cedentes: The breezes (*auras*) give way before Orpheus' attempt to grasp them.

infelix: A key word; Orpheus is unlucky or unfortunate in his fate, for which he alone is responsible.

60   iamque iterum moriens non est de coniuge quidquam

Eurydice suffers a second (*iterum*; cf. 64 *gemina nece*) death: a lamentable, yet somehow fitting outcome given the context of Orphic beliefs in reincarnation. Reed compares Ovid's reworking of Virgil's *Georgic* 4.494–498, which offers a lament from Eurydice. In the present scene, the point at least in part may be that Ovid is presenting the briefly sketched Eurydice in an especially positive light, as someone who merited better than what she has experienced both at the hands of fate and of her newlywed husband; Orpheus will soon enough eschew the company of women, despite Eurydice's apparent virtues.

iterum: cf. 72 *iterum*. The metrical linking of *iamque iterum* almost serves to enact the repetition of the act.

quidquam: Direct object of *questa* in the next verse; Orpheus blames his wife for none of the sad events that have transpired.

61   questa suo (quid enim nisi se quereretur amatam?)

Anderson comments on the swift dactylic rhythm of the verse; Eurydice must return quickly to the lower world, as it were.

questa: From *queror*, and in striking antithesis with the parenthetical *quereretur*, Eurydice had nothing to complain about except that she was loved by Orpheus—a possibly wry comment by the poet.

62   supremumque vale, quod iam vix auribus ille

supremumque vale: cf. 6.509, during the Philomela story; Statius, *Silvae* 3.2.209.

auribus: The ears of the singer fail him at the end.

ille: that is, Orpheus.

63   acciperet, dixit revolutaque rursus eodem est.

revoluta: Orpheus was not supposed to turn his gaze back at Eurydice; the girl, for her part, now turns her back on him as she returns.

eodem: Probably a dative of direction: Eurydice returned to the same place whence she had set out with her husband.

64   non aliter stupuit gemina nece coniugis Orpheus

Arguably, Orpheus has little cause to be amazed at the "twin" or "second" death of his wife, given his failure to follow the injunction not to look back at her.

non aliter: "Not otherwise …"; to be taken closely with 65 *quam* (= "than").

stupuit: On this passage see especially J. Heath, "The Stupor of Orpheus: Ovid's *Metamorphoses* 10.64–71," in *The Classical Journal* 91.4 (1996), 353–370, with consideration of Orpheus' emotional state in this underworld sequence, including some attention to the black humor that is a mark of Ovid's witty style.

65   quam tria qui Stygii, medio portante catenas,

qui: An anonymous victim of Cerberus' ability to petrify. The tradition that Cerberus turned an underworld victim to stone is not otherwise known to extant literature or the visual arts; the point in part may be to accord to the poet/musician Orpheus a novel song.

catenas: Introducing a heavy alliteration (66 *colla canis*) that may reflect the clanking of the heavy chains.

66   colla canis vidit; quem non pavor ante reliquit

colla: Metonymy.

ante: With 67 *quam* (tmesis; the one word *antequam* is "cut," as it were, into two—the term comes from the Greek verb that means to cut or sever).

67   quam natura prior, saxo per corpus oborto;

natura: that is, life; the nature of the human body departed in the wake of the petrifaction.

saxo ... oborto: An ablative absolute that describes the attendant circumstance of the petrifaction; the participle is from *oboriri.*

68   quique in se crimen traxit voluitque videri

quique: Olenos (69), who (unlike Orpheus) shared his wife's fate.

videri: The passive of *videre* can mean "to seem."

69   Olenos esse nocens, tuque, o confisa figurae,

Olenos: The name occurs elsewhere as that of several towns, and also of several mythological personages; the present figure accepted his wife's fate of petrifaction as her punishment for excessive trust in her own loveliness. cf. 8.281, as Ovid describes the reasons for the sending of the Calydonian boar. The story of Olenos and Lethaea is not recorded anywhere else in the surviving literature (though see Reed here, with note of the problems of Propertius, c. 2.28.9–12, which may preserve another citation); the underworld name of Olenos' wife associates her with Eurydice, while the identical first and last letters of the shared names (a favorite trick of both Virgil and Ovid) links Olenos with Orpheus: Orpheus does not wish to live as he once did without Eurydice; cf. the sentiment of not wanting to return to the upper world alone, without his wife (which, in the end is exactly what he was forced to do).

confisa: The verb governs a dative. The synaloepha by which the two syllables of *tuque* and *o* merge into one links Lethaea closely with her defining characteristic (excessive trust in her own loveliness). For the topos see Bömer's commentary here; in the present case, the twist is that the spouse wishes to be implicated in the guilt of his wife.

70   infelix Lethaea, tuae, iunctissima quondam

infelix: Like Orpheus after the loss of Eurydice (59).

Lethaea: The story of this vain woman, as we have noted, is not extant elsewhere; the name connects her to Lethe, the stream of oblivion in the underworld; the name is fitting enough for an underworld denizen, though there may be a particular point to the idea that the stone (71 *lapides*) retains no self-memory of its past. The detail about petrifaction, indeed the specific mention of a Medusan monster, serves to connect Book 10 with Book 5, which opened with the lengthy narrative of Perseus' battle in the banquet hall of Cepheus.

iunctissima: With 71 *pectora*; cf. the notion of a *coniunx*.

71   pectora, nunc lapides, quos umida sustinet Ide.

sustinet: cf. 47 *sustinet oranti ... negare*—a very different use. The Latin poets often repeat the same words in more or less close sequence (with or without a change in sense): the effect is to craft a tightly woven, cohesive narrative.

umida: In marked contrast to the stone; Ida is humid and moist.

Ide: Mount Ida, the sacred home mountain of the Trojans and haunt of the mother goddess Cybele.

72   orantem frustraque iterum transire volentem

The spondaic rhythm of the opening of the line conveys the frustration with which Orpheus fails in his attempt to rectify his blunder; the elision of *frustraque iterum* neatly expresses the repetition of the attempt. Reed points out how the accusative singular participles work together to frame the verse, on the model of Virgil, *Georgic* 4.501–502 *prensantem nequiquam umbras et multa volentem / dicere praeterea vidit; nec portitor Orci / amplius obiectam passus transire paludem.*

iterum: cf. 60 *iterum.* Eurydice can die twice, as it were; Orpheus will not be able to reenter the underworld a second time in a renewed quest to save his wife.

73   portitor arcuerat. septem tamen ille diebus

portitor: Likely Charon; possibly Cerberus.

septem: The number seven was especially significant in Pythagorean mysticism. Reed compares Achilles' mourning at Homer, *Iliad* 24.129.

ille: Perhaps with a hint of "that celebrated one"; the contrast between this Ovidian Orpheus and the Virgilian underworld figure in Elysium is especially striking and powerful.

74   squalidus in ripa Cereris sine munere sedit;

Cereris: A common metonymy for "bread" or "grain." The name of the goddess may also be a deliberate reminiscence of the lore of Persephone and her abduction; references to Ceres and her lost daughter will pepper the present book, a technique by which Ovid draws attention to the connection between the respective closing books of the poem's first and second thirds. Orpheus cares neither for his appearance nor for his health in consequence of his grief over his lost wife.

munere: A reward or boon; the *munus Cereris* = food/sustenance.

75   cura dolorque animi lacrimaeque alimenta fuere.

Another tricolon, as Ovid describes Orpheus' means of sustenance.

dolor animi: "Pain" or "sorrow" of the mind.

lacrimae: The recurring motif of tears.

alimenta: For metaphorical food in Ovid see S. Kaufhold, "Ovid's Tereus: Fire, Birds, and the Reification of Figurative Language," in *Classical Philology* 92.1 (1997), 66–71, 70, where the author considers how figurative language is used often by Ovid to express both narrative development and especially metamorphosis.

fuere: For *fuerunt.*

76 esse deos Erebi crudeles questus in altam

esse: See Reed here for perceptive comments on the choice between this infinitive and the variant reading *inde* (from study of the Byzantine Greek translation of Planudes).

Erebi: First cited in Latin literature in Cicero, as Reed notes; Erebus in Hesiod (*Theogony* 123) is the son of Chaos, whose name could be used to describe not just the underworld, but its darkest and gloomiest regions (see further the entry of Rebecca Katz in the *Virgil Encyclopedia*).

questus: Orpheus' complaint is aimed at Pluto and Proserpina; his own possible culpability in the loss of his wife does not seem to be a factor in his indictment. The verb = *queri.*

77 se recipit Rhodopen pulsumque aquilonibus Haemum.

Rhodopen: The Rhodopeian *vates* and *heros* at last departs for his mountain.

aquilonibus: Aquilo properly = the northeast or north-northeast wind; by a logical enough extension the word can be used (especially in the plural) to describe the storm-laden blasts of northerly winds. There may be an allusion to the tradition that Orpheus was smitten with

Calais, the son of the north wind Boreas (so the Hellenistic poet Phanocles, fr. 1 Powell). The mountain is struck by the blasts of the northerly winds.

Haemum: The mountain took its name from the Greek for "bloody"; one can connect the *nomen-omen* by which the name gives a hint of future events near the locale and Orpheus' eventual violent death.

78   tertius aequoreis inclusum Piscibus annum

tertius: With 79 *Titan.* Three years go by as Orpheus continues his seemingly unending lament for Eurydice. The reference to the third spring and the sun being in Pisces (in March) may connect to the Roman calendar year and the traditional start of the annual cycle in March: now a new beginning will commence, and with baleful consequences. Rather neatly, the word order has the *inclusum …
annum* enclosing the *Piscibus* that mark the time of year by zodiacal reference.

79   finierat Titan, omnemque refugerat Orpheus

Titan: The sun (as often enough in Latin literature; see Reed here for the use of the appellation already in Cicero's *Aratea*). The "titan" in question is Hyperion, the father of Helios; both primeval immortals could be associated with the sun and solar prerogatives.

omnem: With 80 femineam *Venerem.*

80   femineam Venerem, seu quod male cesserat illi,

femineam Venerem: that is, sexual relations with women. The "Misogynismus" (Bömer) or misogyny of Orpheus will be his undoing, as the poet anticipates the opening of Book 11.

male cesserat illi: "Had turned out badly for him." *Illi* is a dative of reference, in this case more specifically a dative of disadvantage.

81   sive fidem dederat. multas tamen ardor habebat

The alternatives are not mutually exclusive.

fidem: His trust or surety, by which Eurydice could be certain that her spouse would remain ever faithful to her memory.

multas: "Many women" or "girls"; the adjective is a substantive (so also *multae* in the next verse).

82   iungere se vati; multae dolore repulsae.

vati: cf. 12 vates.

dolore: The ablative could indicate that many women were rejected to their own sorrow (attendant circumstance), or because of Orpheus' sorrow (causal).

83   ille etiam Thracum populis fuit auctor amorem

Ovid transitions from the Eurydice narrative proper to an extended sequence of stories that are occasioned by Orpheus' rejection of women and his inauguration of the love of boys among the people of Thrace (i.e., Orpheus as instructor in pederasty). At Virgil, *Georgic* 4.516 ff., Orpheus is said to have abandoned the pursuit of love in grief over the loss of Eurydice; there is no particular mention of the love of boys or young men. The Thracians were notoriously wild; Orpheus teaches them a distinctly un-Roman sort of amatory pursuit.

84   in teneros transferre mares citraque iuventam

teneros: With *mares;* "males tender [in years]."

citra iuventam: A difficult phrase to interpret precisely. "On the hither or nearer side of youth" could mean those youths who are just shy of being a *iuvenis,* just on the cusp of youth (Anderson here asserts that "young *men*" are meant—emphasis his; Bömer's commentary here underscores the temporal force of the expression). It seems better to take the phrase as referring to those who are just on the verge of becoming *iuvenes.*

85   aetatis breve ver et primos carpere flores.

breve ver: With a hint of the same theme as for the Eurydice tale: life is brief; love briefer.

carpere: cf. 53 *carpitur,* and the sentiments of Horace's famous dictum. With *carpere flores* cf. Horace, c. 3.27.44.

86–147. *Cyparissus.* The story of the etiology of the cypress tree is obscure based on the evidence of our surviving sources; indeed Ovid is our only extant literary trace. See here especially L. Fulkerson, "Apollo, *Paenitentia,* and Ovid's *Metamorphoses,"* in *Mnemosyne* 59.3 (2006), 388–402 (with interesting and important consideration of how the gods in Ovid are able to experience repentence for their wrongdoings, in contrast to certain humans—with possible connection between Apollo and Augustus). On the theme of Apollo's loves in Ovid's epic, see J. Miller, "*Primus Amor Phoebi,"* in *The Classical World* 102.2 (2009), 168–172, with some consideration of the different aspects of the god. The story may be unique to Ovid, but the topos is a familiar one that recurs in the poet's epic of transformations.

86   collis erat collemque super planissima campi

Ovid sets the scene: there was a mound, and atop the mound a level plain. A brief ekphrasis or descriptive passage, as Bömer notes; the narrative continues its relatively rapid advance, though there is time for another miniature catalog, this time of the trees that assemble to listen to Orpheus' song.

87   area, quam viridem faciebant graminis herbae

The setting, fittingly enough for the first story, is pastoral. *Graminis herbae* is somewhat tautological; the expression is

Virgilian (*Eclogue* 5.26), as Bömer observes here; the material of Orpheus' song will not suit the usual expectations and dictates of pastoral verse.

88   umbra loco deerat; qua postquam parte resedit

umbra ... deerat: The locus of Orpheus' song had no trees and thus no shade, but his arrival will bring a veritable forest of trees to the place due to the power of his verse (90 *umbra loco venit*). Here Ovid may be indulging in a bit of black humor; Ovid has just journeyed to the realm of a rather different sort of *umbra*, and now the presence of the bard who was at least indirectly responsible for Eurydice's second death is a bringer of *umbrae* to the plain where he performs his song. cf. 129.

resedit: cf. 124 *residens.*

89   dis genitus vates et fila sonantia movit,

dis: Ablative of source. The commentators note that the divine parents in question are Apollo and one of the Muses (i.e., Calliope).

fila sonantia: "The sounding threads."

90   umbra loco venit. non Chaonis abfuit arbor,

Chaonis: Perhaps with a hint of a sound effect echo from the very different 30 *Chaos*. The adjective refers to Dodona; the tree is the oak that was sacred to Jupiter. A catalog of trees now commences; the tradition that Orpheus had control over trees that were seduced and uprooted by his music is at least as old as Euripides (*Bacchae* 560–564).

91   non nemus Heliadum, non frondibus aesculus altis,

Heliadum: The daughters of the sun; that is, the sisters of Phaethon, who were transformed into poplars in consequence of their excessive mourning for their lost brother—the reference is ominous. The form is genitive plural.

aesculus: A variety of oak; *OLD* identifies it as possibly either the durmast or the Hungarian oak; cf. Virgil, *Georgic* 2.16, 91 (with Mynors, 1990). But botanical precision and specificity is difficult if not impossible to offer here.

92   nec tiliae molles, nec fagus et innuba laurus,

tiliae: The linden tree, into which Baucis and Philemon had been transformed in Book 8. In a sense Orpheus is summoning all the metamorphoses that had occurred prior to this scene, as he prepares for his own song to start *ab Iove.*

molles: An appropriate appellation given the subject matter of Orpheus' song; *molles* could be used of effeminacy (*OLD s.v.* 13; 15). cf. 125 *mollia.*

innuba: Perhaps also with a pointed reference to the theme of the abandonment of marriage for the love of young males.

laurus: that is, the Daphne of Book 1. Trees are often of feminine gender in Latin. The laurel is unmarried precisely because its creation dates, as it were, to the metamorphosis of Daphne into the tree when she was in flight from an amorous Apollo.

93   et coryli fragiles et fraxinus utilis hastis

A line of balanced antithesis: the hazel wood is fragile, while the ash is suitable for implements of war. The Elder Pliny likely had this line in mind in his *Natural History* (16.228.1–2), where he notes that the ash tree is better than the hazel for spears.

94   enodisque abies curvataque glandibus ilex

enodis: "Free from knots" and thus smooth.

glandibus: "Acorns."

ilex: The so-called holm oak.

95   et platanus genialis acerque coloribus impar

platanus: The plane-tree; cf. Virgil, *Georgic* 2.70.

genialis: "Cheery" and "festive" (*OLD s.v.* 3); Reed notes Virgil, *Georgic* 4.146 as well as *Ars Amatoria* 2.697 as *comparanda* in his commentary.

acer: The initial vowel is short; = the maple tree, not the adjective *acer, acris, acre.*

96   amnicolaeque simul salices et aquatica lotos

amnicolae: "Dwelling by rivers."

aquatica lotos: Also at 9.341; the reference is to the story of Dryope and her unfortunate arboreal metamorphosis; cf. *Heroides* 15.159. All of these allusions to previous tree transformations prepare for the stories of both Cyparissus and Myrrha.

97   perpetuoque virens buxum tenuesque myricae

buxum: The box-tree (an evergreen).

myricae: The tamarisk.

98   et bicolor myrtus et bacis caerula tinus.

bicolor myrtus: The myrtle was sacred to Venus, but—more importantly for the present sequence—it was also associated with Pythagorean burial practices (as noted by the Elder Pliny at *Natural History* 35.160, where Varro is reported to have been interred with myrtle). The two colors refer to the contrasting petals and fruit.

caerula: The color is connected to the sky (*caelum*) as well as the sea, and describes a blueish hue, though its exact chromatic register can sometimes be difficult to determine.

tinus: "The shrub laurustinus" (*OLD*).

99   vos quoque, flexipedes hederae, venistis et una

The vocative address to the ivy lends variety to the still unfinished catalog, and serves to remind the audience that Orpheus is performing a song within a song.

flexipedes: "Having zigzagging shoots" (*OLD*); the word may be an Ovidian coinage.

100   pampineae vites et amictae vitibus ulmi

pampineus: Somewhat tautological; the vines are of course covered with vine shoots or foliage, but what might be repetition in the strict sense only serves to evoke the lushness of the shady setting for Orpheus' new song.

ulmi: Elm trees.

101   ornique et piceae pomoque onerata rubenti

ornique: Ash trees.

piceae: Spruce trees.

pomo: The noun can describe either a fruit tree or (as here) the fruit thereof; it can refer to orchard fruits in particular.

102   arbutus et lentae, victoris praemia, palmae

See Reed's commentary here for consideration of the artistic arrangement of words whereby the adjective and noun *lentae* and *palmae* frame the appositive *victoris praemia*; as he notes, the technique has a Greek precedent, but is a particular favorite of the Latin poets. The effect is in part to lend variety to the lengthy catalog of botanical subjects of the spellbinding Orphic music.

arbutus: The wild strawberry tree. Reed notes that 101–102 is the only example of enjambment in the entire catalog.

victoris praemia: In apposition to *palmae.*

103   et succincta comas hirsutaque vertice pinus

Bömer notes that the catalog ends with a three-verse description of the pine tree; the ethnographical significance of the pine for Ovid (following Virgil) given its connection to the Phrygian Cybele and Attis is thus highlighted as Orpheus prepares to begin a song that will start with the Trojan Ganymede.

succincta comas: The so-called Greek accusative.

hirsuta: The adjective can describe anything that is covered with bristles or somehow shaggy; it can also refer to trees that are thick with foliage.

104   grata deum Matri; siquidem Cybeleius Attis

deum Matri: that is, Cybele. *Deum* is genitive plural. The catalog nears its climactic close on a note of honor to the great Trojan mother goddess Cybele and a detail that alludes to the self-castration of her devotees, just before Orpheus commences his songs about the loves of young men.

siquidem: The conjunction/particle can express the conditional sense of, "if it is really possible that" (*OLD s.v.* 1); it can also be merely causal or epexegetical (i.e., explanatory). It is likely that the poet is introducing a note of question as to the arboreal metamorphosis of Attis.

Attis: The celebrated devotee of the great Trojan mother goddess. This
is the only extant reference to the idea that he was transformed into a
tree; the present passage opens a ring with the transformation of
Atalanta and Hippomenes into lions that draw Cybele's chariot. The
likely influence here is Catullus' galliambic horror story, c. 63; that
poem of fanatical devotion and self-mutilation does not contain any
reference to arboreal metamorphosis, but it provided a powerful
intertextual clarion call for future explorations of Cybele's worshiper
(and cf. especially the implications of 105 *exuit hac hominem*).

105   exuit hac hominem truncoque induruit alto.

exuit: Attis took off his mortal form and became a tree; there is a hint,
though, of his aforementioned traditional self-castration.

106   adfuit huic turbae metas imitata cupressus,

adfuit huic: The last tree is the most important, as Ovid introduces the
cypress, the etiology of which will now be explained.

metas: The image, as Reed notes, is from the Roman circus; the point
is the resemblance of the cypress' form to the goal posts of the
racetrack.

cupressus: A useful study of this tree's significance in Latin poetry see
C. Connors, "Seeing Cypresses in Virgil," in *The Classical Journal* 88.1
(1992), 1–17, with consideration of appearances of this mournful tree
in the *Aeneid.* On the contrast between this metamorphosis and the
eventual fate of the maenads as related in the opening sequence of
Book 11, see von Glinski, (2012: 25).

107   nunc arbor, puer ante deo dilectus ab illo

dilectus: Just possibly a reminiscence of Virgil, *Aeneid* 2.784 *lacrimas
dilectas pelle Creusae,* as Aeneas is advised to forgot about his wife; the
Virgilian narrative is modeled after the poet's own rendition of Orpheus

and Eurydice in the fourth *Georgic*. Reed discusses the anticipation in *deo dilectus* of the announced themes of Orphic music later in the book.

108   qui citharam nervis et nervis temperat arcum

The god is Apollo; in his musical pursuits he is a patron for Orpheus.

nervis et nervis: Anderson notes the play on words with the two types of *nervi*, as the poet narrator artfully mentions the two strings associated with the god Apollo; the lyre and the bow also nearly frame the verse. See further Reed here for the resultant associations of the two Apollonian attributes.

temperat: Exactly = the English verb *temper*; the sense is regulation, moderation, control and maintenance of a state of balance.

109   namque sacer nymphis Carthaea tenentibus arva

Carthaea: A region on the island of Ceos (or Cea) in the Cyclades.

110   ingens cervus erat lateque patentibus altas

The enjambment neatly enacts the shade that the antlers of the animal provide.

ingens cervus: cf. Virgil, *Aeneid* 7.483 *cervus ... ingens*, of Sylvia's stag. The death of that pet at the behest of the Fury Allecto had helped to instigate the war in Latium, a war that ultimately was resolved on the divine plane by the ethnographic revelations of *Aeneid* 12 in Jupiter's colloquy with Juno about the suppression of Troy and ascendance of Italy.

altas: With *umbras* in the next line.

111   ipse suo capiti praebebit umbras.

A neat trick: the plain where Orpheus sits had no shade until the trees were drawn by the melodic power of the singer's voice; the deer of the first story was able to provide its own shade by its mighty horns.

suo capiti: Dative of reference, here a dative of advantage.

praebebit: "Furnish, provide."

112   cornua fulgebant auro, demissaque in armos

See Reed here for the Callimachean model of *Hymn to Artemis* 102.

auro: The ablative can express material or specification; the horns were shining with gold/they were gilded.

armos: Properly the *umerus* of an animal, as it were (*OLD s.v.* 1); in poetry it could also be applied to a man's shoulder.

113   pendebant tereti gemmata monilia collo;

pendebant: The imperfect (and cf., e.g., 115 *movebatur* and *nitebant*) may express the sense that the jeweled necklaces were regularly hanging from the animal's smooth neck.

114   bulla super frontem parvis argentea loris

bulla: cf. 734. This *bulla* is certainly a reference to the ornament worn by Roman youths of high birth; the *bulla* near the close of the book will prove to be more mysterious. The word could refer to any sort of rounded object, both natural (e.g., a "bubble") or artificial. Ovid's audience almost certainly thought of the connection to young Roman aristocrats (especially in a context where young men were an announced theme of Orphic song); the appropriateness of the *bulla* on the deer is open to question, of course.

argentea: cf. 213, where it is used of the colors of lilies.

loris: Apparently a sort of strap that would support the *bulla* (cf. *OLD s.v. lorum* 1d).

115 vincta movebatur, parilesque ex aere nitebant

The text here is fraught with difficulties; is *pariles* the correct reading? *Ex aere?* Pearls (116 *bacae*) are not made of bronze, of course, and it strains credulity to believe that the deer has been decked out in bronzed pearls—though the description of the animal's accoutrements is meant to be somewhat bizarre. The manuscript weight comes down on *parilique aetate*, which has been taken as connected to the *bulla* (i.e., something along the lines of the how the *bulla* was given to the deer at birth—cf. the appearance of the Adonis *bulla* at the end of the book at the moment of his floral metamorphosis). This may well be right, and any resultant metrical seeming infelicity (see Anderson here) might well be intentional to highlight the phrase. In any case, the *bulla* is the most noteworthy of the deer's ornaments (at least in a Roman context).

nitebant: The bronze (?) makes the earrings shine with a metallic gleam. A recurring theme of the book is the image of gleam and shimmer, which in some cases can lead to grim consequences for those attracted by the tempting shine.

116 auribus e geminis circum cava tempora bacae.

bacae: Properly a tree fruit (e.g., a berry), or a pearl or piece of coral. The word is saved to the end of the description; there may be something of an element of mockery in the grandiose description of the decorative accoutrements of the sacred deer of the Carthaean nymphs. cf. the adornment of Pygmalion's statue at 265.

117 isque metu vacuus naturalique pavore

isque: Bömer discusses the weakened force of the demonstrative pronoun, which here has little in the way of special meaning; the verse concentrates, after all, on reflections on the (absence of) fear and dread from the deer's demeanor.

metu: Separative ablative with *vacuus* = "free from fear." The ablative originally expressed separation; this = the basic use of the case.

naturalique pavore: With 118 *deposito;* the animal's natural timidity is put aside as it assumes something of the life of a domesticated pet.

118   deposito celebrare domos mulcendaque colla

celebrare: The deer used "to frequent" the houses of the vicinity.

mulcenda: Gerundive; the image here is one of an animal so adorably affectionate that one simply had to pet its neck. The gerundive expresses obligation or necessity—one simply had to stroke the adorable animal. The animal offered its neck to be petted and caressed.

119   quamlibet ignotis manibus praebere solebat.

quamlibet: "However much" one wanted to pet the deer, the animal allowed it.

ignotis manibus: "Unknown hands": strangers could touch the pet without any harm.

120   sed tamen ante alios, Ceae pulcherrime gentis,

Another apostrophe is employed to add variety to the narrative, this time just as Cyparissus is about to be introduced.

Ceae: Of the island of Ceos in the Aegean Sea. The adjective agrees with *gentis.*

121   gratus erat, Cyparisse, tibi; tu pabula cervum

Bömer notes the double anastrophe of prepositions (i.e., the rhetorical device whereby the usual syntactic order is abandoned) and enjambment of this and the next verse; the effect is to convey something of both the regularity of Cyparissus' service to his pet deer, and, perhaps, something of the absurdity of the situation. Sylvia's care for her pet deer in the *Aeneid* is presented as significantly less ridiculous, and the death of the animal leads directly to the serious consequence of the war in central Italy. The present story will result not in war, but may represent something of Ovid's wry commentary on Orpheus and, by extension, the philosophies that are associated with his name (i.e., they are dismissed as being somewhat ridiculous).

pabula: Ovid had already mentioned the "food" of Orpheus in his grief (75 *alimenta fuere*); the recurring image of sustenance may distantly presage the ultimate Pythagorean revelation of Book 15: one should consider becoming a vegetarian to avoid consuming a former friend who had undergone a metamorphosis via rebirth into a new body.

122   ad nova, liquidi ducebas fontis ad undam

nova: cf. On 121 *pabula;* "new food" may have a range of intended associations.

liquidi ... fontis: Reed notes that the collocation of words is Virgilian (both *Eclogues* and *Georgics*); the image is one of pastoral peace and bucolic serenity.

123   tu modo texebas varios per cornua flores,

modo: "At one time ... at another; now ... now; first ... then" (*OLD s.v.* 6); often there is a second *modo,* but other words can replace it (as here with 124 *nunc*).

texebas: The imperfect may be frequentative; you "kept" doing something.

per cornua: "through/along its horns."

124   nunc eques in tergo residens huc laetus et illuc

residens: cf. 88 *resedit.*

huc . . . illuc: "Hither and thither": the rider playfully enjoys directing his mount in this direction and that.

laetus: Happy and carefree; the force of the adjective will not endure long.

125   mollia purpureis frenebas ora capistris.

A so-called Golden Line, with two nouns and two adjectives "and a verb betwixt to keep the peace." The effect is to highlight something of the ridiculousness of the scene; this is a solemn verse employed in something of an unimportant context.

mollia: cf. 92 *molles.*

purpureis: The color can have ominous undertones that associate the deer with the tragedy of premature death.

ora: Poetic plural. With *mollia ora* Bömer compares 12.577 *dulci . . . ore,* of Nestor; the adjective may imply both the physical characteristic of the deer's soft mouth, and the sweetness and gentleness for which the animal was renowned.

capistris: A sort of halter for controlling the deer's movements; the image becomes rather more ridiculous by the verse.

126   aestus erat mediusque dies, solisque vapore

cf. 174 below, and the temporal setting of the erotic scene of *Amores* 1.5.1 *aestus erat, mediamque dies exegerat horam.* On all of these expressions of time of day, see Rimell (2006: 106–109). The emphasis here is on the extreme heat that inspires rest; the implied eroticism of the hour is part of the background of the image the poet-narrator crafts.

medius dies: that is, noon; cf. 3, 144 and *Ars Amatoria* 3.723.

solisque vapore: Bömer compares Lucretius, *De Rerum Natura* 1.1032 *solis terra vapore*; the phrase is thus old and scientific, and serves to introduce the poet's astronomical dating of the time of year.

127 concava litorei fervebant bracchia Cancri;

concava: "Curving inward."

litorei: "Littoral" or shore-dwelling. Bömer compares 78 above, of the *aequorei Pisces*, as another example of an "Epitheton ornans" or "ornamental epithet."

fervebant: A durative imperfect; the arms of the crab continue to exude heat at the height of the summer.

Cancri: First Pisces was mentioned to give the astronomical, zodiacal time for the start of Orpheus' song; now the mention of Cancer, admittedly within the context of the story within a story, conveys something of a sense of the progression of time, as we move from spring to the heat of summer.

128 fessus in herbosa posuit sua corpora terra

herbosa ... terra: This phrase describing the grassy earth occurs only here in extant Latin.

sua corpora: Poetic plural.

129 cervus et arborea frigus ducebat ab umbra.

umbra: cf. 88 and 90 for possible plays on the meanings of *umbra*; one of the effective techniques Ovid uses throughout the *Metamorphoses* is to play on the dangers that are inherent even in seemingly peaceful, tranquil places (cf., e.g., the serpent in the grass that fells Eurydice).

130   hunc puer imprudens iaculo Cyparissus acuto

The handsome youth Cyparissus forms a pair with Adonis at the end of the book; both men are hunters, and both undergo metamorphoses, despite the rather different circumstances of their last hunting expeditions.

imprudens: So also Hyacinthus as he hastens too quickly to retrieve Apollo's discus. The story of Cephalus and Procris is very similar to this careless accident of the deer slaying; cf. the shared first and last letters of the slayers of wife and pet.

iaculo ... acuto: cf. Virgil, *Aeneid* 11.571, of the infant Camilla.

131   fixit et, ut saevo morientem vulnere vidit,

saevo: "Cruel" and even "savage," in part because no hunter would knowingly slay his favorite pet. With *saevo ... vulnere* cf. *Epistulae ex Ponto* 1.2.15.

132   velle mori statuit. quae nec solacia Phoebus

Cyparissus' reaction to the death of the deer offers something of a comment on Orpheus' response to Eurydice's.

velle mori statuit: With Cyparissus' resolution to die Reed compares the Trojan scion Aesacus at 11.782 (a story of significance to the themes of Book 10), and Myrrha below at 483–487; in the two instances from the present book, there will be a transformation into a tree that is associated with mourning and funereal rites.

Phoebus: With Apollo's love for Cyparissus, and his admonition to his *puer dilectus*, cf. Venus with Adonis near the end of the book.

133   dixit et ut leniter pro materiaque doleret

pro materia: Apollo essentially argues that "it was just a deer." The metamorphosis of Cyparissus into a cypress is reminiscent of the transformation of Apollo's *amour* Daphne into a laurel tree; the present situation is especially ridiculous in comparison to that early episode of the epic. See Reed here for consideration of the question of whether *materia* is meant to have metapoetic considerations (possibly, though certainly not necessarily)—that is, the material or matter of poetic composition; there is of course the striking parallel between the Cyparissus narrative and the Virgilian account of Sylvia's deer, and also something of a connection with the reaction Apollo will soon enough have to Hyacinthus, not to mention his own previous experiences with both Daphne and the ill-fated Coronis.

134   admonuit! gemit ille tamen munusque supremum

munusque supremum: cf. Ovid, *Epistulae ex Ponto* 1.7.29. The adjective underscores that this will be a sort of death.

135   hoc petit a superis, ut tempore lugeat omni.

Cyparissus wants to lament his pet deer for all time; his wish will be granted ("Zypresse als Baum der Trauer":—Bömer).

ut ... lugeat: A so-called substantive clause of purpose, the point of which ultimately is that the action is envisaged as some as yet unrealized occurrence.

136   iamque per immensos egesto sanguine fletus

immensos: cf. the immense air of the opening scene of the book, as the god Hymenaeus descended to earth; the adjective here may convey a sense of the ridiculous.

egesto: Egerere means to extract or use up; to remove or even carry out for burial; Ovid is likely playing on this funereal use of the verb: Cyparissus is preparing his own requiem.

137   in viridem verti coeperunt membra colorem,

viridem: Cf. 87 *viridem*, closing a ring: the locus of Orpheus' story was made green by the grass atop the hillock; now Cyparissus turns green as he joins the forest of trees.

138   et modo qui nivea pendebant fronte capilli

nivea: Snow-white; the word can have associations with the paleness of death; see Reed here for the bibliography on this key color in the Latin chromatic poetic vocabulary (alongside numerous parallel passages). Cf. 247, of the color of Pygmalion's lifeless statue; 272, of the sacrificial animals at the festival of Venus.

139   horrida caesaries fieri, sumptoque rigore

horrida: The adjective means "rough" or "bristly"; here there is a deliberate contrast with *caesaries*, which regularly describes hair that is long and luxurious, with implications of smoothness and sleekness.

rigore: Again, the language can be that of death and *post mortem rigor.*

140   sidereum gracili spectare cacumine caelum,

sidereum: "Starry" in the sense of replete with constellations; cf. the emphasis on Pisces and Cancer.

gracili … cacumine: The top of the cypress tree is slender and slight, with little in the way of weight or substance.

141   ingemuit tristisque deus lugebere nobis

Apollo, like his fellow musician Orpheus, is left to mourn a lover. The present passage stands in striking contrast to the narrative of Apollo with the laurel/Daphne; there the god memorialized his love for a young woman; here the beloved is a boy, in accord with the pederastic theme of Orpheus' story. On this see especially J. Makowski, "Bisexual

Orpheus: Pederasty and Parody in Ovid's *Metamorphoses*," in *The Classical Journal* 92.1 (1996), 25–38, with consideration of Ovid's depiction of Orpheus right after the tale of Iphis and Ianthe at the close of Book 9.

ingemuit: Bömer compares 2.621 for another example of the use of this verb as almost a technical term for the grief of the immortals.

lugebere: With 142 *lugebis*: another Ovidian antithesis. *Lugebere* is an alternative form for *lugeberis*. Bömer notes that *lugere* and *dolere* are essentially synonyms; the former is rather rarer and perhaps indicative of more intense feeling, possibly mingled with the idea that the whole matter is excessive (cf. English "lugubrious"). In any case, Apollo now knows something of the emotion for which he had warned Cyparissus against excessive grief.

142   lugebisque alios aderis dolentibus inquit.

aderis: 'You will be present at …."; cf. the use of the verb in divine epiphanies; in part the point is that Cyparissus will now become immortal, and that he will have the eternal charge of being present for those who suffer loss and who are in a state of grief.

dolentibus: Dative of reference.

143   tale nemus vates attraxerat inque ferarum

The atmosphere has already been funereal; now the trees are joined by wild animals—harmless enough because of the music of Orpheus, but a harbinger of the more savage incident with which the book will close.

144   concilio medius turba volucrumque sedebat.

concilio medius: cf. Virgil, *Aeneid* 5.75–76, as Aeneas proceeds to his father's *tumulus*.

volucrum: Genitive plural.

145   ut satis impulsas temptavit pollice chordas

impulsas: To be taken closely with *chordas;* the strings of the lyre are touched by the thumb of the musician.

pollice: "Thumb."

146   et sensit varios, quamvis diversa sonarent,

quamvis: The conjunction introduces a concessive subjunctive (*sonarent*).

diversa: Neuter plural adjective used substantively as an adverbial accusative; = "differently."

147   concordare modos, hoc vocem carmine movit:

Orpheus commences his song—the second after his appeal to Pluto and Proserpina.

concordare: "To harmonize" (*OLD s.v.* 2b).

modos: "A rhythmic pattern" (*OLD s.v.* 7).

vocem . . . movit: As Bömer observes in his commentary, the expression is without parallel in this sense; one can compare 149 *carmina nostra move.*

148–161. *Ganymede.* The story of the abduction of the Trojan prince was known to Homer (*Iliad* 20.230–237); it stands near the beginning of Virgil's *Aeneid* as one of the main reasons for the wrath of Juno against the Trojans. The Ganymede story also appears on the cloak of Cloanthus that is offered as a prize during the boat race of *Aeneid* 5, where it appears as part of that book's concern with Roman ethnography and the transition from Troy to Italy; see here M. Putnam, "Ganymede and Virgilian Ekphrasis," in *The American*

Journal of Philology 116.3 (1995), 419–440; Putnam discusses at length the importance of the Ganymede story to the Trojan lore that stands at the beginning of "Roman" history when seen in light of its Trojan origins. In Homer the abduction is due to the action of all the immortals in concert; in the *Homeric Hymn to Aphrodite* Zeus alone is responsible. Theognis is the first surviving source to record that Zeus had sexual designs on the boy; aspects of the lore are known both to Pindar (e.g., *Olympian* 1.43 ff.) and Ibycus fr. 269 (289) Page, with numerous other attestations collected by Bömer. See further Gantz (1993: 557 ff).

148   Ab Iove, Musa parens (cedunt Iovis omnia regno),

Ab Iove: The first story will be of a love of Jupiter, and so the god's name is fittingly placed at the start of the song. But the opening is also cosmological, as if Ovid were commencing a creation narrative. See further here Gee (2013: 13). Bömer compares *Fasti* 5.111 *ab Iove surgat opus*; the song of Orpheus opens a meditation on the sometimes seemingly conflicting facets of the Roman ethnographic tradition, in particular the problem of Troy for the Roman imagination. Reed offers extensive notes here on the cosmological precedents and other parallels.

Musa parens: The "parent Muse" would seem to be Calliope (Orpheus' mother), the muse traditionally associated with epic, as befitting a gigantomachy or battle of the gods and the giants—but it will be Jupiter's association with Ganymede, not his more heroic and glorious exploits in victory over the giants, which will be the subject of Orpheus' song. The song of Orpheus offers a parallel to the song of Calliope from Book 5; the traditional world of the Muses—with implications of their patronage over heroic song—has been replaced by the very different hymnody of Orpheus in 10. In the final book of the epic, Pythagorean dogmas and philosophy will provide the third and final eschatological song of the poem, as it were.

149   carmina nostra move. Iovis est mihi saepe potestas

Orpheus states his poetic allegiance: often he has sung first of the power of Jupiter; the god is named three times in two verses.

carmina nostra move: Bömer in his commentary compares Virgil, *Aeneid* 7.641 *Helicona, deae, cantusque movete* for the expression of "moving songs"; the air is epic, though the subject will be quite unlike, for example, the *Aeneid.*

150   dicta prius; cecini plectro graviore Gigantas

graviore: The more serious strains of epic.

Gigantas: The reference is pointed: the opening of Ovid's *Amores* had referred to the poet's attempt to write a gigantomachy, an epic that Cupid converted into erotic elegy.

151   sparsaque Phlegraeis victricia fulmina campis

Phlegraeis: The reference is to Campania's volcanic region, the traditional site of a major engagement of the gigantomachy.

victricia: "Bringing victory." The idea is that the lightning bolts that the god wields accomplish his will by bringing victory as he vanquishes his enemies.

152   nunc opus est leviore lyra; puerosque canamus

leviore lyra: Ablative after *opus est*; literally = "now there is need of a lighter lyre." Orpheus may once have sung of the battle of Jupiter and the giants; now he will begin a poem in a "lighter strain," as he sings of 1) boys loved by immortals and 2) girls struck by forbidden passions.

153   dilectos superis inconcessisque puellas

Ovid associates the *pueri* with divinities as lovers; the *puellae* are to be the subjects of stranger tales and punishment.

puellas: The girls are conceived of as active instigators of unlawful passions; they are thus subject to punishment: Hyacinthus and Adonis may die, but they will be given honored memorials; Myrrha's and Atalanta's fates are somewhat different. Orpheus will sing of girls who were driven mad, as it were, by crazed love affairs; the theme is a foreshadowing of how the poet bard will himself be destroyed by the insane maenads responsible for his dismemberment at the beginning of Book 11.

inconcessis: With 154 *ignibus.* The fires with which the girls burned were not allowed by any standard of convention or morality. As we shall see, in a strict sense only the story of Myrrha would seem to fit the announced theme of the Orphic music. Reed notes that Byblis was similarly introduced at 9.454 *Byblis in exemplo est ut ament concessa puellae*; in a sense Ovid's Orpheus has gone back in time to revisit an earlier example of the same sort of story from the epic.

154   ignibus attonitas meruisse libidine poenam.

attonitas: With 153 *puellas.*

libidine: Ablative of cause.

155   Rex superum Phrygii quondam Ganymedis amore

The line is elegantly balanced, as we move from the solemnity of the king of the immortals to the rather less dignified situation of his infatuation with Ganymede.

superum: Genitive plural. cf. 153 *superis.*

quondam: The poet narrator locates the episode in the misty temporal regions of the distant past (= "once upon a time"); the story of Ganymede stands at the beginning of Roman ethnography, in the early stages of the roughly forward chronology of classical myth that moves forward inexorably to Troy as well as Rome.

Phrygii: The geographic descriptor emphasizes the Trojan nature of the lover and thus highlights the ethnographic question; Ganymede was said to have been abducted from Ida, the sacred mountain of the Trojans.

Ganymedis: The son of Tros and brother of Ilus and Assaracus.

156   arsit, et inventum est aliquid quod Iuppiter esse

Jupiter's obsession with Ganymede encourages him to be something other than what he is, that is, to undergo a metamorphosis.

arsit: The key verb is in the dramatic first position of the line; the Jovian song of Orpheus will be concerned with the notorious love of the god (cf. also the beginning of the *Aeneid* and the reasons for Juno's anger at the Trojans).

inventum est: Bömer observes that the verb has lost much of its sense and amounts almost to *exsistere;* the force, however, may be deliberately on invention and new discovery, as the love of the god for the Trojan boy sets the tone for a new ethnography, as it were, a new beginning for both Troy and, more distantly, Rome (with attendant problems and difficulties).

157   quam quod erat mallet. nulla tamen alite verti

nulla … alite: Perhaps a sort of ablative of price with *verti; dignari* (158) also takes the ablative.

158   dignatur, nisi quae posset sua fulmina ferre.

Jupiter will consent to be self-transformed into an eagle. The present subjunctives are in a present contrafactual conditional sentence.

sua fulmina: The eagle carries the thunderbolts of Jupiter; the point is in part that the Ganymede story represents something of a perversion of the epic theme of the gigantomachy.

159   nec mora, percusso mendacibus aere pennis

The word order mirrors the action; the air is struck by the false wings.

percusso: To be taken with *aere.*

mendacibus . . . pennis: The wings are false because Jupiter is not really an eagle; the theme of mendacity is once again revisited.

160   abripit Iliaden, qui nunc quoque pocula miscet

Iliaden: "The son of Ilus/Ilos" "Anachronistic," Reed notes, if one follows the version that Ganymede was the son of Tros (so Homer) or of Assaracus (so Hyginus); "not anachronistic" if other versions are followed—but the point here may be that *Iliaden* refers more broadly simply to *Ilium*/Troy. While perhaps overly subtle, there also may be a deliberate divergence from the Homeric genealogy (*Iliad* 5.266–267; 20.231–232) as another example of the falsehood theme that has characterized Orpheus' song. The larger issue, though, is once again the poet's pervasive concern with ethnography; this boy lover of Jupiter is a Trojan, no matter the details of his family tree and lineage.

pocula miscet: Ganymede is the cup-bearer of the immortals, and he is imagined as if he were responsible for mixing the water and wine at divine banquets (i.e., as performing the equivalent service for nectar).

161   invitaque Iovi nectar Iunone ministrat.

Reed offers commentary on the essential apotheosis of Ganymede, who becomes a quasi-divine figure as a result of his abduction by the supreme god.

invitaque: Concessive ("though Juno was willing").

nectar: Ganymede serves the nectar of the immortals; at the end of the book Venus will sprinkle nectar on the blood of her boy lover. There is no explicit hint in Ovid of the Hellenistic tradition that associated the boy lover of Jupiter with the constellation Aquarius.

162–219. *Hyacinthus.* The Ovidian account of this floral metamorphosis is the principal surviving version of an old story; cf. Euripides, *Helen* 1465–1478 (with Allan's commentary notes); Nicander, *Theriaca* 902 ff.; the fragmentary *Hyacinthus* of the playwright Euphorion. On one aspect of the story's *Nachleben* see C. Prince, "Ovid Metamorphosed: The Polymorphous Polphony of Widl/Mozart's *Apollo et Hyacinthus*," in *International Journal of the Classical Tradition* 19.4 (2012), 211–239, a detailed examination of how the Ovidian story was transformed into a masterpiece of the musical arts; the death of Hyacinthus is also a frequent subject in the visual arts, and is often alluded to in poetic contexts that discuss the untimely death of beautiful young men (e.g., Keats' *Endymion* 1.327–331; 4.68–72).

162   Te quoque, Amyclide, posuisset in aethere Phoebus,

Te quoque: For the "pathetic apostrophe" of Hyacinthus see Reed ad loc., and cf. the similar Virgilian address of the doomed Palinurus at *Aeneid* 5.840.

Amyclide: "Son of Amyclus" (a patronymic). "Die ovidische Genealogie ist nicht so kompliziert" (Bömer): the Ovidian genealogy is not so complicated.

posuisset: Pluperfect subjunctive in the apodosis of a past contractual condition.

163   tristia si spatium ponendi fata dedissent.

The Fates are grim, because Hyacinthus will die prematurely; it was the young man's destiny to die young, and so the Fates did not give a space to put aside baleful things (*tristia* as substantive neuter plural).

164   qua licet, aeternus tamen es, quotiensque repellit

qua: "To the extent that" (*OLD s.v.* 5).

165   ver hiemem Piscique Aries succedit aquoso,

The line artfully juxtaposes the seasons and patron zodiac signs: spring-winter; winter-spring. Once again the poet narrator focuses on signs of the seasons and the changing tenor of the year.

hiemem: The word means both winter and the storms that are associated with that season.

Pisci . . . aquoso: "The watery Fish," that is, the constellation Pisces.

166   tu totiens oreris viridique in caespite flores.

tu: See Reed for the virtual metonymy because of the question of the young man's blood, which will be transformed into the signal flower.

viridi: cf. 87, 137.

flores: From *floreo, florere.*

167   te meus ante omnes genitor dilexit, et orbe

meus . . . genitor: Phoebus Apollo.

ante omnes: "Before all others."

168   in medio positi caruerunt praeside Delphi

caruerunt: The verb *carere* takes an ablative of separation, here *praeside*; cf. 246.

169   dum deus Eurotan immunitamque frequentat

Eurotan: The river in Laconia where Sparta was situated.

immunitam: "Unfortified."

170   Sparten. nec citharae nec sunt in honore sagittae;

citharae ... sagittae: The accoutrements of music and archery, two of Apollo's usual activities; once again the poet emphasizes the attributes of Apollo, the god not only of poetry and prophecy but also, above all in the historical context, of the Augustan program (Apollo was seen by the regime as the patron deity of the decisive victory of Octavian over Antony and Cleopatra at Actium).

171   immemor ipse sui non retia ferre recusat,

Bömer's commentary discusses the activities typically associated with the *erastes* and the *eromenos*, the lover and the beloved, in Greek culture.

sui: Expressions of remembering and forgetting regularly take the genitive. The commentators note the traditional problem of the immortals in love, who, like humans, forget themselves amid the distractions of their amatory affair.

retia: "Nets" used in hunting.

172   non tenuisse canes, non per iuga montis iniqui

iuga: "Slopes" or "ridges."

iniqui: The slopes were uneven and rough.

173   ire comes, longaque alit adsuetudine flammas.

longa: Of temporal familiarity, but perhaps also with a hint of how much ground was covered in the extended hunting trips. Apollo succumbs to the sort of risk that Ovid himself might caution against in his *Remedia Amoris*. This is Ovid, too, at his witty best, as the god becomes like some victim of elegiac love.

174   iamque fere medius Titan venientis et actae

cf. 126 above.

Titan: = "The sun," which was associated with the Titan Hyperion.

venientis . . . actae: that is, of the sun's rising and setting.

175   noctis erat spatioque pari distabat utrimque;

utrimque: "On both sides."

176   corpora veste levant et suco pinguis olivi

On this scene see especially Rimell (2006: 119–122), who draws comparison between the eroticized athleticism of the present passage and the description of the race between Atalanta and Hippomenes later in the book that rather balances it.

veste: Another separative ablative.

177   splendescunt latique ineunt certamina disci.

splendescunt: The verb is inchoative (cf. 283 *mollescit*); the suffix-*sco* indicates a coming into a particular state of being.

lati: The subtle note about the broad span/width of the discus may be a harbinger of its potentially deadly nature. The fatal discus is known to Hesiod (*Ehoiai* fr. 171 Merkelbach-West); the idea that the Zephyr was jealous of Apollo's attentions to the boy and caused the discus to swerve and hit Hyacinthus is found in the mythographer Palaephatus (46). See further Gantz (1993: 94). The elision of *latique ineunt* is fitting, as Apollo and Hyacinthus literally enter the contest of the broad discus.

178   quem prius aerias libratum Phoebus in auras

libratum: With the notion of balance cf. the emphasis of 174–175 on the balance of the day; it was *almost* (174 *fere*) noon when Phoebus and Hyacinthus were first introduced for their day of discus throwing; Ovid may be playing on the idea of just missing the mark.

179   misit et oppositas disiecit pondere nubes;

nubes: The clouds need not necessarily portend any sort of storm, metaphorical or otherwise.

pondere: Ablative of means; the clouds are broken by the divinely cast weight of the discus.

180   reccidit in solidam longo post tempore terram

reccidit: cf. 18 *reccidimus*; the verb has grim associations in context; also 10 *occidit*, of Eurydice's death.

solidam: The adjective has special force in context; the ground is solid and hard, and so we shall not be surprised, perhaps, when the discus proves to be a dangerous, indeed fatal toy.

181   pondus et exhibuit iunctam cum viribus artem.

viribus: A subtle foreshadowing of the mortal peril posed by the discus.

artem: cf. 247, of a rather different sort of *ars*.

182   protinus imprudens actusque cupidine lusus

imprudens: Like Cyparissus when he shot his pet deer (130).

cupidine: Ablative of cause.

183   tollere Taenarides orbem properabat; at illum

Taenarides: Taenarus was a promontory in Laconia, and the Spartan Hyacinthus is thus fairly called a "son of Taenarus"—but the more pointed association is to the underworld entrance by which Orpheus had descended in quest for Eurydice (13).

184 dura repercusso subiecit pondere tellus

repercusso … pondere: The text printed is an emendation of Koch for the manuscript reading *repercusso … in aere*; cf. 179. On Ovidian repercussions and reverberations see especially Rimell (2006: 120), with discussion of (*inter al.*) Narcissus' image at 3.434; Perseus' shield as he seeks to destroy Medusa at 4.783. Bömer prefers *dura repercussum subiecit ab aere tellus*, which may be best.

tellus: Reed notes that *tellus* may not mean merely earth, but *rocky* earth (which would make more sense in context), with the observation that in Nicander's *Theriaca* (905–906), it is a rock off of which the fatal discus boomerangs at Hyacinthus.

185 in vultus, Hyacinthe, tuos, expalluit aeque

vultos … tuos: Plural for singular; Hyacinthus is wounded in his especially handsome face, and the loveliness is thus marred by the fatal wound. On the discus' destruction of the "prime signifier of … human identity," see von Glinski (2012; 28).

Hyacinthe: Another "pathetic apostrophe" of a doomed young victim of unforeseen tragedy.

expalluit: With the pallor of death. The prefix can indicate intensity.

186 quam puer ipse deus conlapsosque excipit artus;

The boy is effectively juxtaposed with the "very" (*ipse*) god, who reacts instantly to the freak accident. Reed draws attention to Ovid's condensed imitation of the death scene of Virgil's Euryalus at *Aeneid* 9.434–435; in Virgil, Euryalus is like Ganymede—another Trojan *eromenos*.

quam: Anderson draws attention to 222 below, where the easier *atque* is read, and suspects metrical convenience for the use of *quam* here.

187   et modo te refovet, modo tristia vulnera siccat,

refovet: Apollo tries to "warm up" the boy who is already chill with the onset of death. Bömer notes the compound verb which here is used to emphasize how Apollo keeps trying to rouse Hyacinthus, only to fail again and again in his medical ministrations.

tristia vulnera: Poetic plural. The wounds are "grim" or "sad" because they lead to death, of course, but also because they harm the lovely appearance of Hyacinthus' face (cf. 185), and because they lead to a death that is premature and that comes amid the carefree atmosphere of the game (with its erotically charged environment). With the drying of the wounds Bömer compares Virgil, *Aeneid* 10.834 *vulnera siccabat lymphis.*

188   nunc animam admotis fugientem sustinet herbis.

animam: To be taken closely with *fugientem.*

admotis . . . herbis: Apollo was a god of medicine; the divine master of the healing arts will be unable to render effective medical assistance to his beloved.

sustinet: cf. 47 *sustinet oranti* above, of Persephone in the face of Orpheus' prayer for Eurydice.

189   nil prosunt artes; erat immedicabile vulnus.

nil: An adverbial accusative; the medical arts of the god do not avail him at all in his quest to save Hyacinthus (cf. Orpheus' failure).

artes: cf. 181 *artem;* also 247. Apollo may have thrown the discus with *ars,* but his skills are unable to save his favorite.

190   ut, si quis violas riguoque papavera in horto

Ovid prepares for the revelation of the metamorphosis of Hyacinthus;
the brief catalog of flowers reminds one of the forest of trees that had
come to listen to Orpheus' songs.

quis: For *aliquis* (after *si*).

papavera: The poppy. There may be a reference to Virgil, *Aeneid* 4.486
spargens umida mella soporiferumque papavera; the poppy carries
associations of the soporific nature of death, and also (as Reed notes)
has *medicinal* properties, thus creating a sort of tragic irony as the
young man succumbs to his fatal wound.

riguo ... horto: cf. 8.646; 13.797. See Reed here for attempts at
disentangling the complicated intertextual history of the Hyacinthine/
floral metamorphosis imagery from Homer to Virgil.

riguo: "Watered/irrigated."

191   liliaque infringat fulvis horrentia linguis,

liliaque: cf. 212. Reed notes the evocation of the Virgilian Marcellus
passage at *Aeneid* 6.883—yet another prematurely deceased young
man, and one of particular interest to the Augustan succession question;
for Virgil, the archaic imagery of these tragic youths is employed in the
service of exploring the question of how the new political regime had
significant difficulty in ensuring a succession to the principate.

infringat: Present subjunctive in a future less vivid conditional
sentence.

fulvis: "Tawny." This is the first of seven occurrences of the color in this
book (cf. 551; 648 x2; 698; 716; 733). It is applied here in association
with the dead Hyacinthus; later it is used of lions (in conjunction with
Venus' concern for Adonis and his hunting habits); of the apples that

are used by Hippomenes to snare the lovely runner Atalanta; of the
sand (716 *harena*) where Adonis dies (the "arena" connects Adonis'
death scene with the preceding race sequence); of the sky where the
mysterious *bulla* rises in the simile that describes the rise of the Adonis-
anemone. The first and last occurrences, then, are in direct association
with the premature death of young men who were beloved of the
immortals (first in a homosexual union, then in a heterosexual). The
second and second-to-last uses are connected to Venus' concern for
her beloved and his eventual death despite her warnings. The middle
three uses of the sevenfold chromatic progression relate to Atalanta's
seduction and the leonine metamorphosis that provides the climax to
the story; in some sense the yellow apples that win Hippomenes his
beloved will be replaced by the yellow manes of the lions that his
victory will indirectly engender. See further here R. Edgeworth, *The
Colors of the Aeneid*, New York: Peter Lang, (1992), 130–132, with
detailed discussion of the relevant colors. In Virgil the color has
associations with (Roman, in particular) ethnography (cf. Virgil,
Aeneid 1.275, of the pelt of the Romulean she-wolf; 2.722, of the lion
skin that Aeneas uses to shoulder Anchises; 12.792, of the cloud from
which Jupiter addresses Juno before the great revelation of Rome's
Italian future; also 11.776, of the brooch of yellow gold that Chloreus
wears that helps to tempt a distracted Camilla to pursue him to her
doom) as well as the underworld (6.643, of the tawny sand of Elysium).

horrentia: Reed draws attention to the anatomical metaphor of how
the word describes the bristling of hair. *Horrentia* is, however, a
conjecture (or, one might say, correction) of the manuscript reading
haerentia (Reed compares the anemone that ends the book at 731).

192   marcida demittant subito caput illa gravatum

marcida: "Drooping." The dying flower image in Virgil's *Aeneid*
was used to describe the loss of Euryalus (9.433–437) and Pallas
(11.68–72); the ultimate origin of these passages is Homer's description

of the death of Gorgythion, the son of Priam (*Iliad* 8.306 ff.). See further von Glinski (2012: 27), for additional reflection on the whole problem.

subito: The death happened exceedingly quickly; Hyacinthus had gone pale in death as soon as Apollo rushed to help him, and his head has fallen on his neck with stunning swiftness.

gravatum: The heavy word comes hard and heavy at the end of verse; the Marcian manuscript has *quietum*. It is possible that the textual questions (admittedly not particularly serious) of these verses on the floral metamorphosis reflect something of the extensive intertextual imagery of the flower imagery, where a scribe might remember other passages while copying the Ovidian text.

193   nec se sustineant spectentque cacumine terram,

Reed compares the cypress of 140, rather an opposite arboreal reality.

cacumine: Ablative of means: the flowers would look at the ground with their heads.

194   sic vultus moriens iacet, et defecta vigore

vigore: Ablative of specification.

195   ipsa sibi est oneri cervix umeroque recumbit.

sibi … oneri: The double dative, with the reflexive as a dative of reference and the *oneri* as a dative of purpose. The synaloepha or merging of two syllables into one may help to enact the terrible image of how the neck wilts, as it were, onto the shoulder as it proves to be a burden to itself.

196   laberis, Oebalide, prima fraudate iuventa

Reed compares the lament of Apollo here with that of Venus near the end of the book for *her* ill-fated *eromenos*, the doomed Adonis; in the

Ovidian rendering of that love affair, the goddess rather engages in a playacting of Diana, Apollo's divine sister—immortal twins of special significance to the Augustan program—exactly as she did in Virgil's *Aeneid* 1, before the introduction of Dido (who is also compared to Diana, and problematically so).

laberis: Reed notes the use of the same verb to describe the loss of Procris at 11.859—a story, as aforementioned, that has parallels to the Cyparissus tale from earlier in this book; also the death of Virgil's Camilla (*Aeneid* 11.818). The address to Hyacinthus constitutes another pathetic apostrophe; the patronymic has special force in light of the topos of the great tragedy of fathers outliving sons and parents living to know of the death of their children.

Oebalide: Oebalus was a Spartan king.

fraudate: With a type of separative ablative (*prima . . . iuventa*).

197   Phoebus ait, videoque tuum, mea crimina, vulnus.

mea crimina: Cf. the apparent attitude of Orpheus after the death of Eurydice; Apollo blames himself directly for the fatal accident; also 200–201, lines that Merkel proposed for deletion. The juxtaposition of the possessive adjectives is especially fitting in the context of the love affair and the very different fates of god and mortal.

198   tu dolor es facinusque meum; mea dextera leto

dolor: Bömer compares Virgil, *Aeneid* 10.507 *o dolor atque decus*, of Pallas—a likely inspiration for the present lament.

facinus: The primary meaning is any sort of deed or event; the secondary sense (as here) is a crime, indeed often an especially outrageous one.

leto: A poetic word for death.

199   inscribenda tuo est; ego sum tibi funeris auctor.

inscribenda: Gerundive; the right hand "must be inscribed" with your death. The gerundive regularly expresses obligation or necessity.

funeris: First *mea crimina*; then *dolor/facinus*; now *funeris*: something of a tricolon of self-recrimination.

auctor: cf. 214 *auctor honoris.*

200   quae mea culpa tamen? nisi si lusisse vocari

Merkel deleted this line and the next as interpolations; Tarrant (2004) also brackets them as likely spurious, though ultimately the question is subjective.

lusisse: This game has ended rather violently. There may be a play on the idea of *ludus* in reference to poetic composition (cf. Catullus and the neoteric ideal); this metapoetic sense may be especially appropriate given that Apollo was the patron god of verse.

201   culpa potest, nisi culpa potest et amasse vocari.

The perhaps awkward repetitions may be exactly the language one expects from the grief-stricken. For the sentiments cf. the change of mind of Myrrha at 323 below.

amasse: For *amavisse*, the perfect infinitive active.

202   atque utinam pro te vitam tecumve liceret

Reed compares the Virgilian situation of the divine Juturna with her doomed brother Turnus; the sentiment is also not unlike the problem explored by Euripides in the *Hippolytus*, where Artemis is unable to appreciate fully the all too mortal situation of her ill-fated servant. See further Reed's detailed catalog of parallel passages (Greek and Latin) of other immortals left to lament that they cannot die; cf., too, Orpheus' sentiments to the underworld deities about his determination to remain in Avernus if he cannot have Eurydice.

utinam: Introduces a wish, the verb of which (*liceret*) is in the imperfect subjunctive to denote that the hope is incapable of fulfillment in present time.

203　　reddere! quod quoniam fatali lege tenemur,

reddere: Reed compares *Fasti* 5.469 and 6.745, and notes that the verb takes an implied object of *animam*; given the "Orphic" narration there may be a hint of the idea of the surrender of the soul and the possibility of its rebirth in another body (in this case, the flower?).

fatali lege: The *fatalis lex* is the law of fate/destiny, by which one is more or a less a puppet of what has already been determined—and where the salient question is whether or not one knows one's predetermined fate (ignorance of which can provide the illusion of free will). Reed compares 3.316; Virgil, *Aeneid* 12.819. cf., too, the law by which Orpheus was given the chance to return Eurydice to the upper world.

tenemur: cf. 18 *quidquid mortale creamur*.

204　　semper eris mecum memorique haerebis in ore.

memori . . . ore: Reed notes the presentation of Apollo here as a poetic god, one who tells a story (in this case likely an elegiac composition) in verse. The synaloepha of *memoroque haerebis* neatly enacts the clinging connection that will exist between Apollo and his lover.

haerebis in ore: Perhaps with a hint of erotic attachment; for *ore* cf. 209.

205　　te lyra pulsa manu, te carmina nostra sonabunt,

Merkel deleted this and the next three verses.

te ... te: Bömer draws attention to the "pathetische Anapher" or "pathetic anaphora," as the death youth is lamented by the heartbroken god of music and the arts.

206   flosque novus scripto gemitus imitabere nostros.

flos ... novus: In apposition to the understood "you" of the verb *imitabere*.

imitabere: For *imitaberis*. On the passive nature of the inscription and metamorphosis of Hyacinthus, see von Glinski (2012: 30).

207   tempus et illud erit, quo se fortissimus heros

fortissimus heros: Ajax. The idea behind Merkel's deletion of these verses is the suspicion that they were interpolated *after* the later Ovidian narrative of the metamorphosis of Ajax (13.394 ff.).

208   addat in hunc florem folioque legatur eodem.

Hyacinthus is hereby associated with the great hero Ajax, second only to Achilles in the hierarchy of Greek heroes.

209   talia dum vero memorantur Apollinis ore,

ore: cf. 204. The emphasis once again may be on the idea of Apollo as a poetic patron and composer of verse.

210   ecce cruor, qui fusus humo signaverat herbas,

cruor: Repeated at 211; the focus is on the blood that will be the material for the miraculous memorial metamorphosis.

fusus humo: cf. Virgil, *Aeneid* 5.330.

herbas: The verdant setting is now stained with gore; soon enough the mar of the blood will be transformed into a flower that perpetuates the memory of the dead youth.

211   desinit esse cruor, Tyrioque nitentior ostro

Tyrio: "Tyrian," that is, from the region of Tyre and Sidon in Phoenicia. cf. 267 *Sidonide.* The connection to Tyre—the home of Virgil's Dido—adds to the ethnographic flavor; this flower shines more brightly than the purple of that storied land. In Virgil's underworld, Dido's shade is explicitly associated with Homer's Ajax in the Odyssean underworld; there may be a deliberate evocation of Dido here after the mention of Ajax's own forthcoming floral metamorphosis.

nitentior: "More gleaming"; the adjective provides another instance of the recurring theme to the book, a theme that reaches its climax when Atalanta is seduced by the *nitor* of the golden apples.

212   flos oritur formamque capit quam lilia, si non

With this verse cf. 735, of the similar circumstance of Adonis' *post mortem* floral transformation.

lilia: cf. 191; 262. The evocation of Marcellus is likely once again the point of the mention of the flower here.

213   purpureus color his, argenteus esset in illis.

purpureus: The color has funereal associations.

argenteus: "Silvery." cf. 114, where it was used of the *bulla* that Cyparissus' deer wore.

214   non satis hoc Phoebo est (is enim fuit auctor honoris)

Phoebo: Perhaps with special reference to the meaning "bright/ shining," in light of the color imagery of the preceding verse.

auctor honoris: Cf. 199 *funeris auctor*; the question of whether or not the god was responsible for the death of the young boy has been transformed into the question of his engendering of the memorializing of his *quondam* lover.

215   ipse suos gemitus foliis inscribitur et AI AI

AI AI: An expression of grief, which could be associated with the first syllable of the Ajax's name (*Ai-ax*). *Aiai* spells out the vocative of *Aias*.

216   flos habet inscriptum funestaque littera ducta est.

ducta est: The letter was "drawn out," as it were, on the flower.

217   nec genuisse pudet Sparten Hyacinthon honorque

nec ... pudet: Sparta is not ashamed to have been the birthplace of Hyacinthus; it is possible that there may be intentional humor implied in the mention of both the Homeric hero Ajax and Sparta in conjunction with the *eromenos* Hyacinthus. The verb *pudet* is impersonal.

Hyacinthon: The form equals a Greek accusative.

218   durat in hoc aevi celebrandaque more priorum

aevi: A sort of partitive genitive.

celebrandra: The future passive participle/gerundive/passive periphrastic expressing obligation or necessity.

219   annua praelata redeunt Hyacinthia pompa.

redeunt: "Return," that is, in the regular cycle of stars and seasons, the turning of the year.

Hyacinthia: A festival in honor of the youth. For the festival see Flower and Marincola on Herodotus 9.7.1 ("The festival lasted three days, and usually take place in early summer.") For the pervasive influence of ritual festivals on the Orphic narrative of Book 10, see Feldherr

(2010: 271), with consideration of how Ovid devotes significant attention to describing such religious and liturgical events in the present book; the humorous poet thus draws a contrast between the world of solemn spiritual observance and the less than sacred, indeed profane acts often described in the book.

praelata ... pompa: Again, the scansion reveals that this phrase is ablative.

220–243. *The Cerastae and the Propoetides.* Two myths are briefly mentioned/alluded to in closely related succession.

220		At si forte roges fecundam Amathunta metallis

fecundam ... metallis: "Rich in metals." Cyprus was renowned for copper (cf. Cyprus/*cuprum*—Bömer) as well as silver and lead; it was a center of the bronze making industry.

Amathunta: Greek accusative; Amathus was in Cyprus. For Amathus see Harrison on Virgil, *Aeneid* 10.51.

221		an genuisse velit Propoetidas, abnuat aeque

The transition to the next tale of metamorphosis comes with the reactions of certain lands to those born in its environs.

Propoetidas: The name, as Reed notes ad loc., does not occur in extant Greek.

abnuat aeque: "Would equally deny." The subjunctives *roges* and *abnuat* are both present tense in a future less vivid conditional sentence.

222		atque illos, gemino quondam quibus aspera cornu

Two stories are announced: the Propoetides and the Cerastae; both will be told quite briefly, as Ovid transitions to his main concerns.

atque illos: Bömer notes the "brachylogy" or shortened expression; once again, the emphasis is on rapid narrative, and the elision speeds the mention of the "horned ones" Cyprus wishes that it had never produced.

223   frons erat; unde etiam nomen traxere Cerastae.

Cerastae: From the Greek for "horns"; the *cerastes* was the horned serpent, the asp (*Cerastes cornutus*, a somewhat tautological name). *Cerastae* is properly the plural of a Greek masculine singular *Cerastes*, and so one could argue from the historical morphology that *women per se* are not implied by the name—though given the theme of the Orphic song, and the prostitution of the Propoetides, it is possible that women are indeed supposed to be envisaged here.

nomen traxere: A periphrasis for *nominari*, as Bömer notes here. But there may be a point too that the Cerastae have drawn onto themselves not only a name, but also the transformational consequences it implies.

224   ante fores horum stabat Iovis Hospitis ara,

Iovis Hospitis: Jupiter as special protector and patron of hospitality. cf. the shocking revelation of 228 *hospes erat caesus.*

225   ignarus sceleris quam si quis sanguine tinctam

The verse suffers from a difficult textual transmission (Bömer prints *inlugubri celeri* in daggers). *Ignarus sceleris* is an emendation of Madvig for the muddled tradition, and offers probably the best sense possible.

226   advena vidisset, mactatos crederet illic

vidisset . . . crederet: A mixed condition.

227   lactentes vitulos Amathusiacasque bidentes;

Four-word hexameters are not particularly common.

bidentes: Usually applied to sheep destined for sacrifice.

228   hospes erat caesus! sacris offensa nefandis

A neat Ovidian surprise: the one who marveled at the blood on the altar of Jupiter *Hospes* did not realize that the blood was that of the *hospes.*

sacris … offendis: "Sacred things that must not be spoken of": the sacred rites in honor of Jupiter Hospes have been profaned in the most terrible way imaginable.

229   ipsa suas urbes Ophiusiaque arva parabat

ipsa suas: Fittingly the goddess and the reflexive possessive adjective that identifies her haunts are linked closely together. cf. 277 *ipsa suis.*

Ophiusia: That is, Cypriot.

parabat: Probably with inceptive force; Venus was preparing to leave her beloved island. The language underscores the goddess' close connection to Cyprus (*ipsa, suas*).

230   deserere alma Venus, sed quid loca grata, quid urbes

alma: An appropriate epithet for the goddess who is about to express concern for the lands she frequents. The most immediate intertextual echo is of Lucretius, *De Rerum Natura* 1.2, from the proem to the beginning of the poet's didactic epic—another ethnographic reference to the mother of the *Aeneadae,* that is, the Romans.

loca grata: "Pleasing places," that is, those the goddess frequents as her favorite haunts.

231   peccavere meae? quod dixit crimen in illis?

peccavere: Third person plural perfect indicative active.

crimen in illis: Cf. the similar sentiments of 7.794.

232   exilio poenam potius gens impia pendat

gens impia: Perhaps inspired by Virgil, *Georgic* 2.537.

pendat: The basic meaning of the verb is to weigh something in the scales; from this root sense comes the idea of paying something out, indeed in paying a penalty.

233   vel nece vel si quid medium est mortisque fugaeque.

The situation is not dissimilar to that of Book 1, where Jupiter was threatened with the ultimate violation of hospitality by Lycaon.

quid: For *aliquid.*

medium … mortisque fugaeque: The recurring Ovidian theme of how metamorphosis occupies a special (and often terrible) place midway between death and life, as it were. The language is interesting; there is a middle ground, Venus argues, between death and exile—she need not either kill the offenders or drive them from her beloved island. What will really happen is something that will confuse the line between life and death.

234   idque quid esse potest, nisi versae poena figurae?

A line of significance in appreciating the Ovidian philosophy of metamorphosis and transformation; it is a middle ground between exile from what one was and the death of that prior existence.

235   dum dubitat quo mutet eos, ad cornua vultum

quo: "How" or "into what" (she should change them). Bömer's commentary compares 157 and 494.

mutet: Subjunctive in an indirect question.

236   flexit et admonita est haec illis posse relinqui;

flexit: Venus suddenly turned to the horns and conjured an idea for a fitting metamorphosis.

haec: that is, the horns.

illis: Dative of reference with possessive force.

posse relinqui: Infinitive in indirect discourse with *relinqui* as complementary infinitive after *posse*.

237   grandiaque in torvos transformat membra iuvencos.

torvos: The basic meaning is anything that is grim or stern; the adjective can be applied equally to mortals or animals (also of events and occurrences).

transformat: The verb is not common in the *Metamorphoses*; cf. 13.654; 14.74; the adjective *transformia* at 8.871.

238   sunt tamen obscenae Venerem Propoetides ausae

obscenae: A strong adjective, denoting foul and shameful qualities. What is interesting is that the Propoetides are explicitly condemned for having denied Venus' godhood; they are not charged with any particular sexual perversion or crime. The punishment they receive for their blasphemy, in fact, is what may very well prompt sordid and perverse acts.

239   esse negare deam; pro quo sua numinis ira

pro quo: that is, for the denial of the divinity of the goddess. The reaction of Venus to the Propoetides distantly presages the goddess' anger at Hippomenes when he fails to thank her for her assistance in securing the love of Atalanta.

240 corpora cum forma primae vulgasse feruntur;

vulgasse: "To prostitute one's body" (*OLD s.v.* 1b). The Propoetides become the first prostitutes; somewhat appropriately, one might think, prostitution is born on the island that is associated with the goddess of love and sexuality. The form is a syncopation of *vulgavisse* that is metrically convenient.

feruntur: "Are said" (as often).

241 utque pudor cessit sanguisque induruit oris,

induruit: Perfect of *indurescere*; the verb means to begin to become hard or robust; to begin to become set in one's ways, as it were. It is not certain what precisely Ovid means by his description of what happened to the blood of the prostitutes' faces; it may refer to a lack of the shame that would have engendered blushing; cf. Pygmalion's living statue at 293. The theme will also recur in the matter of Myrrha's arboreal transformation; cf. too the mention of petrifaction at the beginning of the book.

242 in rigidum parvo silicem discrimine versae.

parvo . . . discrimine: Ablative of degree of difference. cf. 517; 612.

243–297. *Pygmalion.* Once again, Ovid's account has become the canonical version; it may have been the subject of a third century B.C. telling by Philostephanus. Pygmalion is attested as a Cypriot monarch (so, e.g., the fragmentary historian Hellanicus); the name also appears in Virgil's *Aeneid* as the Tyrian king and brother of Dido who is responsible for Sychaeus' death and her departure for the site of the future Carthage (and there were different traditions here, as indicated by Servius' commentary on *Aeneid* 1.363)—another subtle "appearance" of the spirit of Carthage's queen in this book. Among items in a rich bibliography see here especially D. Bauer, "The Function of Pygmalion in the *Metamorphoses* of Ovid," in *Transactions of the American*

Philological Association 93 (1962), 1–21; J. Elsner and A. Sharrock, "Reviewing Pygmalion," in *Ramus* 20 (1991), 149–153; J. Elsner, "Visual Mimesis and the Myth of the Real: Ovid's Pygmalion as Viewer," in *Ramus* 20 (1991), 154–168—the last two with consideration of Ovid's verbal portrayal of the realm of the visual arts. It is difficult to determine what etymological significance the name may have had to Ovid (and see Bömer's commentary here for some inconclusive speculation).

243   quas quia Pygmalion aevum per crimen agentes

aevum: The space of their lives.

per crimen: Like Orpheus, Pygmalion shuns the company of women; the announced theme of Orpheus' song—the inappropriate loves of women—is here alluded to in passing; the actual story does not fit the declared plan of the Orphic program. In one sense the Pygmalion story offers a variation on the theme of the Iphis/Ianthe tale that ended Book 9; the love of the sculptor for his statue cannot be consummated, and thus immortal intervention will be necessary to permit the love to reach fruition.

244   viderat, offensus vitiis quae plurima menti

plurima: The superlative introduces a subtle but important (and dramatic) expansion of the alleged catalog of female crimes. The antecedent of *quae plurima—vitiis*; Pygmalion was offended by the many vices that nature gave to the feminine/woman's mind.

menti: The noun can mean "intention"; there may be a hint that women are culpable because they intend with full power of the mind and will to commit the misdeeds with which the narrator Orpheus charges them.

245   femineae natura dedit, sine coniuge caelebs

A primer in misogyny; Pygmalion, as we have seen, is offended by the very many vices that nature (perhaps to be capitalized) has allegedly bestowed on the feminine mind. It is important to remember that *Orpheus* is the singer of the Pygmalion song; the lover of Eurydice has embraced the erotic pursuit of boys and has now assumed a negative attitude toward women in general.

coniuge caelebs: Cf. the similar alliterative effect at the end of 246. Another pleonastic or somewhat repetitive expression, as Bömer notes in his commentary; the poet's point is to underscore the celibacy of his central character.

246   vivebat thalamique diu consorte carebat.

carebat: For the verb cf. 168; it takes an ablative of separation. The imperfects that frame the line are likely durative; Pygmalion continued to live his life as the years went by absent from any association with the women he considered offensive for their lifestyle choices.

247   interea niveum mira feliciter arte

niveum: Cf. 138; 247; 272. The adjective agrees with 248 *ebur.* The color here conveys a sense of purity and innocence; the statue is the virtual antithesis of the real women of the island whose company Pygmalion has shunned. Orpheus, too, has shunned the company of women; the two stories will end quite differently.

arte: A new sort of *ars* is introduced: that of sculpture. *Mira* implies an art that is to be marveled at, an object of renown and splendid, breathtaking achievement.

248   sculpsit ebur formamque dedit, qua femina nasci

The first hint that one of the faults Pygmalion might see in women is that none are as beautiful as that which he can create with marble and chisel.

249   nulla potest, operisque sui concepit amorem.

The stories of the Propoetides and the Cerastae formed something of
a pendant to that of Hyacinthus; now the former of those appended
tales leads to that of Pygmalion. But none of the lore Ovid's Orpheus
relates has much of anything to do with his avowed subjects of boys
loved by the immortals and women given over to forbidden passions.

operis sui ... amorem: "A love of his own work"—a love that in this
case is taken to rather extreme extremes.

concepit amorem: Bömer's commentary compares 5.446, and notes
that *amorem concipere* does not recur again until Fronto; part of the
point of the likely novel expression may be that Pygmalion is depicted
as a *model for incest:* he gave birth to the statue, and he will conceive
of a passionate love for his *daughter*, so that he is indeed a true ancestor
for Myrrha, who will reverse the pattern and long for sexual union
with her father. *Concepit* has deliberate shades of the idea of conception
and birth.

250   virginis est verae facies, quam vivere credas

virginis: The emphasis on implied contrast with other women
continues. The genitive expresses a characteristic of the statue's face; it
was that of a true virgin, a living girl. The line has marked alliteration
(*virginis ... verae ... vivere*), which creates the effect of a spell or
charm as the loveliness of the strikingly "real" statue is described.

credas: The subjunctive expresses potentiality, even if one takes it
strictly as present subjunctive in the apodosis of a future less vivid
condition.

vivere: Bömer highlights the rhetorical commonplace of art that is so
vividly realistic that you are led to believe that it really does live, that
it is not a mere imitation of life.

251   et, si non obstet reverentia, velle moveri;

reverentia: Elswhere in the *Metamorphoses* at 2.510; 7.146; 7.609; 9.123; 9.428; 9.556. The word has interesting force in the present context; it can mean shyness or any kind of reserve about something (*OLD s.v.* 2); given the recent discussion of the relationship between Venus and the blasphemous Propoetides, however, it also established Pygmalion as secure in his attitude toward the immortals.

252   ars adeo latet arte sua. miratur et haurit

The opening sentiment of the verse could be used of Ovid's own craft in "concealing" *his* work in the work of Orpheus by narrative game. This is the poet at his playful best, as he draws metapoetic connections between his work and other manifestations of the creative arts.

adeo: "To such a degree" (*OLD s.v.* 4).

miratur: Again, with an emphasis on the wonder that the *objet d'art* engenders in its creator/lover.

haurit: The metaphor inherent to the verb is one of quaffing down a liquid; cf. the English idiom of "drinking something in" *vel sim.*

253   pectore Pygmalion simulati corporis ignes.

simulati corporis: "Of a simulated body."

ignes: Rather different from the fires we were told to expect (154 *ignibus*). Here the celibate Pygmalion finds himself lost in a world that is very different from his previous monastic existence; the implications are onanistic.

254   saepe manus operi temptantes admovet, an sit

operi: Dative; the sculptor moves his hands to or toward his work.

temptantes: "Testing."

an: Introducing an alternative question; Pygmalion is testing whether the statue is a body or ivory.

255   corpus an illud ebur, nec adhuc ebur esse fatetur,

The statue is in something like the condition that Venus had wished for those who had offended her: not entirely one thing or another.

256   oscula dat reddique putat loquiturque tenetque

Tarrant brackets this line as a possible interpolation. The repeated connective enclitics serve to underscore the repetitious, obsessive nature of the sculptor's near veneration of his work of art.

257   sed credit tactis digitos insidere membris

The language is eroticized, as Bömer observes here in his commentary; the tone is in the high style, as the rather solipsistic Pygmalion engages in a relationship with either himself or his child, depending on one's point of view.

sed: Tarrant's suggestion for the manuscript *et*, thus creating a contrast with the sentiment of 255 that Pygmalion no longer believes his creation to be ivory.

258   et metuit pressos veniat ne livor in artus.

veniat: Present subjunctive in a fear clause.

livor: Pygmalion treats the statue as if it/she were capable of receiving a black and blue mark from the repeated manhandling it experiences at the hands of its/her creator/lover.

in artus: In or on the limbs.

259   et modo blanditias adhibet, modo grata puellis

blanditias: "Blandishments," that is, spoken words of flattery and seduction; the word is almost a technical term for erotic exchanges. Here Ovid borrows from the language of elegy; Pygmalion is depicted as if he were an elegiac poet seeking to seduce his *puella,* for whom he will now be described as bearing the classic presents of the elegiac lover.

grata: With 260 *munera*; Pygmalion is like a classic elegiac lover who brings presents that are designed to win the favor of his *domina.*

260   munera fert illi, conchas teretesque lapillos

teretes: "Smooth."

conchas: "Shells," a common enough commodity in Cyprus. Ovid may be consciously imitating Propertius, c. 1.8.39 ff. here, but the language is commonplace enough for elegiac descriptions of a desirous suitor.

261   et parvas volucres et flores mille colorum

parvas volucres: A standard gift of the *amator*; cf. the sparrow of Catullus' Lesbia.

flores: A connection to the story of Hyacinthus; the effect of such little details is to help in the crafting of a cohesive overall narrative.

mille colorum: Also at 11.589, of the colors that Iris masters as goddess of the rainbow.

262   liliaque pictasque pilas et ab arbore lapsas

lilia: Cf. 191; 212.

pila: The first syllable is short; the word = a ball, especially an ornamental or decorative sort of toy. *Pila* could also be used specifically of a ball of cloth made to provoke animals in the arena (*OLD s.v.* 1b), though there is probably no connection to that use here (cf. the luring of Atalanta later in the book).

263   Heliadum lacrimas. ornat quoque vestibus artus;

Pygmalion goes so far as to dress the statue; there is perhaps a more lighthearted, comic element to the description, though there is also the darker sense of the behavior of the obsessed and something of the spirit of what we might expect from the world of horror cinema—the sculptor treats his work as if it were a human being.

Heliadum lacrimas: that is, amber. The reference is once again to the sisters of Phaethon, who were transformed into poplars, their tears into amber. *Heliadum* = genitive plural; they and their ill-fated brother were children of the sun (Greek *Helios*).

264   dat digitis gemmas, dat longa monilia collo,

The adornment is somewhat reminiscent of what was done for the doomed deer of the Cyparissus story. Repetitions, both verbal and thematic, serve often in Latin verse to draw together a narrative more tightly and create added coherence; on the vast subject of repetition (cf. 265 *bacae*), see J. Wills, *Repetition in Latin Poetry*, Oxford (1996).

265   aure leves bacae, redimicula pectore pendent.

bacae: Cf. the deer's earrings at 116.

redimicula: The verb *redimere* means "to encircle"; the noun refers to a sort of band, usually attached to the back of a woman's head covering, which would hang down over the shoulders, back and/or chest.

266   cuncta decent; nec nuda minus formosa videtur.

decent: The verb has only third person forms.

nec nuda . . .: Another elegiac topos; Pygmalion's statue looks beautiful and appears lovely whether clothed or nude. Propertius, c. 1.2.8 *nudus Amor formae non amat artificem* is the classic passage; the mention of the nudity of the statue just before Orpheus describes how Pygmalion sets his artwork to rest on its bed heightens the eroticized tenor of the passage.

267   conlocat hanc stratis concha Sidonide tinctis

The statue is not only dressed, but the artist puts it to bed as well.

concha: The word could be used in particular of the purple-fish or *murex*; also of the shell on which Venus is said to have been wafted to the island of Cyprus after her birth.

Sidonide: cf. 211 *Tyrio*; once again there is a faint hint of the significance of things Tyrian in light of Virgil's *Aeneid*.

268   appellatque tori sociam acclinataque colla

appellat: Ovid never actually names the statue, either ivory or alive; later tradition gives the name Galatea.

tori sociam: cf. 8.521; 10.246 *thalami consors*.

colla: Another poetic plural.

269   mollibus in plumis tamquam sensura reponit.

plumis: "Feathers," as in, the stuffing of the cushions. The infant Adonis will be placed carefully on *molles herbae* by Naiads after his birth from the myrrh tree. Pygmalion is worried about the comfort of his work of art; there is a deliberate contrast between the hardness of the marble and the soft cushions of the bed.

tamquam sensura: "As if she were about the sense/feel . . ." *Sensura* is a future participle active, in agreement with an understood *socia*.

270   festa dies Veneris tota celeberrima Cypro

festa dies: cf. 431, of the rather different circumstance of the Ceres festival during the Myrrha episode. The present book has something of a calendar-like progression; celebrations in honor of the two goddesses, and an allusion to the rituals of the Adonis liturgy, are important features of the narrative. The two festivals for the goddesses will both be marked by a variety of incest, in the present case actively aided and abetted by the deity in whose honor the festival is held. (The incest theme of Book 10 may connect, too, to the abduction of Proserpina in Book 5, with the problem of the erotic relationship of uncle and niece).

tota: With *Cypro*; islands are regularly of feminine gender.

271   venerat, et pandis inductae cornibus aurum

cornibus: The emphasis on the horns of the sacrificial victims connects the Pygmalion story with the preceding tale of the Cerastae. The ablative is descriptive.

aurum: The so-called Greek accusative. The horns of the sacrificial victim are gilded to make the animal more appealing to the goddess. We might contrast the deer of Cyparissus; this animal has not garlands for playful arrangement on its horns, but gilding to mark it as sacred and ready for the knife of the priest.

272   conciderant ictae nivea cervice iuvencae.

nivea: cf. 138 and 247. The color once again carries connotations of purity and innocence (as would be fitting for a sacrificial offering); there is also the attendant idea of the pallor of death. The ablative is once again descriptive (the animals have snow-white necks); there is also a sense of location—they were struck (*ictae*) in the neck by the sacrificial blade. The reference to the sacrifices at the festival reminds the audience of the story of the Cerastae; the Pygmalion story is very different in that the "hero" behaves appropriately in relation to the goddess, but if the subtext is one of incest (especially as the poet prepares for the main narrative of his book, the sordid tale of Pygmalion's descendant Myrrha), then the subtle point may be the same question of hospitality and the violation of laws related to a *hospes*.

273   turaque fumabant, cum munere functus ad aras

cum ... functus: The so-called *cum inversum* construction.

munere: Ablative with a form of *fungi*. The *munus* here is the duty of a worshiper at the festival; Pygmalion is no Hippolytus and renders the due service to the goddess despite his disgust at the behavior of the women of the island. In this disgust he shares something of a view with Venus, at least insofar as her reaction to the behavior of the Propoetides.

274   constitit et timide si, di, dare cuncta potestis,

timide: Pygmalion is consistently presented as a shy artist, a depiction that has been preserved in some of the artistic receptions of the story.

si, di: The opening words of the prayer of the timid supplicant are uttered monosyllabically and hauntingly.

275   sit coniunx, opto, non ausus eburnea virgo

sit ... opto: The language of Pygmalion's entreaty continues to be simple and unaffected.

276   dicere Pygmalion similis mea dixit eburnae.

eburnae: Dative after *similis*. The ivory is significant as more than the raw material for the sculpting of Pygmalion's statue girl. Ivory is also

associated with the Virgilian Gate of False Dreams from the close of
Aeneid 6, and indeed there is a certain element of falsehood in the
Pygmalion story: it does not fit the promised themes of Orpheus'
song. No boy loved by the immortals, and no woman possessed of an
irrational passion here; in an important sense, the only successful
union of *Metamorphoses* 10 is the love of the sculptor for his sculpture,
of the artist for his art. The happy couple, of course, will produce a line
that leads to Myrrha.

277   sensit, ut ipsa suis aderat Venus aurea festis

ipsa suis: cf. 229 *ipsa suas.* The emphasis throughout is on Venus'
possession of the island and the propriety of the worship conducted
there in her honor; this emphasis ties in with Pygmalion's possessive
control of his statue/daughter.

aurea: cf. 230 *alma;* Venus is especially fit to be called "golden" on her
most important festival. Venus is as golden as the horns of the animal
that was slaughtered in her honor.

278   vota quid illa velint et, amici numinis omen,

velint: Subjunctive in an indirect question.

amici numinis: "Of a friendly divine power." The theme of the *omen*
returns; in the present case, the immortal intervention is a blessed
event, though the union of Pygmalion and his vivified statue will lead
directly to the tragedy of Myrrha.

279   flamma ter accensa est apicemque per aera duxit.

flamma ... accensa: cf. Virgil, *Aeneid* 7.74–75.

apicem: From *apex, apicis.*

aera: Greek accusative. The *aer* is the lower air of mortals, in contrast
to the heavenly *aether* that is the proper abode of the immortals.

280   ut rediit, simulacra suae petit ille puellae

ut: "When" or "after" (with the indicative).

simulacra: The language subtly foreshadows the imminent metamorphosis; the statue is now a *simulacrum* of the girl who is his. cf. 14.

281   incumbensque toro dedit oscula; visa tepere est.

tepere: "To become warm." The present bedroom scene stands in striking contrast to the forthcoming encounters of Myrrha and her father during the festival of Ceres.

282   admovet os iterum, manibus quoque pectora temptat;

temptat: "Tests" or "explores." The poet repeatedly emphasizes the notion of touching and testing throughout the story; the language is of course fitting to describe the work of a sculptor.

283   temptatum mollescit ebur positoque rigore

mollescit: The ivory "begins to become soft" (inchoative verb; cf. 177 *splendescunt*; 285 *remollescit*).

positoque rigore: Literally, "and with its hardness having been put aside."

284   subsedit digitis ceditque, ut Hymettia sole

subsedit: The verb can be used of the sexual position adopted by female animals (*OLD s.v.* 1c); there may be intentionally obscene undertones. cf. 498.

Hymettia: Mount Hymettus was near Athens; the locus is celebrated for honey.

285   cera remollescit tractataque pollice multas

remollescit: cf. 183 *mollescit*.

tractataque pollice: The language is especially appropriate in the context of how the craftsman Pygmalion had, after all, fashioned his girl out of rock (cf., too, the petrifaction theme; the present story is rather an inverse of the Medusa/underworld horror tale).

286   flectitur in facies ipsoque fit utilis usu.

The action of the sun on wax is not unlike that of the poet on the victims of metamorphosis. The striking fricative alliteration evokes well the seemingly magical result of the sculptor in wax.

ipso ... usu: "By its very use": a typical Ovidian antithesis.

287   dum stupet et dubie gaudet fallique veretur,

dum stupet: cf. Virgil, *Aeneid* 1.495.

dubie: The adverb is rare in poetry (cf. 7.508), and a favorite of Livy. Pygmalion is shy and not remotely overly confident; he can scarcely believe what is happening.

veretur: The verb expresses dread more than fear; Pygmalion is so smitten with his statue that one of his first reactions to its metamorphosis is dread at the idea that he might be deceived.

288   rursus amans rursusque manu sua vota retractat.

rursus: The repetition of the adverb balances the emotions (*amans*) and the physical reaction thereto (*manu ... retractat*).

sua: With *vota*, as the quantity of the final vowel makes clear; word order, however, allows it to be felt somewhat with *manu* as well, as lover and beloved shade into one.

retractat: "He handles again." The same line-end recurs at 370.

289   corpus erat; saliunt temptatae pollice venae.

temptatae: cf. 254; 282–283; Ovid underscores Pygmalion's action in testing his creation.

saliunt: The verb means to dance or to leap; the poet vividly describes the statue's coming to life under the hands of its creator—the sculptor is now producing a new work of art, as it were.

290   tum vero Paphius plenissima concipit heros

plenissima: With 291 *verba*; cf. the laconic language of his prayer of supplication.

heros: Like Orpheus at 50 (if the reading there is correct); Pygmalion has triumphed in his quest, and is something of a miniature demiurge in his own private world; cf. 294 and how the now living statue sees the lover with the heaven.

291   verba quibus Veneri grates agit, oraque tandem

Ovid wisely refrains from indulging in a long rendition of Pygmalion's thanksgiving prayer; what matters is that he rendered thanks to the goddess, in striking contrast to Hippomenes with Atalanta.

ora: To be taken closely with 292 *ore*; mouth now joins at last to mouth and not marble.

292   ore suo non falsa premit; dataque oscula virgo

non falsa: The falsehood theme: the girl is real, the statue truly transformed, Pygmalion fully in control of his art.

dataque oscula: The elision effectively joins the kisses that are given.

293   sensit et erubuit, timidumque ad lumina lumen

erubuit: Cf. 241 and the possible absence of blushes of shame from the faces of the Propoetides.

timidum: Cf. Pygmalion's timid prayer to Venus.

lumina lumen: "Eyes" and "eye," as often; the repetition serves to highlight the close connection between the romantic couple. Bömer's commentary notes the association of light and life; with the bestowal of the one the other is implied.

294   attollens pariter cum caelo vidit amantem.

The language implies that Pygmalion is the god for the statue that has now acquired humanity; Pygmalion is the first sight the new creation sees at "birth." The final word of the verse highlights exactly what the creator beholds: his creature and beloved.

295   coniugio, quod fecit, adest dea, iamque coactis

adest: Once again of divine epiphany.

coactis: With 296 *cornibus*—a final association with the Cerastae and the very different story of their fate.

296   cornibus in plenum noviens lunaribus orbem

The transition to the next tale commences with the pregnancy of Pygmalion's now lawful, mortal wife—though she is, of course, his "daughter" in an important sense.

noviens: The ninefold months of the pregnancy will be in marked contrast to the nine days of the festival during which Myrrha and Cinyras consummate their illicit union.

297   illa Paphon genuit, de qua tenet insula nomen.

Paphon: The mother of Cinyras, the father of the Myrrha whose sordid story will occupy most of the book. The union of Pygmalion and his statue leads directly to the tragedy of Myrrha, just as the happy nuptials of Iphis and Ianthe at the end of Book 9 presaged the story of Orpheus and Eurydice. Orpheus suffered grievously in the matter of his marriage, and the point of his transition seems to be that a blessed union leads to disaster.

298–502. *Myrrha.* The story of Myrrha's incest with her father Cinyras is the single longest tale in *Metamorphoses* 10. The lore was not original to Ovid; Panyasis apparently composed an epic poem on it, while the neoteric poet Helvius Cinna wrote a *Zmyrna.* Ovid may have been the first to connect the story of the incestuous girl with Pygmalion and his work of the visual arts. Accounts of the tale survive in the prose handbooks of Antoninus Liberalis (34); Pseudo-Apollodorus (3.14.4.2 ff.); and Hyginus (*Fabulae* 58). Much has been written by scholars on Myrrha; see further especially B. Nagle, "Byblis and Myrrha: Two Incest Narratives in the *Metamorphoses*," in *The Classical Journal* 78.4 (1983), 301–315 (with good consideration of parallel episodes in Books 9 and 10 of the poem); M. Putnam, "Ovid, Virgil, and Myrrha's Metamorphic Exile," in *Vergilius* 47 (2001), 171–193 (with study of Ovid's epic debt to his predecessor); von Glinski (2012: 43–44). For the connection between Cinyras and Adonis (and certain aspects of the localization of the Adonis death sequence), see J. Reed, "Antimachus on Adonis?," in *Hermes* 124.3 (1996), 381–383. In Pseudo-Apollodorus (3.14.3–4), Cinyras married the daughter of Pygmalion (Metharme) and became the father of Adonis; he also notes that according to the epic poet Panyasis, Cinyras was an Assyrian who had been the father of Smyrna (= Myrrha). This Smyrna was like one of the Propoetides in that she refused to give Aphrodite her proper due (cf. the story below of how Hippomenes offends Venus because he forgets to thank her for her assistance in securing the love of Atalanta); she was thus struck by the goddess with a perverse love for her father Cinyras.

Dante places Myrrha among the falsifiers (*Inferno* 30.22–45). In the visual arts, the birth of Adonis from the maternal myrrh is a frequent subject; the worlds of opera and ballet have also responded to Myrrha's tragedy.

298   Editus hac ille, qui si sine prole fuisset,

sine prole: Appropriately enough, the emphasis from the start is on the bearing of children; Pygmalion gave birth to his own daughter, in a sense, and he conceived a child with his own daughter—incest will prove to be ingrained in the family identity.

fuisset: Pluperfect subjunctive in a past contractual conditional sentence.

299   inter felices Cinyras potuisset haberi.

felices: "Blessed" or "fortunate."

haberi: "To be reckoned" or "considered."

300   dira canam; procul hinc, natae, procul este, parentes!

One wonders why daughters and parents are expelled from a song that is ostensibly being sung to trees (at least in terms of explicitly defined audience members).

dira: Cf. 426.

procul hinc: Elevated language, as Bömer notes in his commentary the tone is high, in contrast to at least the greater part of the content.

natae … parentes: Again, it might seem a reasonable question to ask if any daughters or parents were present for Orpheus' songs. The dismissal of parents is especially appropriate, of course, given the incest at the heart of the tale.

301   aut, mea si vestras mulcebunt carmina mentes,

mea: cf. 302 *mihi*; Orpheus as narrator takes full responsibility for the tale he is about to sing, with marked emphasis on the self.

mulcebant: "Soothe" or "soften." The future here and at 303 *credetis* is in the protasis of a future more vivid condition that, as often, has an imperative (cf. 302 and 303 *credite*) or other expression of futurity (302 *desit*, a jussive subjunctive or "milder" imperative). It is possible that the poet is making something of a comment on the nature of an audience that would be interested in hearing such a sordid tale as that of Myrrha.

302   desit in hac parte mihi fides, nec credite factum,

fides: "Trust" or "faith." The falsehood theme returns; the lull of music may please the mind and heart, but Orpheus urges either that no one believe the story of Myrrha to be true—or at least that they believe that there was indeed a penalty for her actions.

303   vel, si credetis, facti quoque credite poenam.

si credetis: Future indicative in the protasis of a future more vivid condition; the apodosis of such constructions can take any form that denotes futurity (e.g., as here, the imperative).

facti ... poenam: A foreshadowing of the eventual metamorphosis of Myrrha.

304   si tamen admissum sinit hoc natura videri

The protasis once again raises the idea that Orpheus' song is a lie.

admissum: The word can be used of any crime or wrongdoing.

305   gentibus Ismariis et nostro gratulor orbi,

Schrader deleted this line, "scarcely I know whether rightly" (Tarrant).

Ismariis: A reference to Mount Ismarus in southern Thrace, and so by poetic extension, = "Thracian."

gratulor: The verb is strikingly repeated to highlight the horror of Myrrha's crime and the resultant blessedness of those lands free from its stain.

306   gratulor huic terrae, quod abest regionibus illis

huic terrae: The area around Haemus and Rhodope (cf. 77). The ethnographic theme continues in the poet narrator's emphasis on the impact of sin and wrongdoing on the reputation of the lands where it occurs.

307   quae tantum genuere nefas. sit dives amomo,

tantum ... nefas: "So great an unspeakable thing." *Nefas* has special meaning in a context of metamorphosis, since transformation usually brings with it the suppression of voice: the *nefas*, fittingly enough, remains unspoken.

amomo: A spice plant from the east, almost a watchword for luxury and wealth.

308   cinnamaque costumque suum sudataque ligno

Ovid engages in something of a new catalog of trees, as he prepares to introduce the fateful myrrh.

costum: A plant known for its rich aroma.

ligno: Ablative of source.

309   tura ferat floresque alios Panchaia tellus,

Panchaia: A mysterious, legendary land of wealth and poetic fame; Ovid may have had in mind Virgil's *turiferis Panchaia pinguis harenis* (*Georgic* 2.139); cf. 478 below. The ethnographic theme returns yet again, here with specific reference to orientalism; part of Ovid's point is to emphasize that these strange events such as the metamorphosis of Myrrha into a myrrh tree and such problems (from a Roman perspective) as Orpheus' pederasty take place outside Rome, in eastern realms—a recurring theme of interest in Augustan Rome given the imperial propaganda surrounding the defeat of Antony and

Cleopatra and the conquest of the east. The geographical theme is once highlighted, this time with specific reference to certain realities of Augustus' Rome.

310   dum ferat et murram; tanti nova non fuit arbor.

A wry comment on the previous arboreal metamorphoses of the book; no tree was ever born at such a price as the myrrh.

dum: Introducing a proviso clause with the subjunctive (*ferat*).

et: Adverbial; = "also."

tanti: Genitive of price. No new tree ever came at such a high price as the myrrh.

311   ipse negat nocuisse tibi sua tela Cupido,

nocuisse: The verb regularly take a dative object.

tibi: With 312 *Myrrha*; first the tree (310), then the personal pronoun, finally the name.

Cupido: Still useful on Ovid's treatment of the god and his mother is W. Stephens, "Cupid and Venus in Ovid's *Metamorphoses*," in *Transactions of the American Philological Association* 89 (1958), 286–300, a careful examination of different appearances of the two immortals in Ovid's poetry.

312   Myrrha, facesque suas a crimine vindicat isto;

isto: Often forms of *iste, ista, istud* carry a pejorative force.

vindicat: Here means "to free from blame" or "to absolve" (*OLD s.v.* 4b); the basic meaning of the verb is to lay claim to something (here Cupid asserts control, as it were, over his shafts; they had nothing to do with Myrrha's infatuation, and if they had, he would know).

313   stipite te Stygio tumidisque adflavit echidnis

stipite . . . Stygio: A *stips* can mean a stick that is used for kindling or fuel; here the Furies are imagined as using some underworld twig or branch to start the fire that burns in Myrrha's heart. Bömer notes here that *stips* here is almost identical to *fax*; the point is that Cupid's traditional torch had nothing to do with Myrrha's love for her father. One might note that while Pygmalion may have been aided in his love for his statue by Venus, no immortal power was credited with the instigation of the infatuation.

echidnis: Vipers and serpents were regularly associated with the Furies (cf. 314; 349); the serpents are swollen with their deadly venom. Bömer notes in his commentary that swelling is typically associated with serpents.

314   e tribus una soror. scelus est odisse parentem,

tribus: There were traditionally three Furies: Allecto, Megaera, and Tisiphone.

odisse: Perfect infinitive active.

315   hic amor est odio maius scelus. undique lecti

odio: Ablative of comparison.

lecti: With 316 *proceres.*

316   te cupiunt proceres, totoque oriente iuventus

Cyparissus has affinities with Adonis, and Myrrha with Atalanta (so also Pygmalion and Hippomenes, both of whom win their erotic quests, albeit with vastly different consequences).

proceres: The first men of the land, the leading nobles.

317   ad thalami certamen adest. ex omnibus unum

adest: Another epiphany, this time of the youths who arrive for the challenge of winning Myrrha. Anderson notes that Ovid never says that Myrrha is beautiful; true enough, but it is reasonable to suppose that she was, and that if she were not distinguished for her looks, the poet would have made it a point to tell us.

certamen: Cf. the forthcoming race to win Atalanta's hand.

318   elige, Myrrha, virum—dum ne sit in omnibus unus.

elige: Imperative, as often with a vocative.

virum: "Husband," as often.

dum: Introducing a clause of proviso with the subjunctive.

unus: With 317 *unum* in another typically Ovidian antithesis.

319   illa quidem sentit foedoque repugnat amori,

quidem: "To be sure."

foedo: A strong adjective; the erotic attachment of Myrrha to her father is especially repugnant.

repugnat: Myrrha fights back; she is no unwitting victim of her infatuation. Ovid's depiction of Cinyras' daughter owes much both to the Medea of tragedy (another *M-a* figure); and to Virgil's Dido.

320   et secum quo mente feror? quid molior? inquit

mente: "Intention" as well as "mind."

feror: "Am I carried"; the verb connotes a lack of ability on the part of the girl to control her actions. With Myrrha's expression here cf. *Heroides* 18.30.

inquit: Bömer and the other commentators discuss different aspects of Myrrha's monologue, including comparison of the similar soliloquies of her incestuous doublet Byblis as well as Medea and, later in the present book, Atalanta.

321   di precor, et pietas sacrataque iura parentum,

di: Vocative plural.

pietas: Of special relevance given the imminent affair between father and daughter; Myrrha's relationship with Cinyras is a perversion of the sacred trust between parent and child.

parentum: Genitive plural.

322   hoc prohibete nefas scelerique resistite nostro,

Anderson notes the swift dactylic rhythm of these lines, as Myrrha hastens through her rationalizations and reflections on incest.

prohibete nefas: Also at Virgil, *Aeneid* 5.197, during the regatta. Once again the unspeakable nature of the incest is underscored.

sceleri . . . nostro: Myrrha is amply aware of the forbidden nature of her desired union. The case is dative after *resistite.*

323   si tamen hoc scelus est. sed enim damnare negatur

si tamen hoc scelus est: Cf. Apollo's reaction to the death of Hyacinthus at 200–201 above.

sed enim: "But truly" or "but indeed," as Myrrha introduces a justification for her questionable wishes.

324   hanc Venerem pietas, coeuntque animalia nullo

hanc Venerem: that is, the incestuous union of Myrrha and her father.

pietas: Myrrha invokes exactly the concept that should protect a proper relationship between a father and his child.

coeunt: "Come together," that is, in sexual union; cf. 327 *init.*

325   cetera dilectu, nec habetur turpe iuvencae

dilectu: The reading of the eleventh century manuscript M (i.e., the "Marcianus"), preferred by both Anderson and Tarrant (who wonders if *delectu* may be the correct *lectio*); P has *dilectu*; the remaining witnesses, *delicto.* This sense of *dilectus* = OLD s.v. 3, "choice (between two or more possibilities), discrimination, distinction"; it is possible that *delicto* is correct, and the point that other animals have sexual couplings absent any notion of sin or morality.

habetur: "Is it considered." *Turpe* is yet another especially strong adjective, especially for what amounts to self-condemnation; throughout, the emphasis is on Myrrha's awareness of the seriousness of her situation.

326   ferre patrem tergo; fit equo sua filia coniunx,

The perversion of *pietas* is expressed by a perversion of the image of Aeneas carrying his father from the ruin of Troy.

fit: "Becomes"; *fieri* functions as the passive of *facere.*

327   quasque creavit init pecudes caper, ipsaque, cuius

ipsa: With 328 *ales.*

328   semine concepta est, ex illo concipit ales.

The avian world provides the last of Myrrha's animal *comparanda.*

329   felices quibus ista licent! humana malignas

felices: Cinyras would have been counted among the *felices* had he not had a daughter like Myrrha; Myrrha, for her part, notes that the *felices* are those who are allowed to commit incest with impunity. The poet narrator's emphasis on what is allowed in the animal kingdom in his description of what Myrrha says to justify and rationalize her wishes connects to the metamorphosis theme; so many humans have been transformed into animals and birds, and Myrrha here is depicted as feeling jealousy over what they are allowed to do.

ista: The demonstrative need not have a pejorative or notorious connotation, but here the common shade of meaning is pointedly felt. cf. 335 *isto.*

malignas: With 330 *leges;* the descriptor is especially strong.

330   cura dedit leges, et quod natura remittit

Myrrha argues that nature grants remission of the "sins" that human laws have condemned.

331   invida iura negant. gentes tamen esse feruntur

invida iura: The laws are almost perceived to be jealous things that begrudge mortals their chance at happiness.

feruntur: "There are said to be."

332   in quibus et nato genetrix et nata parenti

et nato … et nata: The almost jingling rhythm of the line helps to underscore Myrrha's attempt to argue that anyone should be allowed to join with anyone.

genetrix: The word has particular association with Venus, the mother of the Romans.

333   iungitur, ut pietas geminato crescat amore.

geminato … amore: "Love that has been twinned," that is, the *amor* between parent and child joined with that between lover and beloved. The ablative is a sort of ablative of attendant circumstance.

334   me miseram, quod non nasci mihi contigit illic

The metrical pattern emphasis the girl's state of mental disarray; Bömer's commentary quotes Jackson Knight's observation that this is "a rugged hexameter … there is scarcely any caesura in the third foot."

me miseram: Accusative of exclamation.

nasci: "To be born"; infinitive of *nascor.*

contigit: "It befell."

illic: "There, in that place."

335   fortunaque loci laedor! quid in ista resolvor?

fortunaque loci: "The luck of the locale" or "fortune of the place."

laedor: = "I am harmed."

ista: Probably with *fortuna* understood; the demonstrative can have pejorative force. Myrrha blames her situation on the mere accident of geography. Throughout the book, there has been a marked emphasis on *place* and location; Ovid adds a playful version of his geographical theme here to highlight something of the absurdity of Myrrha's reasoning.

336   spes interdictae, discedite! dignus amari

interdictae: See Reed here on the legal language; Ovid once again employs the language of the law courts, with a certain degree of humor—there is nothing lawful about what Myrrha is contemplating. *Spes interdictae* = a vocative.

dignus: With 337 *ille,* that is, Cinyras.

amari: "To be loved" (present infinitive passive).

337   ille, sed ut pater, est. ergo si filia magni

ille: The demonstrative can mean "the famous one"; cf. *magni* (with 338 *Cinyrae*). Myrrha's sire is not merely a father, but a king.

ut pater: "As a father" (sc., should be).

magni: The deliberate contrast is between the girl's incestuous thoughts and the heroic, regal status of her father; there is something of a reflection on the corruption here of the nobility of epic verse by a perverse sort of elegiac lament.

338   non essem Cinyrae, Cinyrae concumbere possem.

essem . . . possem: Imperfect subjunctives in a present contrafactual or contrary to fact conditional sentence.

Cinyrae . . . Cinyrae: Myrrha repeats the name of the object of her unlawful affections.

339   nunc, quia iam meus est, non est meus, ipsaque damno

meus . . . meus: Effective Ovidian antithesis.

damno: Dative of purpose; part of a double dative with 340 *mihi*. In this case the dative of purpose is also a dative of disadvantage.

340   est mihi proximitas; aliena potentior essem.

Anderson notes the dactylic rhythm of 340–342, which serves to highlight how Myrrha wishes to escape her situation; she will, in fact, become the myrrh tree that is associated with some of the most distant eastern realms of the Roman geographical conception, safely distant, one might hope, from the heart of empire.

aliena: "As a foreigner/foreign woman."

341   ire libet procul hinc patriaeque relinquere fines,

libet: Impersonal verb = "It is pleasurable."

hinc: "From here," "hence." With *procul hinc* cf. the Orphic admonition for certain members of the audience to depart (possibly so that they would not receive any untoward ideas about what they should do in their own lives from the poet narrator's rendition of what happened once in Cyprus).

patriae: "Native land," but with special reference to the reason for Myrrha's wish to depart from her home. The concept of exile recurs from the story of the Propoetides; Venus had considered banishing those women for their denial of her divinity.

342   dum scelus effugiam; retinet malus ardor amantem,

dum: The conjunction introduces a clause of provision/proviso clause, and governs the present subjunctive *effugiam*.

malus ardor: As Bömer notes, the collocation is without ready parallel; in *ardor* there is a continuing emphasis on fire (cf. *Ardere*).

amantem: The lover, that is, Myrrha.

343   ut praesens spectem Cinyran tangamque loquarque

ut: The *malus ardor* detains Myrrha, and the natural result of her presence is that she may behold, touch, address, and even kiss (344) her father.

The repeated connective conjunction *-que* creates a jingling effect that evokes Myrrha's obsessive, vigorously enthusiastic reaction to the proximity of the object of her infatuation.

344   osculaque admoveam, si nil conceditur ultra.

ultra: that is, "beyond" what a daughter can be expected to share with her father in both word and gesture. The repetition (cf. 345) underscores the limits that Myrrha is crossing.

345   ultra autem sperare aliquid potes, impia virgo,

impia virgo: The self-recriminatory address highlights two crucial aspects of Myrrha's state; she is in danger of violating the *pietas* that a daughter owes to her father, and she is of a marriageable age. With *virgo* cf. 360 *virginei*. Both Seneca (*Agamemnon* 19) and Valerius Flaccus (*Argonautica* 4.13–14) imitate Ovid's use of *impia virgo*.

346   nec quot confundas et iura et nomina sentis?

confundas: Subjunctive in an indirect question after *quot*.

iura: The legal imagery continues.

nomina: that is, of father and daughter.

347   tune eris et matris paelex et adultera patris?

tune: The powerful repetition of this vocative at 348 forms a sharp rebuke to the girl; Myrrha has blurred the lines of family relationships, and must be metaphorically shaken back to her senses.

paelex: An especially harsh appellation.

adultera: "Mistress." The word may have had particularly strong resonance in Augustan Rome, given the attempts of the *princeps* to revive adultery legislation.

348   tune soror nati genetrixque vocabere fratris?

soror nati: Reed notes here how the wording of the question anticipates the end of the story.

vocabere: Alternative form of *vocaberis*.

349   nec metues atro crinitas angue sorores,

For the serpentine Furies cf. 313–314.

atro: The color is especially baleful.

crinitas: "Having long hair"; in this case, the coiffure of the Furies consists of serpents.

350   quas facibus saevis oculos atque ora petentes

facibus: From *fax*, "a torch"; cf. the torches associated with Cupid and the bestowal of erotic infatuations.

atque ora: The elision gives metrical enactment to the relentless pursuit of eyes and face, as the words run into each other.

351   noxia corda vident? at tu, dum corpore non es

at: Introduces a strong adversative: Myrrha reminds herself that she has yet to act on her ill-conceived passions. cf. 355.

corpore: In contrast to 352 *animo*. Ovid plays throughout the Myrrha episode on the distinction between mental and physical wrongdoing.

352   passa nefas, animo ne concipe, neve potentis

ne concipe: A negative imperative; the use of *ne* with a present imperative is both archaic and poetic (cf. Virgi, *Aeneid* 2.48 *equo ne credite*). The classical prose construction is *noli* with an infinitive, or *ne* with the perfect subjunctive.

neve: The normal connective for multiple negative commands.

potentis: With 353 *naturae*. The bond between father and daughter is powerful.

353   concubitu vetito naturae pollue foedus.

pollue: Another especially strong word to describe what Myrrha is contemplating.

foedus: An alliance or solemn bond; there may be a play on the adjective *foedus* with its sense of that which is disgusting and appalling.

354   velle puta; res ipsa vetat. pius ille memorque est

The paratactic rhythm of the line that the commentators note here fits with the disordered state of Myrrha's mind.

pius ille: Cinyras understands the dictates of *pietas* better than his daughter does. The word may have had special resonance for Ovid's audience in light of the importance of *pietas* in the Virgilian *Aeneid* and the idea of *pius Aeneas.*

355   moris—et o vellem similis furor esset in illo!

moris: With a hint of the *mos maiorum* and the traditions of Roman *mores;* the verse is balanced between the world of *mos* and that of *furor.*

vellem ... esset: Imperfect subjunctives in present wishes that are incapable of fulfillment.

356   dixerat, at Cinyras, quem copia digna procorum

at: Cf. 351. Myrrha has her own concerns; Cinyras, for his part, has been worried about which of the outstanding suitors should be chosen for his daughter; once again, the conjunction introduces a strongly adversative contrast.

357   quid faciat dubitare facit, scitatur ab ipsa

faciat: Present subjunctive in an indirect question.

scitatur: An impersonal passive construction.

358   nominibus dictis, cuius velit esse mariti.

nominibus dictis: "With the names having been spoken"; that is, Cinyras lists the possible candidates for marriage to his daughter by name. Cf. 366 *nomine dicto;* 439.

velit: Present subjunctive in an indirect question.

359   illa silet primo patriisque in vultibus haerens

silet: Cf. 389, of Myrrha's similar silence with her nurse.

vultibus: Plural for singular.

360   aestuat et tepido suffundit lumina rore.

aestuat: Myrrha blazes or burns with passion; the verb can have particular application to the ardent desire of lovers (*OLD s.v.* 3).

tepido: Very different from the tepid state of the Pygmalion statue as it began to warm; these are the hot tears of a girl possessed of an unnatural passion.

rore: that is, her tears.

361   virginei Cinyras haec credens esse timoris

virginei: Cf. 366.

haec: Neuter substantive, referring to the silence and the tears.

timoris: Genitive of characteristic.

362   flere vetat siccatque genas atque oscula iungit.

siccatque genas: The father dries his daughter's cheeks of their tears.

oscula: Cf. 344. The joining of the kisses, appropriately enough, comes with a metrical linking of conjunction (*atque*) and noun.

363   Myrrha datis nimium gaudet consultaque, qualem

datis: Supply *osculis.*

nimium: "Excessively."

consulta: Myrrha is asked what sort of husband she would prefer.

364   optet habere virum, similem tibi dixit; at ille

optet: Present subjunctive in an indirect question.

at: The strongly adversative conjunction highlights the different understanding of the father and daughter to the answer Myrrha provides.

365   non intellectam vocem conlaudat et esto

A marvelous Ovidian trick: the meaning must be that the father thoroughly (*con-*) praises the utterance (*vocem*) he did not understand, though conceivably it could also mean he did *not* praise thoroughly the utterance that he *did* understand. The double meaning of Myrrha's words to her father is thus reflected in his response. Ovid is here once again at his witty, indeed irreverent best, as father and daughter engage in words of double meaning and thinly veiled import.

esto: The future imperative, which carries with it solemn, indeed legal or religious force. Myrrha's crime will grow all the more serious as she abandons the precept her father enjoins on her here.

366   tam pia semper ait, pietatis nomine dicto

pia ... pietatis: With heavy emphasis on the key concept in the relationship between father and daughter.

nomine dicto: Cf. 358 *nominibus dictis*; 439.

367   demisit vultus sceleris sibi conscia virgo.

sibi conscia: Once again, the poet narrator emphasizes how Myrrha is aware of exactly what she is contemplating.

virgo: Cf. 345 *impia virgo*; 368.

368   noctis erat medium, curasque et corpora somnus

Cf. the midday hour of 126 and 174.

curasque et corpora: Note the elision; cares and bodies slide into each other in a lull of sleep.

369 solverat; at virgo Cinyreia pervigil igni

virgo: Ovid continues to emphasize Myrrha's virginal state. For the appellation *Cinyreia* with *virgo* Bömer compares 660 *Schoeneia virgo*, of Atalanta; the tone is deliberately epic and solemn to provide greater contrast with the sordid subject matter.

pervigil: Myrrha keeps watch through (*per-*) the hours of the night.

370 carpitur indomito furiosaque vota retractat.

carpitur: Always a significant verb; Myrrha is slowly and constantly eaten away by the fire of her undying passion for Cinyras.

indomito: The metaphorical fire of Myrrha's passion is untamed; there may be a hint of the idea of real lights to illumine the nights for those who would keep watch.

furiosa: The language of fury recurs throughout the episode.

vota retractat: Cf. 288.

371 et modo desperat, modo vult temptare, pudetque

The rhythm is brisk and swift; the language expresses the almost frenzied actions of the maddened girl as she longs for that which she (as yet) cannot have.

modo ... modo: "Now ... now."

temptare: Very different from the same use of the verb to describe Pygmalion with his statue.

372 et cupit, et quid agat non invenit; utque securi

agat: Subjunctive in an indirect question.

utque: Introducing a simile.

securi: "An ax."

373   saucia trabs ingens, ubi plaga novissima restat,

trabs: The basic meaning is a tree-trunk; the word can come to be used of any piece of lumber. The image of the falling tree recalls Virgil, *Aeneid* 5.446 ff. with its simile of the collapse of a tree on Ida, as well as other passages of similar import in Homer, Apollonius Rhodius, Catullus and Virgil. In one sense the comparison of Myrrha to storied trees of epic is another example of the poet narrator's delight in contrasting the situation of the crazed Myrrha with nobler, more elevated poetic moments.

novissima: "The last." In *plaga novissima* there may be a hint of the final blow that would bring death, that is, via suicide.

374   quo cadat in dubio est omnique a parte timetur,

quo: "Where."

timetur: The verb is used impersonally. *Omnique a parte timetur* may be a reminiscence of Propertius, c. 1.11.18. The synaloepha (whereby two syllables are merged into one) neatly expresses how the fear that Myrrha feels is pervasive, total and all-encompassing.

375   sic animus vario labefactus vulnere nutat

vario ... vulnere: The wound is "various" because it is both complicated in its nature, and recurrent: proximity to her father worsens the passion (cf. 340).

376   huc levis atque illuc momentaque sumit utroque.

levis: In elegiac contexts the adjective can mean "fickle."

momenta: Exactly = English "momentum."

377   nec modus aut requies, nisi mors, reperitur amoris;

Mention of *requies* leads at once to the thought of the ultimate remedy of death; exile does not seem to be one of Myrrha's options. In *requies amoris* there is a return to the theme of the *remedia amoris*; only death will resolve this infatuation.

mors: Repeated at 378; together with *requies* the strong emphasis of the verses is on how death is the only means Myrrha can see to escape.

378   mors placet. erigitur laqueoque innectere fauces

Hanging was considered an especially shameful form of death.

placet: Cf. the very different use of the same form at 524.

laqueo: Dative after *innectere*.

379   destinat, et zona summo de poste revincta

zona: The removal of the *zona* could be taken as a sign of the loss of virginity (*OLD s.v.* 2b), a use that is known to Ovid (*Epistulae ex Ponto* 2.116).

380   care vale Cinyra; causam te intellige mortis.

Cinyra: Vocative.

te: In apposition to *causam ... mortis*.

381   dixit et aptabat pallenti vincula collo.

aptabat: The imperfect may be inchoative: she began to fit the noose around her pale (*pallenti*) neck; the adjective describes Myrrha's paleness in all aspects: her natural color; the blanch of fear; the (proleptic) pallor of the death that seems imminent.

382   murmura verborum fidas nutricis ad aures

murmura: The word will recur at 702, of the sounds made by lions.

nutricis: The faithful nurse is a stock figure of tragedy; Myrrha's nurse also has affinities with Virgil's depiction of Dido's sister Anna.

383 pervenisse ferunt limen servantis alumnae;

ferunt: "They say."

384 surgit anus reseratque fores mortisque paratae

mortisque paratae: The six-syllable line-end neatly balances that of 382, as Ovid contrasts the guardian nurse with the scene of her charge's suicide. Cf. Also 390 *tardae conamina mortis,* as Myrrha reacts to the nurse's rescue.

385 instrumenta videns spatio conclamat eodem

conclamat: The prefix can be intensive.

386 seque ferit scinditque sinus ereptaque collo

A dramatic tricolon of action, the first two reactions being classic instances of lamentation, as the nurse beats herself and tears her clothing.

erepta: "Snatched from" (with *vincula* in the next line).

387 vincula dilaniat. tum denique flere vacavit,

vincula: The noose Myrrha has prepared for her suicide.

denique: "At last, finally."

vacavit: "She was free/there was time for her."

388 tum dare complexus laqueique requirere causam.

Another tricolon is concluded, now that the danger of death as passed: the nurse gives Myrrha time to weep; she bestows embraces of comfort and support; and, at last, she seeks the reason for the suicide attempt.

389   muta silet virgo terramque immota tuetur

silet: Cf. 359, of the same behavior of Myrrha with her father.

immota: Myrrha keeps her eyes fixed to the ground.

tuetur: "Looks at." *Tueor* is a deponent verb.

390   et deprensa dolet tardae conamina mortis.

tardae: Possibly = "drawn out" or "delayed" (*OLD s.v.* 2); it agrees with *mortis.* The adjective more appropriately describes the *conamina;* as Bömer notes, this is an example of "enallage," or what might be considered a misuse of "correct" agreement for the sake of rhetorical effect. In this case, the force of the rhetorical device is to highlight how Myrrha should have died long before the present moment that finds her on the precipice of harm.

391   instat anus canosque suos et inania nudans

The nurse resumes her gestures of lament.

canosque suos: Her white hair; *capillos* can be understood.

inania: With *ubera* in the next verse.

392   ubera per cunas alimentaque prima precatur

cunas: A cradle; the word can be applied metaphorically to describe infancy and one's formative years.

alimentaque prima: The milk with which she had nourished the infant Myrrha: the nurse bears her breast and prays by the sustenance she once provided her young charge.

393   ut sibi committat quidquid dolet. illa rogantem

ut sibi committat: A substantive clause after a verb of prayer and entreaty.

quidquid dolet: "Whatever is grieving her."

illa: Myrrha; to be taken with *aversata* in the next verse.

394   aversata gemit; certa est exquirere nutrix

aversata: "Having turned away."

certa est: The nurse is resolved to learn the truth.

exquirere: "To discover" (*OLD s.v.* 3).

395   nec solam spondere fidem. dic inquit opemque

spondere: The nurse is willing to give a pledge of her trustworthiness and surety to her charge.

inquit: The caesura after the verb serves to highlight the *opem*, the key word that describes the fateful assistance that the nurse will bestow on her crazed charge.

396   me sine ferre tibi; non est mea pigra senectus.

pigra: "Sluggish." Reed collects a number of passages in Greek and Latin verse on the slow and unsteady nature of old age. Bömer's commentary compares parallel passages with *tarda*; the point of the adjective here is to emphasize not so much the mere fact of slowness that could be associated with old age, but exactly the force of English "sluggish."

397   seu furor est, habeo quae carmine sanet et herbis;

seu: The nurse refines her point; if someone has bewitched Myrrha and caused a state of madness, she has spells and other magical charms/remedies to heal her charge.

quae: Introducing a generic relative clause.

carmine: The word can refer to a magical spell or charm; cf. Ovid's mysterious *carmen et error* that led to his banishment. Reed compares 15.20–22, where *carmen* and *herba* are invoked as antidotes to the problem of love (*per alleviare una crisi d'amore*). The present passage owes something to the Virgilian depiction of Dido and the magical rites that she employs in the matter of her infatuation with Aeneas.

398   sive aliquis nocuit, magico lustrabere ritu;

lustrabere: If Myrrha has been cursed in some way, the nurse will perform a purificatory ritual. The form is an alternative to *lustraberis.*

399   ira deum sive est, sacris placabilis ira.

deum: Genitive plural.

sacris: "Sacred rites" and rituals; sacrifices and prayers by which the anger of the immortals might be appeased. The form is the ablative of means.

400   quid rear ulterius? certe fortuna domusque

rear: First person future indicative active of *reor.*

ulterius: That is, beyond what she has already enumerated, with continuing emphasis on how Myrrha is crossing beyond the *fines* of natural and social law.

401   sospes et in cursu est; vivit genetrixque paterque.

cursu: OLD s.v. 8b, as Reed notes here.

genitrix: That is, the mother of Myrrha, though with reference, too, to the goddess Venus as the ultimate progenitor of Rome (and, of course, of the love that led to Myrrha).

paterque: The nurse's reassuring words end with the cause of the problem.

402   Myrrha patre audito suspiria duxit ab imo

patre audito: Cf. 358 *nominibus dictis*; 366 *nomine dicto.* Ovid repeatedly emphasizes the question of name and title; at 439 *nomine mentito*, the nurse will lie to Cinyras about the name of the girl who is to be procured for his bed.

suspiria: "Sighs" that betray the girl's emotional state. Bömer's commentary provides parallel passages for *suspiria* as "signum amoris"; the communication of the girl that helps to betray her secret is a visceral reaction of her deeply felt emotion, not the language of her recent monologue.

imo: The enjambment stretches out the emotion, which wells up from the deepest part of the girl's heart.

403   pectore. nec nutrix etiamnum concipit ullum

etiamnum: "Even now, still."

concipit: Another key word; Pygmalion had begun to conceive a love (*concipere amorem*) for his statue, which was in effect his offspring. That union has led to the girl who has now conceived a love for an unspeakable thing, and the nurse cannot conceive of it (*concipere nefas*).

ullum: With 404 *nefas.*

404   mente nefas, aliquemque tamen praesentit amorem.

mente: The poet narrator has frequently underscored how the girl *intends* or *wills* what she is doing; her action is one over which time has been spent in deliberation. Here, the nurse is unable to absorb in her mind exactly what game is afoot, though she knows it is amatory.

aliquem ... amorem: "Some love," though not an unspeakable (*nefas*) one.

praesentit: Cf. *Heroides* 11.33 ff. The prefix expresses how she realizes in advance of any definitive knowledge that *amor* is the problem that has driven Myrrha to embrace suicide.

405   propositique tenax quodcumquest orat ut ipsi

propositique tenax: A sort of genitive of specification; in poetry the genitive is found frequently with adjectives. The phrase is borrowed from Horace, c. 3.1 (where see the commentary notes of Nisbet and Rudd); the elevated tone of Horace's first Roman ode is here employed in the very different context of the nurse's appeal to her charge Myrrha that she reveal to her (*ipsi*) what is troubling her.

406   indicet, et gremio lacrimantem tollit anili

indicet: Of an informer or "tattletale."

gremio . . . anili: "The lap of an old woman." The nurse's age is a major feature of the poet's description of Myrrha's partner in crime; the contrast with the girl's youth is deliberate.

lacrimantem: that is, Myrrha, who is dissolved in tears; cf. 419.

407   atque ita complectens infirmis membra lacertis

atque ita: The elision neatly enacts the nurse's embrace of Myrrha.

infirmis: Ovid continues to emphasize the nurse's aged state (and cf. 414). See here A. Nikolopoulos, "*Tremuloque gradu venit aegra senectus:* Old Age in Ovid's *Metamorphoses,*" in *Mnemosyne* 56.1 (2003), 48–60, for discussion of the depiction of the elderly in the poem—in Ovid, the old are sometimes found to be quite powerful indeed, despite their seemingly sluggish and impaired movement.

408   sensimus inquit; amas. sed et hic mea (pone timorem)

The language is short and sweet; paratactic and direct: the nurse at once offers to assist in what she imagines is a relatively routine infatuation or love interest.

et hic: "Also here . . ."

timorem: With a hint that fear is a particular trait of a skittish young girl.

409   sedulitas erit apta tibi. nec sentiet umquam

sedulitas: Sedulous care and painstaking, rigorous attention to detail. Cf. 438 *male sedula nutrix.*

apta tibi: The nurse will do exactly what is necessary to help in the particular case of Myrrha's love; the words are soon to take on a meaning she (rather remarkably) does not as yet understand.

410   hoc pater. exsiluit gremio furibunda torumque

pater: Once again in the dramatic last place in the sentence.

gremio: "From the lap"; the ablative is of separation.

furibunda: One of the strongest words in the Latin poetic repertoire to describe the maddened state of the girl.

torum: Myrrha presses the bed with her mouth (411 *ore premens*); the *torus*, of course, is the locus of her eventual sin. The commentators note the parallel to Virgil's Dido (*Aeneid* 659 *os impressa toro*); Ovid may be playing on the same name of Pygmalion, Myrrha's Cypriot ancestor, and the Tyrian king who was Dido's wicked sibling—thus a reason for the association of the two women throughout.

411   ore premens discede, precor, miseroque pudori

misero: "Miserable" or "wretched" because it demands the abandonment of Myrrha's intensely felt passion. *Miseroque pudori* depends on 412 *parce.*

412   parce ait; instanti discede, aut desine dixit

instanti: The nurse continues to press the matter.

discede … desine … dixit: The alliteration neatly evokes the force of the strong imperatives and the force of Myrrha's plea.

413   quaerere quid doleam; scelus est quod scire laboras.

A crucial line for the study of Myrrha's psychology; she knows that what she desires constitutes a *scelus*.

doleam: Present subjunctive in an indirect question after *quid*.

414   horret anus tremulasque manus annisque metuque

horret: Another of the many "bristling" words in a book replete with arboreal metamorphoses and the hazards of wild fauna.

tremulas: The nurse's hands tremble both because of her age and her fear for Myrrha's situation.

annisque metuque: Ablatives of cause.

415   tendit et ante pedes supplex procumbit alumnae;

alumnae: Myrrha, her charge.

procumbit: The nurse essentially prostrates herself in supplication before the girl.

416   et modo blanditur, modo, si non conscia fiat,

blanditur: At first she utters words and performs gestures that are designed to cajole and coax Myrrha.

conscia: A sharer (*con-*) in the knowledge (*scia*).

417   terret et indicium laquei coeptaque minatur

indicium: "Revelation" or "disclosure" of the suicide attempt (*laquei*).

coepta: "The beginnings" of the suicide that the nurse interrupted.

418   mortis, et officium commisso spondet amori.

officium: In effective contrast with *indicium:* the nurse is more than ready to assist Myrrha in the pursuit of her passion—though she is still in ignorance of the identity of the girl's *objet d'amour.*

commiso ... amori: The love to which Myrrha is committed, whatever that love might be.

419   extulit illa caput lacrimisque implevit obortis

lacrimis: Tears once again dominate the narrative of the etiology of the myrrh tree.

obortis: From *oboriri.* The tears that are falling begin to fill the bosom (420 *pectora*) of the nurse.

420   pectora nutricis conataque saepe fateri

conataque ... fateri: Myrrha is unable to speak because of her grief and distress (as well as fear and shame at the revelation); she is reminiscent of those Ovidian characters who lose the power of human voice because of metamorphosis into animal or plant form.

421   saepe tenet vocem pudibundaque vestibus ora

pudibunda: "Shameful" or "disgraceful"; cf. 410 *furibunda.* Myrrha covers her face with her clothes (perhaps to conceal any telltale blushing).

422   texit et o dixit felicem coniuge matrem!

felicem ... matrem: Accusative of exclamation. Once again the poet narrator returns to the question of what it means to be *felix;* the present passage is in distinct contrast to the idea at 299 that Cinyras might have been considered fortunate had he not had any children.

coniuge: An ablative of specification.

423   hactenus, et gemuit. gelidus nutricis in artus

hactenus: that is, *hac-tenus*; "thus far," "up to this point": Myrrha need say no more.

gemuit: Bömer offers parallels of the groans and laments of lovers (cf. the *suspiria* when Myrrha heard the name of her father), with special reference once again to Virgil's Dido.

gelidus: With 424 *tremor*.

424   ossaque (sensit enim) penetrat tremor, albaque toto

penetrat: The fear goes through the bone to the very marrow, as it were.

tremor: The delayed noun for *gelidus* closes a neat ring: the "chill fear" penetrates to the limbs and bones, which are enveloped syntactically by that which drills into them.

toto: With 425 *vertice*; the hair on the nurse's whole head bristled at Myrrha's words.

425   vertice canities rigidis stetit hirta capillis.

stetit: Exactly the same as the English idiom of hair standing on end.

hirta: "That which is covered by hair" (*OLD*).

426   multaque ut excuteret diros, si posset, amores

diros: cf. 300.

excuteret: Literally, that she might "shake out" the dire, accursed love. Cf. 739; the verb will recur at the very end of the book, in a quite different sense.

427   addidit; at virgo scit se non falsa moneri,

Once again Ovid underscores Myrrha's awareness of the reality of the situation, as well as the young woman's virginal state.

at: A strongly adversative word; that is, a more intense conjunction than *sed.*

428   certa mori tamen est, si non potiatur amore.

certa mori: Like Dido at Virgil, *Aeneid* 4.564; the poet narrator continues the frequent references to Virgil's Carthaginian queen, who in his epic stands rather in opposition to the image that Camilla presents in the second half of the poem—cf. Myrrha and Atalanta in Ovid's book.

potiatur: The verb *potiri* takes the ablative.

429   vive ait haec, potiere tuo—et non est ausa parente

haec: that is, the nurse.

potiere: the verb takes the ablative (*tuo ... parente*); the repetition of the verb is very much in Ovid's style.

430   dicere conticuit promissaque numine firmat.

numine: A strong word: the nurse shores up her promises with a nod of divine favor, as it were.

431   festa piae Cereris celebrabant annua matres

piae Cereris: Cf. 270, of the festival of Venus where Pygmalion made his prayer. The mention of the goddess Ceres returns the audience to the memory of the Proserpina story from Book 5, as another third of the epic hastens to a close.

432   illa, quibus nivea velatae corpora veste

nivea: Snow-white, with connotations of purity.

corpora: Accusative of respect

433   primitias frugum dant spicea serta suarum

primitias: The "first fruits" or first offerings.

spicea: "(Of wreaths) made from ears of corn" (*OLD s.v.* b). The end of the verse has striking alliteration.

434   perque novem noctes Venerem tactusque viriles

Venerem: A good example of metonymy; the name of the goddess is used as a suitable name for the sexual act.

tactusque viriles: cf. 7.239–240. As Bömer notes in his commentary, the poet employs a hendiadys, from the Greek for "one through two"; the *Venus* and the "touches of a man" are essentially the same thing. In one sense the intended effect is to give first the almost epic splendor of the name of the goddess, and then the definition of what exactly the invocation of the name means in the present context.

435   in vetitis numerant. turba Cenchreis in illa

in vetitis: "Among those things that are forbidden." Anderson raises the suspicion that Ovid invented the circumstances for the incest, which is not elsewhere attested in any of the surviving sources; if so, the reason would be to connect the episode with the story of the abduction of Proserpina in Book 5.

Cenchreis: The wife of Cinyras enters the story at last; Ovid introduces here as the spouse of the king (and thus rival of Myrrha), not as the girl's mother.

436   regis adest coniunx arcanaque sacra frequentat.

adest: The verb is used here not of an immortal of course, but the briskly paced book is marked by a number of sudden appearances.

arcanaque sacra: The rites of a mystery religion. The present scene may be meant deliberately to evoke the Eleusinian Mysteries, which celebrate the return of Proserpina to the upper regions from her yearly sojourn in the underworld; there may be an intentional comment, too, on the incest theme that is implicit in such

narratives as those of the union between Proserpina and both Pluto
and Jupiter.

frequentat: cf. English "to frequent" something; the nine-day festival
no doubt requires nine days of liturgical rituals.

437   ergo legitima vacuus dum coniuge lectus,

legitima ... coniuge: Ablative of separation; the bed is free from its
lawful occupant. Bömer notes that the phrase occurs only here;
legitima uxor only in classical poetry at *Amores* 2.545; the point of
course is that a *coniunx* is usually *legitima* by mere implication, with
no need of a legalistic qualifier, as it were; Myrrha has blurred the
whole question, and so the narrator must distinguish between lawful
and unlawful spouses.

438   nacta gravem vino Cinyran male sedula nutrix

nacta: From *nancisci.*

gravem vino: A poetically elevated way to describe the state of the
king's intoxication.

male sedula: Cf. 409. The nurse is *male sedula* precisely because her
sedulous, dutiful service to Myrrha will result in the incestuous union
of daughter and father.

439   nomine mentito veros exponit amores

nomine mentito: The recurring theme of the power of a name; cf. 28,
where the same verb was used in connection with the story of Pluto
and Proserpina—the falsehood theme once again as well. Anderson
comments that Myrrha "pretends insanely that is *not* herself," though
in one sense the point is precisely that Myrrha does *not* pretend—she
takes advantage of the darkness of the night and the absence of light,
the convenient circumstance of the festival of Ceres—with the
introduction of light into the bed chamber, there is absolutely nothing

that conceals the girl from recognition by her father. The point, in part, is to play on the recognition theme from both tragedy and especially New Comedy.

exponit: She expounds upon, or, as it were, "places before" the king the true love of the girl whose name she conceals with a lie.

amores: The plural is regular.

440   et faciem laudat; quaesitis virginis annis

faciem: "Face"; the nurse tells Cinyras first that there is a girl who truly loves him, and then proceeds to praise her physical appearance.

virginis: With pointed force; Myrrha is merely a girl, and, further, she is the daughter of her prospective lover.

441   par ait est Myrrhae. quam postquam adducere iussa est

Myrrhae. quam: The father thinks the two are different, but the juxtaposition of the name and the relative pronoun is deliberately pointed.

442   utque domum rediit, gaude, mea dixit alumna;

ut: "When." This use of *ut* takes the indicative.

443   vicimus! infelix non toto pectore sentit

vicimus: For an interesting exploration of a possible historical allusion here see W. Clarke, "Myrrha's Nurse: The Marathon Runner in Ovid?," in *Classical Philology* 68.1 (1973), 55–56, with reference to the famous announcement of the Athenian victory over the Persians at Marathon.

sentit: Ovid continues his careful delineation of the psychological of the "heroine" of Orpheus' song: she knows even now that rejoicing is not entirely fitting.

444   laetitiam virgo, praesagaque pectora maerent,

praesaga: A significant word in Ovid's poem of change; cf. the related *vatum praesagia* of 15.879, the final verse of the epic. It is probably no accident that it occurs here, in this narrative of Orpheus.

virgo: The poet narrator continues to emphasize the girl's virginal state.

445   sed tamen et gaudet; tanta est discordia mentis.

discordia mentis: Cf. 9.630.

446   tempus erat quo cuncta silent, interque Triones

For more on the perverse nuptials see especially the article of S. O'Bryhim, "Myrrha's 'Wedding' (Ov. *Met.* 10.446–70)," in *The Classical Quarterly* N.S. 58.1 (2008), 190–195. For the idea that Myrrha's union with her father represents a certain type of underworld visitation, see J. Dyson, "Myrrha's Catabasis," in *The Classical Journal* 94.2 (1998–1999), 163–167.

Triones: Strictly speaking these are oxen that are employed in agricultural works; the term became most famous for its use to describe the constellations Ursa Major and Ursa Minor.

447   flexerat obliquo plaustrum temone Bootes;

temone: The "pole or yoke-beam of a cart, chariot, etc.; also, of a plough" (*OLD*).

Bootes: Or Arctophylax, literally "The Bear Warden" or "Guardian of the Bear"; see here Kidd's commentary on Aratus, *Phaenomena* 91–95. Bootes, as Kidd notes, was conceived because of the linkage of the conspicuous star Arcturus with the seven stars of Ursa Major, when those stars were known as the Wagon or Wain; the *plaustrum* thus here is the Great Bear. The constellation is thus something of a composite ("not an obvious group," Kidd notes), and so it is not entirely surprising that the "constellation" is referred to by a variety of names, and that (as likely below at 450), Bootes and Icarius become synonymous; cf. Propertius, c. 2.33.24). Bootes thus became associated with other mythological personages (not only Icarius, but also Arcas, the son of Callisto, who was transformed into a she-bear).

448   ad facinus venit illa suum. fugit aurea caelo

The story has been long; Myrrha's arrival at the scene of the crime is told with effective concision; cf. 454 *it tamen.*

aurea: With 449 *luna.*

caelo: Separative ablative.

449   luna, tegunt nigrae latitantia sidera nubes,

nigrae: The clouds are dark as if with an impending storm or tempest.

sidera: "Constellations," as often; here they are hiding (*latitantia*), lest they witness Myrrha's incestuous union.

450   nox caret igne suo; primus tegis, Icare, vultus

caret: The verb takes an ablative of separation (*igne suo*); the night is deprived of its own light (i.e., from the moon and the stars).

Icare: that is, Bootes or the bright star Arcturus in the constellation Bootes ("ein Stern am Sternbild des Bootes," as Bömer puts it; see further Kidd's commentary on Aratus, *Phaenomena* 91–95). Icarius (or Icarus) was transformed along with his faithful daughter Erigone and the hound Maera (destined to be the Dog Star). It is likely that the similarity of the dog's name to Myrrha gave Ovid one reason for the description of the flight of the stars; Icarius and Erigone also provide a *melior* comparison of how a father and her daughter should act.

vultus: Poetic plural.

451   Erigoneque pio sacrata parentis amore.

Erigone: The daughter of Icarius, who committed suicide after the death of her father; the contrast with Myrrha's behavior is striking. *Post mortem* Erigone was rewarded by Dionysus with a memorial catasterism or stellar metamorphosis as the constellation Virgo. The story of the family is preserved, for example, in the mythographer Hyginus' *Fabulae*; Icarius was said to have introduced the art of viticulture to provincials at the behest of Dionysus; the villagers were upset when they became drunk and mistook intoxication for poisoning. They killed Icarius, and his daughter committed suicide out of grief. The suicide motif thus recurs; the implication is that Myrrha *should* have followed the example of Erigone, if only in the taking of her own life.

452   ter pedis offensi signo est revocata, ter omen

Stumbling on a threshold was a sign of ill omen and bad luck.

omen: Cf. the same image from the opening of the book, as Hymenaeus did not bring his *felix omen* to the nuptials of Orpheus and Eurydice.

453   funereus bubo letali carmine fecit;

bubo: The horned owl was often considered a bird of ill omen.

letali carmine: A dreadful or lethal song; the noise of the owl is considered a harbinger of imminent death.

454   it tamen, et tenebrae minuunt noxque atra pudorem,

The darkness of night seems to diminish the sense of shame.

nox: The adjective *atra* is a regular enough description of the night in Latin poetry; perhaps the noun should be capitalized to refer to the vaguely personified goddess Night.

455   nutricisque manum laeva tenet, altera motu

laeva: With deliberate reference to the adjective's sense of "unfavorable" and "adverse" (*OLD s.v.* 4).

456   caecum iter explorat. thalami iam limina tangit,

thalami … limina: The nurse's conveyance of Myrrha to Cinyras' bed chamber is a perversion of the Roman nuptial liturgy.

iam: Bömer's commentary discusses the anaphora of the adverb in this sequence, and also the parallels to the description of Byblis' actions at 9.466 ff.

457   iamque fores aperit, iam ducitur intus; at illi

ducitur: Ducere is used of a man's marriage to a woman (*vs. nubere* of a woman's to a man).

458   poplite succiduo genua intremuere fugitque

succiduo: Not a particularly common adjective; Bömer notes that it occurs elsewhere in Ovid only at *Heroides* 13.24.

intremuere: Third person perfect indicative active alternative form for *intremuerunt*.

459   et color et sanguis animusque relinquit euntem.

animus: Myrrha's courage begins to falter.

euntem: Accusative participle from *ire*.

460   quoque suo propior sceleri est, magis horret et ausi

quo: Ablative of degree of difference; = "by which the more."

suo: With particular emphasis on how the crime is hers and hers alone.

sceleri est: The synaloepha or merging of the two syllables into one enacts the closeness of Myrrha to the crime she has contemplated for so long.

461   paenitet et vellet non cognita posse reverti.

paenitet: The verb governs the genitive object *ausi* (460).

462   cunctantem longaeva manu deducit et alto

cunctantem: A significant participial form in Augustan poetry. Both this verse and 463 open with a participle, the first in the present, the second (*admotam*) in the perfect as Myrrha is moved from the couch.

alto: Perhaps to reflect Cinyras' regal status; cf. the very different description of 465.

463   admotam lecto cum traderet accipe dixit

accipe: The succinct, almost brusque language continues.

464   ista tua est, Cinyre devotaque corpora iunxit.

ista: With unintentionally (at least on the part of the nurse) pejorative sense.

devotaque corpora: The language evokes the Roman tradition of *devotio*.

465   accipit obsceno genitor sua viscera lecto

obsceno ... lecto: The "lofty couch" of the king has been replaced with an obscene bed as Myrrha joins with her father in perverse union. For the framing of the incestuous couple by the *obscenus lectus* see D. Lateiner, "Mimetic Syntax from Word Order, Especially in Ovid," in *The American Journal of Philology* 111.2 (1990), 204–237, 221, with extensive consideration of how Ovid uses language to imitate speech and action.

466   virgineosque metus levat hortaturque timentem

virgineosque metus: Once again, Myrrha's virginal state is emphasized.

467   forsitan aetatis quoque nomine filia dixit,

See here especially M. Lowrie, "Myrrha's Second Taboo: Ovid's *Metamorphoses* 10.467–468," in *Classical Philology* 88.1 (1993), 50–52, which provides a study of how Ovid details the "multiple transgressions" that characterize Myrrha's behavior.

forsitan: The adverb introduces a sordid speculation on Orpheus' part. For *forsitan* with the indicative Bömer compares 5.333; cf. the opening of the Atalanta and Hippomenes narrative at 560 below for the more usual construction.

aetatis … nomine: "With the name of her age," that is, with an affectionate diminutive appropriate to her youth; the emphasis on naming continues. The theme of what one should be called is related to ethnographic concerns: the name of a people and a place.

468   dixit et illa pater, sceleri ne nomina desint.

The emphasis on onomastics reaches its perverse climax; both Cinyras and Myrrha use the titles of the familial bond.

illa: Bömer notes that the remote demonstrative is here rather akin to *ea*; the point, though, may be to refer to Myrrha as something like "that infamous one."

469   plena patris thalamis excedit et impia diro

plena: "Pregnant."

impia: With 470 *semina*. The child of this union is the offspring of a perversion of the *pietas* that should govern the relationship between a father and daughter.

470   semina fert utero conceptaque crimina portat.

First the descriptions and authorial comments were made (*impia; diro*); then the physical realities they label (*semina; utero*).

concepta: And so her ancestor Pygmalion had "conceived" a love for his statue, which he had created and in a very real sense fathered; the daughter of Cinyras has inherited something of the incestuous history of the family.

471   postera nox facinus geminat, nec finis in illa est,

postera nox: Nowhere else in classical poetry, as Bömer notes, while *postera lux* is not at all unusual (half a dozen times on Ovid); the crime of Myrrha is a nocturnal one, from which the constellations have averted their gaze.

geminat: "Doubles," perhaps with a play on the notion of twinning.

illa: sc. *nocte.*

472   cum tandem Cinyras, avidus cognoscere amantem

cum tandem: Cf. 480.

amantem: Cf. 466 *timentem*; there is subtle hint in the text that Myrrha's fear diminished with each encounter.

473   post tot concubitus, inlato lumine vidit

inlato lumine: "With a light having been brought in," that is, a torch or other source of illumination.

474   et scelus et natam; verbisque dolore retentis

The language effectively paints the picture of the daughter and the crime as one and the same.

dolore: Ablative of cause; Cinyras' strongly felt emotion took away his power of speech.

475   pendenti nitidum vagina deripit ensem.

pendenti ... vagina: Cinyas' sheath for his sword was hanging near the bed. The scene owes much to Virgil's description of Pallas at *Aeneid* 10.474–475 *At Pallas magnis emittit viribus hastam / vaginaque cava fulgentem deripit ensem.* The two passages both occur at almost exactly the same verse in their respective epics (surely no coincidence); at one level, there is a seemingly ludicrous reappropriation of the earlier, martial passage to a scene from the incestuous bed chamber. At another, there is a careful evocation of Virgil's young hero just before the introduction of the Adonis sequence; Virgil's Pallas, like Adonis and Hyacinthus, is memorialized by a flower image. See further R. Smith, *Poetic Embrace and Poetic Allusion in Ovid and Virgil*, Ann Arbor: The University of Michigan Press, (1997), 71–72, for a brief and useful study of the common poetic use of the flower image to describe the premature death of young men.

nitidum ... ensem: The sword gleams in the *inlato lumine* (473); the adjective will recur later, in the context of the golden apples that seduce Atalanta.

476   Myrrha fugit tenebrisque et caecae munere noctis

caecae munere noctis: "The boon of the blind (i.e., dark) night." Ovid's Orpheus effects a contrast between the light that Cinyras brought into the *thalamus* and the darkness into which Myrrha now flees in shame and terror.

477   intercepta neci est, latosque vagata per agros

intercepta: "Taken away" (with ablative of separation; cf. *OLD s.v.* 2).

vagata: From *vagari*.

478   palmiferos Arabas Panchaeaque rura relinquit.

Cf. 309. Yet again, the emphasis is on geography and space, in this case rather remotely conceived, quasi-magical lands of the distant East, territories that also formed part of the somewhat poetically embellished dream of the *Pax Augusta* and its sway over the known world.

palmiferos: "Palm-bearing," as the story hastens to its arboreal climax.

479   perque novem erravit redeuntis cornua lunae,

That is, for nine months, or the duration of her pregnancy. Cf. 434 and the nine nights of the festival of Ceres that was the occasion for the perverse spectacle.

480   cum tandem terra requievit fessa Sabaea;

cum tandem: Cf. 472.

Sabaea: The romanticized mention of eastern lands is in part a reflection of how myrrh was imported to Rome from the Arabian peninsula.

481   vixque uteri portabat onus. tum nescia voti

uteri … onus: that is, the unborn child.

nescia voti: Myrrha does not know what she should pray for, that is, a safe delivery, or the death of mother and child.

482   atque inter mortisque metus et taedia vitae

mortis metus: Myrrha is afraid of life, even as she is sick of the existence in which she finds herself.

taedia vitae: Taedium can refer to a disgust with life or a repugnance at its vicissitudes. Cf. 625.

483   est tales complexa preces: o si qua patetis

complexa: From *complecti.*

qua: That is, *aliqua.*

patetis: Answered by 488 *patet.*

484   numina confessis, merui nec triste recuso

merui: Once again, the poet Orpheus underscores Myrrha's awareness
of her guilt.

triste: The *supplicium* (485) is *triste* because it may amount to nothing
less than death—or perhaps something even worse.

485   supplicium. sed ne violem vivosque superstes

The narrative returns to the theme of how metamorphosis is a sort of
middle ground between life and death; Myrrha does not wish to
violate either the living by remaining alive as a human, or the dead by
being a shade in the underworld.

superstes: In apposition to the implied first person singular in *violem*;
as a "survivor" Myrrha would be an affront to the living, and if dead
(486 *mortua*) she would be a disgrace to the dead.

486   mortuaque exstinctos, ambobus pellite regnis

ambobus ... regnis: That is, earth and the underworld. *Ambo* follows
the same declensional pattern as *duo* and is one of the few vestiges in
Latin of the "dual" form that is more frequently encountered in Greek.

487   mutataeque mihi vitamque necemque negate.

A line of powerful and effectively juxtaposed alliterations, as Myrrha
closes her solemn appeal for a status between life and death. In an
important sense, what Myrrha requests is a reflection in itself of the

larger problem of the fate of the soul *post mortem*, where one finds the
competing theologies, as it were, of a permanent afterlife; of the rebirth
of souls into new bodies; of no existence or sensation whatsoever after
death. Myrrha wants to be driven into exile from both life and death.

mutataeque mihi: Dative of reference (here either of advantage or
disadvantage, depending on one's point of view).

488   numen confessis aliquod patet; ultima certe

patet: Responding to 483 *patetis*.

ultima: With 489 *vota*; the "ultimate votive offerings" are the prayers
made by those on the cusp of an existence in which supplication and
entreaty will be impossible.

489   vota suos habuere deos. nam crura loquentis

deos: Anderson notes here that in the *Metamorphoses* of the
mythographer Antoninus Liberalis the god responsible for answering
Myrrha's prayer is Zeus; Hyginus, in contrast, credits Venus, while
Pseudo-Apollodorus, like Ovid, does not specify the responsible deity
or deities. The absence of specificity, and the narrative detail about
how final prayers find their own divine patrons, points to how the
transformation of Myrrha is something of an unquestioned necessity:
this girl *needs* to disappear, as it were, into the eternally lachrymose
myrrh tree, which will have its associations not with victory (cf. the
laurel), but with funerals and the preservation of the dead for burial.

crura: The transformation begins with the legs of the girl; the
metamorphosis will be arboreal, and so fittingly enough first the
impact on the legs is described, as Myrrha is rooted to the ground.

loquentis: Myrrha will lose the power of speech (a recurring topos and
point of emphasis in Ovidian descriptions of metamorphosis; the
transformation begins as the girl is still speaking).

490   terra supervenit, ruptosque obliqua per ungues

ruptosque ... ungues: The transformation is violent and grisly.

obliqua: With 491 *radix.*

491   porrigitur radix, longi firmamina trunci,

longi ... trunci: cf. 493 *magnos ... ramos*; the emphasis is on the large size of the tree.

firmamina: A "support or prop"; the word is not common (though not, as Bömer reminds us, a *hapax legomenon*, a word "read once" only in the extant literature); in a sense, Myrrha becomes a metaphorical mother of a new lineage, rooted firmly in consequence of her arboreal metamorphosis; the contrast with the virginal Daphne and the birth of the laurel is pronounced.

492   ossaque robur agunt, mediaque manente medulla

ossa: Myrrha's bones provide the matter for the strength of the trunk of the tree and its characteristic hardness.

agunt: Agere can mean "to produce" (*OLD s.v.* 11); there may also be a deliberate play on the botanical sense of the verb, which can describe the sending forth of shoots or buds (*OLD s.v.* 10).

medulla: "Marrow."

493   sanguis it in sucos, in magnos bracchia ramos,

sucos: The "sap."

494   in parvos digiti, duratur cortice pellis.

pellis: The word can be applied either to animal or human flesh, though in the latter case it often implies a somewhat rough and uncultivated state; the point may be that Myrrha has been dehumanized by her experiences and has entered an animal-like state that is now being transformed into yet another reality.

duratur: The emphasis on the hardness of the tree relates to the escape from emotion that Myrrha in some sense seeks; this flight from sensitivity relates to her willingness to violate the expectations of paternal *pietas*. Still, the soft inner heart remains (cf. 493); Myrrha's metamorphosis is decidedly more complex than many others in the epic—fittingly enough for the girl who wishes to exist between two worlds, as it were.

495   iamque gravem crescens uterum praestrinxerat arbor

gravem . . . uterum: She is, after all, still pregnant. Adonis will literally be the child of the myrrh tree.

praestrinxerat: "Had grazed."

496   pectoraque obruerat collum operire parabat;

parabat: Perhaps with inceptive force; the tree was beginning to cover over Myrrha's neck. The passage owes something to 9.324–393 and the similar story of Dryope. The description of this stage of the metamorphosis hints at the suppression of the power of speech (cf. the Dryope narrative) that stands at the heart of many of Ovid's metamorphoses.

497   non tulit illa moram venientique obvia ligno

non tulit: "She did not brook" (any delay, *moram*).

obvia: Literally "in the way of"; Myrrha rushes forth to the best of her ability to meet the approaching bark.

498   subsedit mersitque suos in cortice vultus.

subsedit: Perhaps with sexual connotations; cf. 284.

mersitque suos ... vultus: Myrrha is ashamed of her deeds and seeks escape from the reproving gaze of others. The reflexive possessive adjective has special force—this is Myrrha's crime and Myrrha's shame.

499   quae quamquam amisit veteres cum corpore sensus,

veteres ... sensus: Her human feelings. There is likely a direct reference here to her incestuous feelings for Cinyras; the arboreal metamorphosis has resolved her illicit passion at last.

500   flet tamen, et tepidae manant ex arbore guttae.

The lachrymose girl continues to cry in her new manifestation. The tears are clearly not to be taken so much as part of her *veteres sensus*, but rather as the essential, defining characteristic of the girl. Cf. the desire of Cyparissus to lament for all time on account of the death of his deer.

tepidae: The tears themselves reflect the emotional state of the girl; her salient characteristic continues even in her new state of existence.

501   est honor et lacrimis, stillataque robora murra

honor: An interesting and important detail; Ovid's (Orpheus') Myrrha is depicted in complex terms: she is not without honor, or more precisely, her tears are not devoid of honor. In part this reflects the fact that her deeds deserve to be the source of mourning; there may be an implicit comparison between her arboreal crying and the tears she shed *before* her final decision to pervert her relationship with Cinyras.

stillata: The verb means to drip or to fall in drops.

502   nomen erile tenet nulloque tacebitur aevo.

erile: That which belongs to a master or mistress.

tacebitur: An impersonal passive use. Metamorphosis regularly deprives its victim of the power of speech; in the case of Myrrha, there will be silence in no age. The impersonal construction is important; it is not so much that *Myrrha* will not be silent—she has, after all, been stripped of the ability to talk—but the tears that still fall create their own sound, as it were, for all time, and the very existence of the tree is a memorial to the whole sordid affair.

503–559. *Adonis and Venus.* Apart from the late first/early second century B.C. *Epitaph* of Bion (on which see especially Reed's Cambridge edition (1997)), there is no earlier extant version than Ovid's for this exceptionally popular tale, though a fragment of Panyasis does preserve evidence of the story of Adonis' birth from the myrrh tree. See further V. Emeljanow, "Ovidian Mannerism: An Analysis of the Venus and Adonis Episode," in *Mnemosyne* 22.1 (1969), 67–76, which special consideration of Ovid's language, and with material that is useful for a study of the playful and wittier aspects of the poet's art.

503   At male conceptus sub robore creverat infans

male conceptus: A strong commentary on the nature of Myrrha's affair with Cinyras.

infans: Literally, the one who cannot speak; the would-be newborn will grow within the bark of the tree, and will in a sense end life as it began, its humanity transformed into botanical life. The language continues the emphasis of the story on the power of speech.

504   quaerebatque viam qua se genetrice relicta

quaerebat: Conative (or perhaps inceptive) imperfect; the infant kept trying to find a way to escape his maternal tree (with durative/frequentative force as well).

genetrice relicta: "With his mother having been left behind"; there is something of an image of the infant almost recoiling in shame from his mother and desperate to escape her presence.

505 exsereret; media gravidus tumet arbore venter.

gravidus tumet ... venter: The tree is pregnant. The description of the tree's travails as Adonis reaches the moment of his birth is in the form of a Golden Line, which again renders a tone of solemnity to the aftermath of the rather sordid affair.

506 tendit onus matrem, neque habent sua verba dolores,

Once again the emphasis is on the suppression of speech that arboreal transformation entails. Myrrha can still cry, but she cannot utter the plaintive and painful laments of those in childbirth (but cf. 508–509).

tendit onus: Standard enough language for pregnancy (parallels in Bömer).

507 nec Lucina potest parientis voce vocari.

Lucina: The goddess of childbirth, who was usually identified with either Juno or Diana. Early inscriptions record the form of her name as *Loucina.*

508 nitenti tamen est similis curvataque crebros

nitenti: "To one struggling," that is, to one in the labors of birth. *Similis* is a key word; the myrrh tree is *similar* to a woman giving birth, since of course the woman in this case no longer exists. The tree is now depicted as giving forth frequent groans (*crebros/gemitus*); the point is that like any tree on the verge of falling or splitting, there is a sound—but it is nothing like the cries of a woman in actual labor, rather a sad perversion of the usual experience of childbirth. For the use of "anthropomorphizing language" *post*-metamorphosis, see von Glinski (2012: 13).

509   dat gemitus arbor lacrimisque cadentibus umet.

umet: Cf. 505 *tumet.* Once again, Myrrha is defined by her tears; Cf. 514. The tree is wet with the falling tears of myrrh.

510   constitit ad ramos mitis Lucina dolentes

constitit: The force of the prefix is to emphasize that Lucina was "with" Myrrha in the agonies of her delivery.

mitis: Lucina takes pity on the suffering Myrrha in her labor pains.

ramos ... dolentes: The "suffering branches": the tree continues to be effectively described as if it were a woman enduring an especially painful delivery (in this case made all the worse by the arboreal circumstances).

511   admovitque manus et verba puerpera dixit;

admovit: The goddess moves her hands to the bark of the tree and acts as a divine midwife in the delivery process.

verba ... dixit: Almost as if the words of the goddess constituted a magical spell.

puerpera: As a substantive the word refers to a woman who has either very recently had a child (*puer* + *parire*), or a woman who is in the process of delivering one; the adjectival form is extremely rare.

512   arbor agit rimas et fissa cortice vivum

rimas: Fissures or cracks.

vivum: With 513 *onus.* All the force of the line comes at the end, as the tree successfully delivers its offspring, which is rather coldly referred to as a "burden" in light of the sufferings it has caused its now arboreal mother.

513   reddit onus, vagitque puer, quem mollibus herbis

vagit: The cry of an infant; free from his maternal myrrh, Adonis now has something of the power of speech.

mollibus herbis: Fittingly enough, given that one needs to avoid the image of the infant falling down on hard ground. But the description also points to the narrative's emphasis on the exceeding loveliness of Adonis; the handsome, lovely infant deserves a soft bed of grass that is spread, as it were, by water nymphs.

514   Naides impositum lacrimis unxere parentis.

Naides: Water nymphs, who are appropriately described as washing the newborn. Cf. the Naiads who accompanied Eurydice on the day of her marriage/death.

unxere: For *unxerunt.* The water nymphs use myrrh to anoint Adonis, as if he were already dead on the very cusp of life. Myrrh was used in burial practices; Adonis' very origins provide a harbinger of his ultimate fate.

515   laudaret faciem Livor quoque: qualia namque

laudaret: Potential subjunctive.

Livor: Cf. 6.128–129. *Livor* is the personification of Envy and Resentment. "Both disguises and the traditional insignia of divine identity are random and interchangeable, functioning as a costume which does not penetrate to the layer of identity" (von Glinski, 2012: 74).

516   corpora nudorum tabula pinguntur Amorum,

A comparison to the visual arts in this book that is so concerned with artistic representations and depictions.

Amorum: "Cupids."

517   talis erat; sed, ne faciat discrimina cultus,

discrimina: "Distinction" or "difference." Cf. 242; 612.

518   aut huic adde leves aut illis deme pharetras.

A foreshadowing of the hunting habits of Myrrha's offspring; cf. also
525, as the quivered Cupid wounds his mother. A hint of incest, too:
Adonis could be like Cupid, were he simply to have a little quiver, or
were the other to be deprived of his; Venus will become infatuated
with Adonis, and so she will become infatuated with someone who
looks like her son.

leves: "Light," because, after all, they are small.

519   labitur occulte fallitque volatilis aetas,

The line is borrowed from *Amores* 1.8.49.

labitur: The years "glide" or slide by in their swift course; cf. Lucretius,
De Rerum Natura 4.1123.

fallit: The years deceive because they surprise one by their action;
there is no really perceptible change in appearance from day to day,
and yet almost as if by magic there is suddenly the onset of a different
phase of life.

aetas: "Age" or "years"; the passage of time.

520   et nihil est annis velocius. ille sorore

annis: Ablative of comparison.

sorore: An ablative of source or origin, which is of course a natural use
of the separative function of the case.

521   natus avoque suo, qui conditus arbore nuper,

avoque suo: That is, Cinyras; another ablative of source.

nuper: The repeated adverb creates the effect of a swiftly progressing narrative.

522   nuper erat genitus, modo formosissimus infans,

formosissimus: Exceedingly handsome or beautiful.

infans: The first in a trio of life stages: *infans, iuvenis, vir;* cf. the threefold repetition of the adverb *iam* at 523.

523   iam iuvenis, iam vir, iam se formosior ipse est;

se: Ablative of comparison; Adonis is more beautiful than himself—a typically Ovidian paradox.

524   iam placet et Veneri matrisque ulciscitur ignes.

placet: The verb regularly takes the dative. Cf. the use of the verb at 378, where death was pleasing to Myrrha; she has now delivered a son, and the son will snare Venus in a tragic love affair thanks to the carelessness of Cupid with his shafts. Venus had, after all, engendered the success of the passion of Pygmalion for his statue, and now matters will come full circle in the goddess' doomed involvement with the son of Myrrha.

et: "Even." The force of the adverb is that the goddess is not immune to the charms of the exceedingly handsome young man.

matrisque ulciscitur ignes: He avenges the passion of his mother because he will be a source of sorrow and misery for the goddess.

525   iamque pharetratus dum dat puer oscula matri,

Bömer compares the celebrated scene from Virgil, *Aeneid* 1.657 ff. of interaction of Venus and Cupid in the matter of the love to be engendered between Dido and Aeneas, but, as he notes, there is no apparent parallel to the present depiction of affection between mother and son; in the kisses of the boy there may be a hint of the incest theme.

pharetratus . . . puer: Cupid.

526   inscius exstanti destrinxit harundine pectus.

inscius: Both mother and son are sometimes depicted as either capricious or unaware of the consequences of their actions; cf. 528.

exstanti: The shaft is pointing or projecting out as Cupid moves to kiss his mother.

harundine: For the virtual equivalent to *sagitta* Bömer compares 1.471 and 11.325.

527   laesa manu natum dea reppulit; altius actum

laesa: From *laedi*; the goddess was wounded or harmed by the shaft.

natum dea: Son and mother are effectively juxtaposed, just before the verb *reppulit* describes Venus' action in pushing away the careless minor god.

528   vulnus erat specie primoque fefellerat ipsam.

fefellerat: From *fallere*.

ipsam: That is, Venus., with deliberately intensive force—one might never have expected the very goddess of love and loveliness to be a victim of the passions her son and she regularly plot and execute. The goddess herself was deceived; the falsehood theme returns, this time with the goddess as victim. Venus had caused the whole problem, in a sense, by her assent to the prayer of Pygmalion that he might win the chance to love his statue (i.e., his ivory daughter, complete with all the association of ivory as a conduit for false dreams) as a human being; that decision of Venus has led directly to Myrrha's incestuous passion for her father, the conception and birth of Adonis, who now is the *objet d'amour* or love object of the goddess most responsible for his conception (subtle hints there, too, of incest!). The goddess will work her revenge out, ultimately, only in the matter of Atalanta and Hippomenes—in the case of the former, a Diana-like girl who will be yet another casualty of the more or less low level tension between the goddesses whose very existences stand at variance and odds with each other.

529   capta viri forma non iam Cythereia curat

forma: Ablative of cause.

Cythereia: The epithet of Venus takes its name from Cythera, an Aegean island that was sacred to the goddess. Appropriately enough, the miniature catalog begins with an appellation for the goddess that identifies her with a particular place.

530   litora, non alto repetit Paphon aequore cinctam

alto: "Deep."

Paphon: With a reminiscence of the child of Pygmalion and his statue; Ovid continues to link his stories closely together. Once again, there is an emphasis on place and the importance of location, as the poet narrator details what no longer enchants or concerns the goddess in her smitten state.

aequore cinctam: "Sea-girt."

531   piscosamque Cnidon gravidamque Amathunta

piscosam: "Rich in fish."

Amathunta: The accusative of *Amathus*, a town in Cyprus.

532   abstinet et caelo; caelo praefertur Adonis.

caelo praefertur Adonis: An inappropriate and thus ominous status for the mortal, who is preferred even to Olympus. The repetition of *caelo* underscores the questionable behavior of the goddess as she makes Adonis the center of her existence.

533   hunc tenet, huic comes est, adsuetaque semper in umbra

hunc … huic: Once again the repetition is effective; all that Venus cares about now is the exceedingly handsome Adonis.

umbra: Perhaps with a hint of foreshadowing of the other sort of *umbra.*

534   indulgere sibi formamque augere colendo

indulgere: The image is of the carefree goddess at leisure in the shade.

formam augere colendo: In marked contrast to the usual life of the hunt; for Venus and Adonis, a significant portion of the time is spent at rest and with attention to appearance.

535   per iuga per silvas dumosaque saxa vagatur

dumosa: The adjective evokes the image of a briar patch, rocky territory that is thorny and overgrown with bushes and lack of cultivation.

vagatur: A new sort of carefree lifestyle, as the goddess roams about with her mortal lover on hunting expeditions; cf. *vagata* of Myrrha.

536   fine genus vestem ritu succincta Dianae.

fine: Very rare as a preposition, in this case governing the genitive *genus* (from *genu,* the knee).

Dianae: Venus is playacting Diana. The image is borrowed from the first book of the *Aeneid,* where the goddess behaves similarly in her appearance to her son Aeneas in Carthage, where she announced the story of Dido, whom Virgil also compares to Diana (however problematically and inappropriately) as she enters the temple of Juno at Carthage and is first seen by the Trojan hero; with *ritu succincta Dianae* cf. 9.89. The present detail is a highly significant indication of the essential conflict between the rival goddesses, immortals who represent such vastly different perceptions of acceptable and desirable behavior.

537   hortaturque canes tutaeque animalia praedae,

hortaturque canes: At first we might think the point is that the goddess is driving on hunting hounds after some ferocious beast (and cf. 710, where Adonis' dogs track the fateful boar); soon we realize that the concern is that Adonis (and Venus) pursue only safe prey, and that the point of the dogs is that they may serve to make the hunter safer; in the end Adonis' hounds will do him little good.

tutae ... praedae: The key detail of the hunting exploits of the goddess and her lover; there is to be no real risk, no peril or hazard incurred on the expeditions.

538   aut pronos lepores aut celsum in cornua cervum

pronos: "Close to the ground." Bömer in his commentary collects the parallels for depictions of the behavior of hares and their traditional timidity. Ovid is being his humorous self here, as he describes the goddess urging her pseudo-heroic lover to hunt small animals.

cornua cervum: The line-end is likely borrowed from Virgil, *Aeneid* 10.725 *conspexit capream aut surgentem in cornua cervum*; cf. Martial, *ep.* 13.94.1. The hunt is to be concerned with safe prey, whether one is concerned with animals that hug the ground or with taller fauna.

539   aut agitat dammas; a fortibus abstinet apris

dammas: The word can be applied generally and without taxonomic precision to any sort of smaller deer; the noun is of common gender and is sometimes spelled *dama*.

apris: Wild boars: the animal that will eventually kill Adonis is named first in the miniature catalog of dangerous beasts. Bömer lists the many parallels for the topos in poetic descriptions of the storied ferocity of wild animals. Diana, of course, was the Mistress of Animals; Venus, in contrast, would prefer to have nothing to do with animals that can actually fight back against a hunter (or huntress). The two rival goddess are at last in direct conflict.

540   raptoresque lupos armatosque unguibus ursos

raptores: "Predatory."

ursos: One might cf. the hunting expedition of Arcas in the Callisto story, where the son inadvertently hunts the bear into which is mother has been transformed.

541   vitat et armenti saturatos caede leones

armenti: "Of the flock": the lions are sated with the slaughter of sheep and domesticated animals.

caede leones: Cf. Horace, c. 3.2.11–12. The lions are "saturated with the slaughter."

542   te quoque ut hos timeas, si quid prodesse monendo

quid: For *aliquid* (after *si*).

monendo: Gerund in an ablative of means.

543   possit, Adoni, monet fortisque fugacibus esto

fugacibus: A dative of reference; Adonis is urged to be valiant only in the matter of animals that readily run away from the first approach of the hunter.

esto: The future imperative; Venus' command is meant to be especially solemn and binding. It will in essence be ignored.

544   inquit, in audaces non est audacia tuta.

audaces ... audacia: Another typically Ovidian paradox; further, there can be no true *tuta audacia*—the poet indulges in more humor in advance of the death of the goddess' lover.

545   parce meo, iuvenis, temerarius esse periclo,

parce: The verb regular takes the dative (here *meo ... periclo*). Bömer's commentary collects the many poetic parallels for the use of the imperative form of the verb with an infinitive. Venus essentially wants Adonis to behave like the rabbits and other trivial, harmless game whose conquest she enjoins.

iuvenis: Cf. 523 *iam iuvenis, iam vir:* the Orphic/Ovidian narrator had indicated a transition from youth to manhood, while Venus uses the endearing language of Adonis as youth.

546   neve feras quibus arma dedit natura lacesse,

arma: The metaphorical weapons of tusks and teeth; the *ungues,* for example, with which the bears are armed.

547   stet mihi ne magno tua gloria. non movet aetas

magno: Ablative of price.

non movet aetas: Cf. 615. The emphasis is once again on age and youth; Venus' point is that the animal kingdom is not impressed by Adonis' young age and feels no need to be sensitive to it.

548   nec facies nec quae Venerem movere leones.

quae ... leones: If we are to take the relative clause as the last part of a tricolon of those things that do not move wild animals, then this constitutes a reference to the lions that convey the goddess' chariot (with a conflation of Venus and Cybele): the transition to the inserted tale of Atalanta and Hippomenes is thus presaged. Otherwise, one may punctuate as Anderson does: *nec facies nec, quae Venerem movere, leones*, where *quae* refers to further unspecified qualities of Adonis that move the goddess and not the animal kingdom.

549   saetigerosque sues oculosque animisoque ferarum.

Tarrant brackets this verse as a likely interpolation.

550   fulmen habent acres in aduncis dentibus apri,

The goddess dwells yet again on the animal that will bring death to Adonis.

aduncis: "Curved" or "hooked"; the adjective is regularly used in descriptions of parts of the bodies of animals.

551   impetus est fulvis et vasta leonibus ira,

vasta … ira: The anger of lions is the focal point that brings the narrative to the story of the huntress and her ultimate leonine metamorphosis.

552   invisumque mihi genus est. quae causa roganti

roganti: Adonis asks his divine lover why lions are hateful to her.

553   dicam ait et veteris monstrum mirabere culpae.

monstrum: Properly of any portentous thing; in this case, the reference is pointedly applied to the animal metamorphosis that constitutes the climax of the forthcoming story.

mirabere: That is, *miraberis.* The alternative form is metrically convenient.

554   sed labor insolitus iam me lassavit, et ecce

labor insolitus: A typically Ovidian detail: the goddess is tired out by the unaccustomed exercise. "Ruhepause auf der Jagd als erotisches

Thema" (Bömer); = the pause for rest on the hunt as the erotic theme. Dido and Aeneas consummated their own love affair in the context of a hunt; the hunt is a theme behind the drama of Camilla, a narrative replete in its own erotic associations.

555   opportuna sua blanditur populus umbra

blanditur: Cf. the action of the nurse with Myrrha; the tree offers the seductive image of shady rest during the apparently exhausting hunt.

sua ... umbra: The tree provides its own shade; the poet may once again be playing on the different meanings of *umbra*.

populus: "A poplar tree."

556   datque torum caespes; libet hac requiescere tecum

caespes: Properly the topmost layer of a grassy surface, the "turf."

hac: With 557 *humo.*

557   —et requievit—humo pressitque et gramen et ipsum,

requievit: The subject is likely Venus, though the point is essentially the same with either goddess or mortal lover as the one who first takes rest in the shade of the tree. The emphasis on rest continues in the repetition of *requiescere, requievit*; the rest will be all too short lived, and the forthcoming action equally brief and fatal to its actor.

ipsum: That is, Adonis.

558   inque sinu iuvenis posita cervice reclinis

The image owes something to the description of Venus with Mars at the start of Lucretius' *De Rerum Natura*; this is an all too fleeting moment of safety and security for the mortal lover before his encounter with the boar results in an outcome no less deadly than that of the great Calydonian boar hunt of Book 8.

559   sic ait ac mediis interserit oscula verbis:

The story is introduced with erotic undertones that mirror the ultimate problem of Atalanta and Hippomenes, who prove unable to control their lustful passion.

560–707. *Atalanta and Hippomenes*. Ovid has already introduced Atalanta (in Book 8), as a contestant in the Calydonian boar hunt (8.317–323). The present story within a story makes no direct reference to the previous narrative, which had ended with no clear resolution of Atalanta's fate: it was as if she had wandered off after Meleager's death, with the poet ready to move on to other characters and tales. We shall see in the present sequence how Ovid responds to a number of literary concerns in a relatively short compass of lines: 1) the confused preexisting tradition of *two* Atalantas, one associated with the boar hunt and the other with the celebrated race with the golden apples; 2) Virgil's depiction of the huntress-heroine Camilla in the *Aeneid*, which provided a literary model for Ovid's Atalanta; 3) most importantly, the significance of the character in the overall structure of Ovid's epic, where her stories come at both the very midpoint of the poem and the close of its second third.

The story of Atalanta's race first appears in surviving classical literature in Hesiod, in fragments of his *Catalogue of Women*. The narrative of the race is substantially extant (fr. 75 and fr. 76 Merkelbach-West; fr. 48 in Most's Loeb edition). The account in Hesiod provides a clear source for Ovid's version here: the agreement to run a race for the prize of Atalanta's hand or the penalty of death, the throwing of the apples by the suitor to distract the swift girl—even an unintentionally dramatic ending as the papyrus fragment breaks off just as the victorious would-be husband is left panting at the finish line. For general study of Atalanta in Ovid especially, as well as other sources, see West, 1983: 49–50; 135; Gantz, 1993; Fratantuono, 2005, 2008,

2011; Hunter, 2005: 213–216; Barchiesi, 2006; Ziogas, 2013 (this last item with special reference to Ovid's borrowings and inheritance from Hesiod). On the significance of the allusion to Atalanta in context with other famous apples of mythology, see L. Fratantuono, "Apples for Atalanta: A Reading of *Priapea*, c. 16," in *Bolletino di studi latini* (2014), 21–32. In the notes below Ovid's reception of his diverse material, and his method of presenting what was already in his day a tangle of sometimes contradictory material, is explored in light of the importance of Atalanta to the climax of the second movement of his tripartite poem.

Atalanta has been widely celebrated in the visual and musical arts; cf. Reid (1993: 237–240).

560   Forsitan audieris aliquam certamine cursus

forsitan: An old word, found in both poetry and prose from an early date. Ovid's Venus opens her story with words designed to build suspense: the swift huntress will not be named for five lines (565 below). Cleverly, the assonance and alliteration of *audieris aliquam* and *certamine cursus* highlight the two women on Ovid's literary mind: Atalanta, whose story he will now "complete," and Camilla, the character from Virgil on whom he models his mysterious girl.

audieris: The verb introduces an indirect statement with infinitive (561 *superasse*) and subject accusative (*aliquam*). *Audieris* is a shortened or "syncopated" form of *audiveris*, the perfect subjunctive. Latin uses either the perfect or the present subjunctive independently to express potentiality: "perhaps you may hear/may have heard." There is no significant difference between the use of the present and perfect subjunctives in this construction; the perfect might convey more of a sense of the completion of the act, but English translations would not usually reflect the subtlety.

certamine: The ablative can be used to denote specification: Atalanta surpassed men in racing contests (genitive *cursus* dependent on *certamine*). With *cursus* compare 570 *cursu* below: Latin epic poets often repeat words in close sequence to create the effect of a tightly compressed and coherent narrative, and this story has an unusually high concentration of such repetitions (so also, for example, 561 *veloces* and 571 *veloci*; 560 *certamine* and 572 *certaminis*; 563 *pedum* and 570 *pedibus*), which may help to create the image of a breathless narrative for the drama of the race.

561   veloces superasse viros: non fabula rumor

Ovid here distinguishes *fabula* and *rumor.* Venus opens her story with an almost casual comment about the rumor that there was once a girl who could outrace all men, however swift; the goddess declares here that the rumor is no story, but true—with a hint of a joke on the part of the poet, who is, of course, telling a *fabula.* Latin poets sometimes introduce mythological stories and "etiologies" or explanations of natural events and wonders with the language of hearing, rumor, and story: "there are those who say … they say that … the story is told that …"

superasse: A syncopated form of *superavisse,* the perfect infinitive active. The abbreviated form is metrically convenient and appears often in poetry. The perfect infinitive expresses action in primary sequence that was completed before the time of the main verb.

562   ille fuit—superabat enim—, nec dicere posses,

ille: The demonstrative, as ever, "points out" the noun to which it refers; Latin has no definite article, but the use of *ille* led to the familiar articles of the Romance languages: cf. French *le.*

fuit: Latin has no simple past (i.e., aorist) tense, and so the perfect must function as both a "true perfect," that is, an expression of present time and completed aspect ("he/she/it has been"), and as a simple past: "he/she/it was"; the latter is the preferable interpretation here.

superabat: The imperfect indicative can be durative or frequentative: "she kept surpassing them." As often, the imperfect tense also adds liveliness to the narrative, a feature of the language that Ovid will exploit during his stirring account of the race.

enim: This conjunction regularly offers an explanation for something, in this case why the story of Atalanta was not a mere *fabula:* "for she really did surpass them."

posses: The imperfect subjunctive in secondary or historic sequence. Most manuscripts of the epic, however, read the present subjunctive *possis* here, which, if the correct reading, would add a certain vividness and immediacy to the narrative, even if not strictly "correct" according to the sequence of tenses.

563   laude pedum, formaene bono praestantior esset.

pedum: Genitive plural of *pes, pedis.*

bono: The adjective is used, as often, substantively, and balances *laude* (ablatives of cause). Often such a substantive use with a defining genitive of characteristic is best translated by a single English word: *formae bono* = her loveliness; see further on 573 below.

-ne: The conjunction marks the alternative indirect questions: you would be unable to tell *whether* she was more outstanding for x or y.

praestantior: Comparative adjective; *prae-stans* is an appropriate descriptor for the winner of a race (Atalanta literally "stands before" all competitors).

564   scitanti deus huic de coniuge coniuge dixit

Ovid continues to build suspense. The dative present participle *scitanti* refers to Atalanta and agrees with *huic*; the god is almost certainly

Apollo, the patron of oracles and prognostication. The alliteration of the line creates a jingling effect that mirrors the language of oracular pronouncements; the heart of Atalanta's two stories in Ovid is the problem of her romantic associations, whether with Meleager (in Book 8) or, here, with Hippomenes—hence the triple repetition of the word "spouse" in lines 564–565.

565   nil opus est, Atalanta, tibi. fuge coniugis usum!

Atalanta is named at last. *Opus est* here governs an ablative (564 *Coniuge*); some manuscripts read *non* instead of *nil*, perhaps because of scribal concern that the verb *est* needed a negative adverb and not the indeclinable noun *nil*, which functions here as an accusative of respect: "with respect to nothing is there need of a spouse," if one were to try to imagine the logic of the Latin—that is, "you do not need a husband, Atalanta." *Fuge* is particularly apt for a swift runner to use as an imperative to her would-be challenger.

usum: cf. 37; 651; 737. Orpheus asks for the *usus* of Eurydice; Hippomenes must be taught the *usus* of the golden apples by which he will win Atalanta. The Adonis-flower (that is, the anemone) will have but a *brevis usus* before it succumbs to the wind.

566   nec tamen effugies teque ipsa viva carebis.

carebis: The verb *careo* regularly takes an ablative object, here *te,* which functions as an ablative of separation—the original use of the ablative case ("ablative" is from *ablatus*, "having been taken away").

"You yourself, living, will lack yourself." A typical Ovidian antithesis, which introduces the eventual climax of the story and Atalanta's metamorphosis into a lioness. The elision of *teque* and *ipsa* contributes to the humor: Atalanta will not flee from a husband, and she will lack her own self (both after she is wedded and, especially, after she is transformed into a wild animal): the personal pronoun *te* and the intensive adjective *ipsa* are metrically linked in the Latin, just as Atalanta, trapped in the lioness, will both have and not have her very self.

567   territa sorte dei per opacas innuba silvas

territa: Perfect passive participle, in coordination with 568 *vivit;* compare 570 *victa* below, where the same participle is used with an understood form of the verb "to be."

sorte: Sors can mean a fortune or "lot": Atalanta's lot is to be better off if single. Atalanta is terrified at her lot because the god revealed that she would not escape her fate: she will marry, and go to her doom. *Sorte* = ablative of cause.

dei: Latin regularly refers to the Delphic oracular pronouncements as the word of "the god"; Apollo is not specified, as at 564 above. In his depiction of Atalanta, Ovid will exploit her associations with Diana, the virgin goddess of the hunt and Apollo's twin sister.

opacas: The woods are shady and dark, and thus provide an attractive hiding place for Atalanta as she seeks to do the impossible: escape her oracular destiny.

innuba: Not a common word in Latin. Elsewhere in the epic Ovid uses this adjective to describe only the laurel/Daphne (92 above) and the Sibyl (14.142), both of whom have connections to Apollo, the brother of Diana (the goddess with whom Atalanta has the greatest affinity). See further on 585 *intemptata.*

568   vivit et instantem turbam violenta procorum

vivit: Cf. 566 *viva:* Ovid underscores how Atalanta is *alive,* even as she is, in a sense, already doomed to her fate, which will be a sort of living death.

instantem: Present participle of *insto:* the image is of the crowd of suitors pursuing Atalanta into her forest lair.

violenta: Ovid here subtly continues to build his portrait of Atalanta: she is *violent* in her banishment of suitors: a potentially interesting detail about the psychology of Ovid's heroine. The *turba procorum* recurs at 574.

569   condicione fugat, nec sum potienda, nisi inquit

condicione: Ablative of means: Atalanta drives off the suitors by means of a condition.

sum potienda: The passive periphrastic or gerundive construction once again, where the future passive participle is used with a form of the verb *sum* to express obligation or necessity: "I am not to be obtained" (*potior*).

fugat: Word play: Atalanta fled into the woods, though the oracle made clear she would not flee from her fate; here she seeks to drive the persistent suitors into flight.

570   victa prius cursu. pedibus contendite mecum.

victa: As at 567 *territa*, the auxiliary verb is omitted. In Ovid's account, Atalanta decides on the challenge. Her swiftness is emphasized by both Catullus and Propertius near the beginning of both their collections of poems: Catullus c. 2b and Propertius c. 1.15 mention the quick-footed girl in amatory contexts (see further here Fratantuono 2008).

571   praemia veloci coniunx thalamique dabuntur:

praemia: The plural is probably poetic, though there may be an implication of a dowry.

coniunx: The repeated emphasis on the spouse, literally the one "joined with" another, continues; Ovid's point is to prepare for the ultimate revelation that Atalanta and Hippomenes will be a pair of yoked lions. Here, the *coniunx* is Atalanta, while above it referred to the girl's potential spouse.

thalami: Properly the nuptial chamber or bedroom, sometimes used by metonymy to mean the marriage itself. The plural is sometimes used "poetically" for the singular.

572   mors pretium tardis: ea lex certaminis esto!

mors pretium: The words are set up in apposition, and, as usual, the verb to be is omitted: death is the price for those who wager and lose. *Mors* continues the emphasis on Atalanta's violent nature: she seeks to escape her fate by the dramatic pronouncement of death as the likely punishment for those who would try to marry her. *Pretium* creates an antithesis with *praemia*, and there is also a hint of the irony of how the *praemium* of Atalanta as wife will mean a sort of death for the husband, who will undergo animal metamorphosis with his new spouse.

lex: Cf. 574 *legem.*

esto: The future imperative, which is used in especially solemn and dramatic contexts. "Let that regulation for the contest stand!"

573   illa quidem immitis; sed (tanta potentia formae est)

quidem: The particle emphasizes the entire sentiment (*OLD s.v.* 2).

formae: Cf. 563 above, where the poet offered the alternatives of Atalanta's exceptional swiftness and breathtaking loveliness. Here, the crowd of suitors is moved by the latter and willing to test the former (at the risk of life). The parenthetical sentiment is especially appropriate for the goddess of love.

574   venit ad hanc legem temeraria turba procorum.

legem: Ovid reiterates and underscores the firm and presumably unbending nature of the contest (572 *lex*, with future imperative *esto*).

temeraria: The crowd of suitors is reckless and impetuous; there may be a hint that Atalanta's loveliness was such that many a passerby of the (daily?) contest may well have added rash boldness to fortuitous attendance.

turba procerum: Cf. 568.

575   sederat Hippomenes cursus spectator iniqui

Hippomenes: The ultimate victor among the suitors is named for the first time; cf. Pseudo-Virgil, *Catalepton* 9.25–26 *non illa, Hesperidum ni munere capta fuisset, / quae volucrem cursu vicerat Hippomenen.*

cursus ... iniqui: The race is uneven because no one, it would seem, can hope to outperform Atalanta.

576   et petitur cuiquam per tanta pericula coniunx?

per tanta pericula: Ovid may have been inspired by Virgil, *Aeneid* 9.200 *solum te in tata pericula mittam* and 483 *nec te sub tanta pericula missum,* in both contexts of Nisus and Euryalus, contestants in the foot race of *Aeneid* 5, and both ultimately doomed in the ill-fated night raid of Book 9. The race Hippomenes enters will bring destruction on himself, despite his triumph over Atalanta.

577   dixerat ac nimios iuvenum damnarat amores;

dixerat: So he had spoken—but his words will soon enough be the source of regret (cf. 580 *dixit*).

ac: He not only uttered his rhetorical question about seeking a spouse at the risk of such great peril, "and, what is more," he damned the young men for being excessively concerned with love (i.e., lust) for the alluringly beautiful runner.

damnarat: That is, *damnaverat.*

578   ut faciem et posito corpus velamine vidit

posito ... velamine: The provocative phrase is also used by Ovid at
Amores 1.5.17 *ut stetit ante oculos posito velamine nostros,* of the
elegiac lover's partner in his noon hour tryst; more ominously, it is
also repeated from *Metamorphoses* 3.192 *nunc tibi me posito visam
velamine narres,* where Diana uses it in her address to Actaeon before
turning him into a stag: Atalanta has affinities with the goddess of
the hunt, and Hippomenes (so also his erotic conquest) will be
transformed into a wild animal.

579   (quale meum, vel quale tuum, si femina fias),

quale ... quale: The goddess' language draws a close association
between lover and beloved; she considers Adonis and herself to be the
most beautiful of all males and females.

femina fias: Cf. *Ibis* 455 *deque viro fias nec femina nec vir, ut Attis.*
There may be a hint of the liminal state of gender ambiguity that Ovid
imputes to Atalanta in the Calydonian boar hunt.

580   obstipuit tollensque manus ignoscite dixit,

tollens ... manus: A gesture of supplication, for forgiveness from those
he had mocked.

581   quos modo culpavi; nondum mihi praemia nota,

quos: That is, the other suitors. Initial relative pronouns are often best
translated in English as demonstratives = "Those (whom)."

modo: "Only recently, just now" (*OLD s.v.* 5).

praemia: Cf. the different reward of 571. The plural may be taken as
poetic, but Hippomenes does wish to underscore just how much of a
treasure and reward he now realizes is at stake in this race.

582   quae peteretis, erant. laudando concipit ignes

peteretis: Imperfect subjunctive in a generic relative clause, as Hippomenes observes that the characteristics of the *praemia* for which the suitors were willing to risk execution had not been known to him when he made his initial, sarcastic observations.

laudando: Gerund used as an ablative of means.

concipit ignes: Cf. the same phrase at *Metamorphoses* 7.9, of Medea— another baleful allusion. The prefix can be taken as intensive.

583   et ne quis iuvenum currat velocius optat

quis: After *si, nisi, num,* and *ne,* the *ali*-disappears.

iuvenum: Partitive genitive or genitive of the divided whole.

currat: Present subjunctive in a clause of fear (584 *timet*).

velocius: Comparative adverb.

584   insidiasque timet. sed cur certaminis huius

insidias: The word can refer to a snare for wild animals (*OLD s.v.* 3), and may distantly presage the eventual leonine metamorphosis; in context it describes Hippomenes' fear of a trap, that is, some trick or ruse by which Atalanta can defeat any competitor.

certaminis huius: "Of this contest," that is, of this race.

585   intemptata mihi fortuna relinquitur? inquit

intemptata: A deliberate echo of Horace, c. 1.5.12–13 *miseri, quibus / intemptata nites* (of Pyrrha and her affect on those who have not experienced her perilous charms). Cf. 567 *innuba*; the "untried fortune of this contest" is a not so veiled reference to Atalanta, its prize; the language may subtly underscore the runner's virginal state (so 587 *virgo,* as Atalanta darts past).

inquit: "He said"; Latin did not originally have quotation marks, and so this verb often served the place of such a punctuation device.

586   audentes deus ipse iuvat. dum talia secum

audentes deus ... uvat: A reminiscence of Virgil, *Aeneid* 10.284 *audentis Fortuna iuvat,* the powerful half-line of Turnus as he prepares to launch an attack on Aeneas and his Trojans.

dum talia secum: For how the action overtakes the distracted Hippomenes, see von Glinski (2012: 147). *Talia* is neuter plural substantive.

587   exigit Hippomenes, passu volat alite virgo.

exigit: To be taken closely with 586 *secum:* Hippomenes was pondering these thoughts to himself (*OLD s.v.* 10c); the Ovidian inspiration is likely from *Aeneid* 4.474–476 *ergo ubi concepit furias evicta dolore / decrevitque mori, tempus secum ipsa modumque / exigit* (of Dido), which serves to further the ominous undertones of the scene.

passu ... alite: "With winged step." *Volat* and *virgo* are effectively alliterative, as the girl speeds by the lovestruck suitor.

588   quae quamquam Scythica non setius ire sagitta

A brief simile: Atalanta in flight is no tardier than a Scythian arrow. Ovid associates *Scythicae sagittae* with the locus of his exile (*Ep. Pont.* 1.7.9; 2.1.65); the image is once again grim.

non setius: The phrase is Virgilian (*Georgic* 3.367; *Aeneid* 5.862; 9.441), and the Ovidian image is likely inspired by the Virgilian description of the hunting practices of the Scythians (*Georgic* 3.371–375). Ovid most probably means for the audience to imagine that Atalanta is not slower than a Parthian shaft; Virgil's Camilla also has Parthian associations.

quae: That is, the virgin Atalanta.

setius: Comparative adverb.

589   Aonio visa est iuveni, tamen ille decorem

Aonio: In striking geographical contrast to the "Scythian" arrow to which Atalanta was compared. The reference is to Boeotia or Thebes; it is unlikely there is any allusion to the Heliconian mount of the Muses to which the descriptor is sometimes applied.

decorem: The noun is strikingly used twice at line-end (cf. 590); the word choice is inspired by Turnus' application of the same label to Virgil's Camilla, the *decus Italiae* (*Aeneid* 11.508).

590   miratur magis; et cursus facit ipse decorem.

A choice has been made: loveliness is prized over speed and agility (cf. 562–563). The image of the girl made more beautiful by the act of running is borrowed from Ovid's description of Daphne (*Metamorphoses* 1.530 *aucta forma fuga est*) while she is being pursued by Diana's brother Apollo.

cursus ... ipse: "The very course" makes her lovely; all the emphasis is on the *decus* of Atalanta—the very word also used by Turnus to describe Camilla as the *decus Italiae.*

591   aura refert ablata citis talaria plantis,

talaria: Almost a technical term for the famed winged sandals of the god Mercury. If there was a connection between Camilla and Mercury, then Ovid has carried the parallel over to his own recreation and reimagining of the Virgilian Camilla. Atalanta, like Camilla, is something of a psychopomp or "conveyor of souls" (i.e., to the underworld): a figure who, like Mercury, can be associated with the leading of souls to their deaths.

plantis: The sole of the foot.

592 tergaque iactantur crines per eburnea, quaeque

Ovid continues to paint his image of the girl in her swift flight: the locks of her hair are tossed on her ivory-white back as she runs.

terga: Poetic plural.

eburnea: Cf. Pygmalion's ivory statue, and the falsehood theme that recurs throughout the book; the emphasis once again is on the power of the visual arts.

quaeque: Latin is fond of this sort of inceptive relative; in English we would prefer a demonstrative after the referent (593 *genualia*).

593 poplitibus suberant picto genualia limbo;

genualia: The word occurs only here in extant Latin, and seems to describe some sort of decorative accoutrement for the knees—likely an adornment for aesthetic appeal and not anything meant to improve the runner's speed.

picto … limbo: In Virgil's *Aeneid* Dido is similarly dressed with an "ornamental border" (*OLD s.v.* a).

594 inque puellari corpus candore ruborem

Ovid introduces a new chromatic image for his description of Atalanta: her ivory color (592 *eburnea*) now takes on a ruddy hue (*ruborem*) as she proceeds on her course. See further here von Glinski (2012: 147–148), who discusses both the "literal and figurative" senses of the color change that comes over Atalanta.

puellari: Not a common adjective; Manilius has it of the girl Europa (*Astronomica* 4.684), and Ovid of Proserpina before her abduction (*Metamorphoses* 5.393; cf. *Fasti* 4.463 *inde puellaris nacta est vestigia plantae*), a passage that almost certainly inspired the present scene in light of the importance of the connections between Books 5 and 10. Before her abduction, Ceres' daughter gathers both violets and lilies (5.392 *ludit et aut violas aut candida lilia carpit*); Cf. the contrasting color imagery of Ovid's description of Atalanta in flight; in both cases, a girl is on the verge of being conquered (and cf. the chromatic registers that predominate in this book of floral metamorphoses). Atalanta's *puellaris candor* may refer to her relatively young age: the bright gleam of youth (but just how old is she?). There may also be a hint of the gender ambiguity that was noted about her in Book 8 with reference to the liminality of her age.

595   traxerat, haud aliter quam cum super atria velum

haud aliter quam cum: "Scarcely otherwise than as when . . ." Another simile is introduced, this time from the contemporary world of Ovid's Rome: the color that comes over Atalanta's pale flesh is like that of the chromatic effect produced by a purplish awning on a white (i.e., likely marble) courtyard.

596   candida purpureum simulatas inficit umbras.

A line of rich resonance and poetic effect: the color *purpureus* is difficult to define precisely, it could refer to English "crimson" just as much as "purple." Once again the colors reflect the similar variety of shade and hues elsewhere in the book in the description of the flowers that memorialize the prematurely dead.

597   dum notat haec hospes, decursa novissima meta est

hospes: Hippomenes is depicted as the guest of the grisly spectacle—another hint of the hospitality theme. Cf. 620.

decursa: From *decurrere*, which can be used to describe downward motion both literal and metaphorical; it does have the specialized meaning of running a race (*OLD s.v.* 5). Statius imitated the present passage at *Silvae* 1.2.85 *immiti cupidum decurrere campo Hippomenen,* where the adjective *immitis* that Ovid applied to the girl is transferred to the race course she demanded as the locus for her testing of prospective lovers.

598   et tegitur festa victrix Atalanta corona;

victrix: Cf. 599 *victi.*

festa ... corona: In striking, indeed perverse contrast to the circumstances of the suitors.

599   dant gemitum victi penduntque ex foedere poenas.

Ovid mitigates the mythographic tradition in which Atalanta actually chases after the would-be lovers and kills them herself with a spear; she is, nonetheless, a bringer of death (cf. Virgil's Camilla) to young men, with no hint that she feels sorry for any of the contestants except Hippomenes. See Anderson here for the opposite view, whereby Atalanta is presented more sympathetically in the matter of her reaction to the doomed suitors.

gemitum: The groan of both their impending fate and the agony of their death.

600   non tamen eventu iuvenis deterritus horum

iuvenis: Rather like Adonis, another reckless *iuvenis.*

eventu: "The outcome," to be construed closely with the genitive *horum* it governs.

deterritus: Cf. 597 *decursa* for the prefix, which here is used in another passive verb form, as Hippomenes watches the result of the race course he now wishes to hazard.

horum: Of the unlucky losers.

601   constitit in medio vultuque in virgine fixo

in medio: In the midst of the throng, likely of the audience, in which other potential suitors can be imagined.

vultuque in: The elision enacts the fixation of face on the girl; Hippomenes cannot take his eyes off his desired prize.

602   quid facilem titulum superando quaeris inertes?

titulum: Of a title of victory.

superando: Ablative of the gerund or verbal noun.

inertes: Of the vanquished runners, who are dismissively labeled as inconsequential and easily defeated.

603   mecum confer ait. seu me fortuna potentem

confer: "Compete," with the core sense of comparison. *Ferre* and its compounds have an imperative in *fer*; cf. *dic; duc; fac.*

604   fecerit, a tanto non indignabere vinci;

fecerit: Future perfect in a conditional protasis (as often).

tanto: "By so great a one" (as me).

indignabere: For *indignaberis.*

605   namque mihi genitor Megareus Onchestius, illi

Once again there is an emphasis on parentage and provenance; once again the genealogies and lineages are confused (Reed notes that at Pseudo-Apollodorus 3.15.8a Megareus appears as the *son* of Hippomenes; here Megareus is the father, and Onchestius the geographical adjective that denotes the birthplace of the parent).

mihi: Dative of the possessor.

606 est Neptunus avus, pronepos ego regis aquarum,

Neptunus: Neptune had associations with horses; cf. the first part of *Hippo*menes' name (from the Greek for "horse"). For the lineage one might compare Virgil's Messapus, the hero who was immune to fire and iron; this Neptunian descendant will fare less well than his relative from the *Aeneid*.

607 nec virtus citra genus est. seu vincar, habebis

virtus: Cf. 616.

citra genus: Hippomenes is careful to note that his qualifications do not extend only to genealogy, but to questions of personal character and heroic intention. With *citra* cf. the sentiments of 84 *citra iuventam*, of the age of the *eromenoi* of whom Orpheus promises to sing. During the Calydonian boar hunt Atalanta had been described as having something of a liminal look between boyishness and girlishness; she, too, could have been classified as *eromenos*-like in appearance, though here we find a very different young woman, and Hippomenes takes on the role of an elegiac suitor—a would-be lover ready to take on a challenge and undergo a gauntlet (cf. the opening of Propertius, c. 1.1).

608 Hippomene victo magnum et memorabile nomen.

Hippomene victo: "On account of the defeat of Hippomenes."

memorabile nomen: The phrase is borrowed from Virgil, *Aeneid* 2.583, where Aeneas reflects that there will be no real honor in the killing of a woman (i.e., Helen). The climactic end of Hippomenes' speech is a subtle and powerful intertextual reference to that scene from the night Troy fell; Hippomenes casts himself in the part of Aeneas as he contemplates the death of the woman who has in his view brought death to so many. Virgil's Helen, like Ovid's Atalanta, has affinities with his Camilla; see further L. Fratantuono and J. Braff, "*Communis Erinys:* Helen in the Latin Poets," in *L'Antiquité classique* (2012). cf. *Metamorphoses* 6.12. Lucan has the same phrase of the now dead city of Troy at *Bellum Civile* 9.964.

609   talia dicentem molli Schoeneia vultu

molli ... vultu: Atalanta has already begun to soften in her attitude toward this particular young man; cf. 614.

Schoeneia: "The Schoenean one," that is, the daughter of Schoeneus. In Hesiod (fr. 73 Merkelbach-West), Atalanta is similarly identified; Schoeneus was the son of Athamas and Themisto. Hesiod says that Atalanta was like a Harpy in her swift speed—and so not surprisingly, at Hyginus, *Fabulae* 206, Schoeneus is identified as the father of Harpalyce. As we have noted, there there *two* Atalantas in origin, the daughter of Schoeneus and the daughter of Iasus, a descendant of Arcas (the progenitor of the Arcadians); Pseudo-Apollodorus knows both of them. His Iasian Atalanta was exposed to animals because his father desired a son; she lived a private life in the forest, where she slew Centaurs who tried to rape her. She took part in the Calydonian boar hunt, and introduced the idea of the celebrated foot race as a response to her father's wish that she marry after she was reunited with him on her return to public life. Melanion (or Milanion) won the race; the newlywed couple underwent leonine transformation after they angered Zeus by having sex in a temple precinct.

610   aspicit et dubitat, superari an vincere malit.

aspicit: With emphasis on the power of sight in arousing erotic appeal; cf. the centrality of the visual arts to the Pygmalion story.

dubitat: Introducing a clause of doubting that governs the present subjunctive *malit*.

611   atque ita quis deus hunc formosis inquit iniquus

deus hunc: It is telling that Atalanta is made to juxtapose the mention of an immortal and the demonstrative pronoun that describes Hippomenes, and that the first word after *hunc* is the signal descriptor *formosis:* Hippomenes is one of the handsome and lovely youths Atalanta imagines some god to hate.

formosis: Dative after *iniquus.*

612   perdere vult caraeque iubet discrimine vitae

carae … vitae: "Of a dear life," that is, of a life is of a life that should be dear to Hippomenes, and is certainly dear to Atalanta; more broadly, of the commonplace of life as desirable and (at least usually) preferable to death.

discrimine: Cf. 242; 517.

613   coniugium petere hoc? non sum, me iudice, tanti!

hoc: The demonstrative has dramatic force and import; not just any nuptial union, but *this particular* one.

me iudice: "If I am to judge/with me as judge."

tanti: Genitive of value or price; cf. 618.

614   nec forma tangor (poteram tamen hac quoque tangi),

forma: Ablative of cause.

tangor … tangi: Effective antithesis of the two passive forms of the verbs; the indicative, as Anderson notes, is not unusual in such a potential expression, though there is also a likely added vividness to the expression—Atalanta has more than noticed Hippomenes' handsome appearance.

615   sed quod adhuc puer est: non me movet ipse, sed aetas.

The emphasis on age continues; Atalanta tries to argue with herself that she is moved not by the youth's handsome appearance, but by his barely having had any experience of life.

puer: Atalanta's reflection on Hippomenes as *puer* is reminiscent of the *puer dilectus* imagery of Orpheus' song of, for example, Ganymede; the present relationship will be quite different on several levels, not least outcome.

non me movet ipse, sed aetas: Cf. 547.

616   quid quod inest virtus et mens interrita leti?

quid quod: "What of the fact that?" The triple repetition in this and the next two lines is especially striking, as Atalanta works through her own rationalizations about Hippomenes.

inest: The verb implies that Hippomenes' *virtus* is almost a natural, innate characteristic of his being; he is a hero, and like Meleager in Book 8, he will not shirk from heroic endeavors. Both men will be doomed for their association with the beautiful runner.

virtus: Cf. 607.

mens interrita: Cf. 15.514.

617   quid quod ab aequorea numeratur origine quartus?

A line that may reveal an interesting detail of Atalanta's psychology; she notes the specific number of his place in the Neptunian lineage, perhaps with a hint that she is impressed by his line of divine descent.

618   quid quod amat tantique putat conubia nostra

Atalanta moves from praise of lineage to admiration of his love . . . an interesting order of priorities.

tanti: Cf. 613.

conubia nostra: The phrase is Catullan (cf. 64.158); also Virgilian (*Aeneid* 4.213, 316; 9.600; 12.42).

619   ut pereat, si me fors illi dura negarit?

ut pereat: Of result; Hippomenes is imagined by Atalanta as thinking so much of the idea of marrying her that he is willing to risk death if fortune should deny him victory in the race.

fors ... dura: "Cruel fortune."

illi: that is, Hippomenes.

620   dum licet, hospes, abi thalamosque relinque cruentos.

hospes: Cf. 597. The form is vocative, as Atalanta now addresses Hippomenes directly with a strongly worded, grim command.

abi: Imperative of *abire*.

thalamos ... cruentos: Thalami can be used of marriage by metonymy; there may be a hint here of the fate of the husbands of the Danaids. The key word comes last; the metaphorical marriage chamber of Atalanta is stained with blood. *Cruentos* introduces a heavy alliteration that continues in the next verse, as the girl describes what erotic pursuit of her entails.

621   coniugium crudele meum est; tibi nubere nulla

nubere: Of a woman's marriage to a man. With *nubere nulla* cf. *Fasti* 3.196. The alliteration of *nubere nulla* and *nolet* in the next verse is striking, as Atalanta practically pleads with Hippomenes to give up his infatuation with her.

622   nolet, et optari potes a sapiente puella.

nolet: Potential subjunctive.

a sapiente puella: An interesting comment by the swift girl; the implication may be that Atalanta does not consider herself to be a *sapiens puella.*

623   cur tamen est mihi cura tui tot iam peremptis?

The swift runner now begins to change her thinking; this phenomenon has been seen repeatedly in the book, as character after character undergoes a most definite sort of metamorphosis of emotion and sentiment, and an ever transforming array of reactions to circumstance.

cura tui: Objective genitive, with reference to Hippomenes.

tot iam peremptis: Ablative of attendance circumstance. The *peremptis* = all the suitors who have already lost and been killed.

624   viderit! intereat, quoniam tot caede procorum

viderit: Perfect subjunctive. Elsewhere in the epic this initial form occurs at 9.519, where Byblis is thinking of her brother Caunus; the force of the perfect subjunctive is to underscore the imagined completed state of the action.

intereat: Jussive subjunctive: "Let him perish."

caede: An especially strong word. That which should have warned (625 *admonitus*) Hippomenes is highlighted first in Atalanta's explanation. The mention of the suitors connects to 356 and how Myrrha, too, was desired by many—though with vastly different outcomes.

625   admonitus non est agiturque in taedia vitae.

taedia vitae: Cf. 482, and see Reed ad loc.; the point would seem to be that Atalanta views Hippomenes as having something of a death wish. The plural is poetic.

626   occidet hic igitur, voluit quia vivere mecum

Another Ovidian antithesis: Hippomenes will die because he wishes to live with Atalanta; in an important sense, the young woman is all too correct. This and the next line are elegantly balanced, with mentions of Hippomenes' unworthy death at the start of both, and Atalanta as Hippomenes' love at the close; note also the alliteration of *voluit ... vivere* and 627 *pretium patietur*, which adds to the sense of balance.

627   indignamque necem pretium patietur amoris?

indignam: "Unworthy," with the full range of emotions—Atalanta's thoughts that Hippomenes can find a *puella sapiens* who would marry him without expecting him to risk his life for his bride (cf. Orpheus' willingness to harrow hell for Eurydice); Hippomenes' age and handsome appearance.

pretium ... amoris: In apposition to *indignamque necem*.

628   non erit invidiae victoria nostra ferendae.

invidiae ... ferendae: Atalanta will not be able to bear her own victory. With *invidiae* cf. 642 *invida*. The dative is a sort of dative of purpose; Atalanta's victory (note that she does not doubt her ability to defeat Hippomenes, just as she has defeated every other suitor thus far) will produce a hatred or ill-will that she cannot tolerate (gerundive *ferendae* expressing obligation or necessity). Reed's commentary here identifies this use as = *OLD s.v.* 2a, where the "odium" especially affects the recipient, in this case the swift girl.

629   sed non culpa mea est. utinam desistere velles,

Once again, the poet narrator dwells on the question of fault and the introspection of his characters; Atalanta comes to the conclusion that she is not to blame for the risks that Hippomenes is essaying to undertake.

velles: Imperfect subjunctive in a wish incapable of fulfillment in present time (so also 630 *esses*).

630   aut, quoniam es demens, utinam velocior esses!

Atalanta has no doubt that she will win the race. The repetition of *utinam* underscores the almost pleading wistfulness of the girl as she laments what she considers the certain death of Hippomenes.

esses: Imperfect subjunctive in a wish (governed by *utinam*) that is incapable of fulfillment in present time.

631   at quam virgineus puerili vultus in ore est!

Atalanta observes that Hippomenes is of an age where his appearance has elements of both the feminine and the masculine; the same was true of her at 8.322–323. Reed comments on the essentially narcissistic qualities of the girl that are expressed here in her admiration of the handsome form of the young suitor; Atalanta is, as it were, beholding a mirror image of herself.

632   a, miser Hippomene, nollem tibi visa fuissem!

a: An interjection that verbalizes what amounts to a sigh; Reed comments on the likely borrowing from the usage of the neoteric poets.

nollem ... fuissem: Atalanta wishes that she had never been seen by Hippomenes; the emphasis is once again on the potentially destructive power of vision.

633   vivere dignus eras. quod si felicior essem

dignus: Once again, Atalanta's focus is on worth.

felicior: Another recurring theme; cf. the comment on how Cinyras would have been able to have been counted among the fortunate, had he not been the father of Myrrha (299).

essem: Imperfect subjunctive in the protasis of a present contrafactual conditional sentence.

634   nec mihi coniugium fata importuna negarent,

negarent: Imperfect subjunctive in the protasis of a present contrafactual conditional sentence.

importuna: "Unfavorable" or "adverse." In origin the word referred to unseasonable, stormy conditions and carried a nautical metaphor.

635   unus eras cum quo sociare cubilia vellem.

sociare cubilia: Cf. Statius, *Thebaid* 1.460.

vellem: Imperfect subjunctive in the apodosis of a present contrafactual conditional sentence. Ovid expresses the vacillating nature of Atalanta's character by his attribution of numerous conditional and wishful subjunctives to her speech on the cusp of the race.

636   dixerat, utque rudis primoque cupidine tacta,

Atalanta's unfamiliarity with the stirrings of erotic passion is underscored.

rudis: The adjective carries special force in light of the image of Atalanta as huntress from her first appearance in Book 8.

tacta: With a hint of proleptic force; Atalanta has been touched by her first desire, and, in the case of this suitor, the touch will soon be more than metaphorical.

637   quod facit ignorans amat et non sentit amorem.

A line of rich psychological import; Atalanta is in love, and yet she does not feel the love.

quod facit: So the reading of G, *vs. quid facit* of the rest of the manuscript witnesses; see here Reed for a defense of *quid,* with reference *inter al.* to the *Bryn Mawr Classical Review* article of Tarrant's Oxford text by M. Possanza. The point is perhaps not all that different either way; the question of *why* Atalanta does what she does may be of greater interest to moderns, but the Augustan poet may be making a simpler point than that of questioning motivations: Atalanta does not know what she does.

facit: The indicative in the indirect question adds a sense of greater vividness to the scene.

638   iam solitos poscunt cursus populusque paterque,

paterque: Schoeneus (cf. 609). The alliterative power of *populusque paterque,* together with the use of the enclitic connectives, helps to underscore the insistence of the girl's father and the crowd that has assembled for the anticipated grisly spectacle. (Enclitics are words that literally "lean" on another word; in this case-*que* can never stand on its own, but must be attached to another word).

639   cum me sollicita proles Neptunia voce

sollicita . . . voce: "With pleading voice."

proles Neptunia: With deliberate emphasis on the young suitor's status as the son of a god, appropriately enough just as he invokes Venus for help. Reed comments on the "magniloquent" use of the adjective instead of a personal genitive; the descriptor points to the imminent victory of the young hero, but the connection of a mention of Neptune with Venus points, too, to the Virgilian scene of the two deities in the divine preliminaries to the loss of Aeneas' helmsman Palinurus in *Aeneid* 5.

640   invocat Hippomenes Cythereaque comprecor ausis

comprecor: The prefix carries intensive force; there may also be a hint of how Hippomenes is calling on the goddess to assist in a shared action with him.

ausis: Dative of reference, to be construed with 641 *nostris.*

641   adsit ait nostris et quos dedit adiuvet ignes.

Hippomenes' prayer bears comparison to Pygmalion's.

adsit: The subject = 640 *Cytherea* (i.e., Venus). This and *adiuvet* are both subjunctives, expressing the wish of the would-be lover.

642   detulit aura preces ad me non invida blandas;

detulit aura preces: "Ohne Parallelle" (Bömer), or "without parallel": there is no extant parallel for the precise expression, though the sentiment is related to the idea of how the breezes scatter prayers (or parts of prayers); cf. Arruns' request that he might both slay Camilla *and* return home safe and inglorious in *Aeneid* 11, and so there may be a hint of future trouble despite apparent victory. See further Reed here for the question of the wind as intermediary between mortal and goddess.

invida: Cf. 628 *invidiae.* The etymology is from *in-video*, with connotations of the evil eye and imputation of baleful sentiment and harmful intention.

643   motaque sum, fateor, nec opis mora longa dabatur.

nec opis mora longa dabatur: Venus has little time in which to help Hippomenes; the race must commence.

fateor: The paratactic structure that Bömer notes here is a reflection of the goddess' close relationship to Adonis and the direct, almost casual manner in which she addresses her beloved. Time is also, of course, of the essence.

644   est ager, indigenae Tamasenum nomine dicunt,

indigenae: The locals call the place Tamasenus; once again there is an emphasis on location and place.

Tamasenum: The adjectival form of the place name Tamasus.

nomine: The ablative has the force of specification, as Venus identifies the locale where the magical apples that will aid Hippomenes are to be found.

645   telluris Cypriae pars optima, quem mihi prisci

Cypriae: The only appearance of the adjective in Ovid, as Bömer notes; once again, the emphasis is on place (*Tamasenum; Cypriae*), and on the central part of Venus in the whole drama. The present sequence is a doublet of the Pygmalion episode where the young man prayed to the goddess to win his beloved; that successful appeal led to the union that ultimately produced the incestuous Myrrha, and now a similar successful prayer will be linked to the narrative of the death of the goddess' beloved, the son of the sordid girl whose birth Venus helped to ensure.

pars optima: Cf. 14.604, during the description of the deification of Aeneas.

quem: The referent is 644 *ager*; the far better attested reading *quam* would be taken with reference to the feminine noun *tellus*.

prisci: "Ancient" and venerable. The locus of the apples is sacred in its hoary antiquity and religious sanctity; there is a connection to the secluded holy place that will be the scene of the sexual profanation and resultant leonine transformation of Atalanta and Hippomenes that serves as the climax of the story.

646   sacravere senes templisque accedere dotem

sacravere: Third person plural perfect indicative active.

dotem: The Cypriots of old assigned this prize land to be the dowry of the goddess.

templis: With 647 *meis*; the plural here is for once not poetic but literal.

647   hanc iussere meis; medio nitet arbor in arvo,

iussere: Once again, the third person perfect plural indicative = the alternative form of *iusserunt.*

nitet: "Gleams" or "shines"; cf. 666 *nitidi.* The tree has a shining gleam because of its fruit.

648   fulva comas, fulvo ramis crepitantibus auro.

The description of Venus' sacred tree owes something to that of the Golden Bough in Virgil's *Aeneid* 6.

fulva . . . fulvo . . . auro: Cf. 733. The signal color returns, this time in a striking anaphoric use that evokes the image of the Virgilian Bough amid richly textured, complex allusions to the other uses of the adjective in the present book as well as elsewhere in the Latin poetic tradition; cf. its aforementioned use in Virgil to describe the sand of Elysium; also the brooch of Chloreus that will distract Camilla in exactly the way these apples distract Atalanta.

crepitantibus: "Crackling." The same effect is used by Virgil in his description of the Bough.

649   hinc tria forte mea veniens decerpta ferebam

mea: With 650 *manu.*

decerpta: Cf. *carpere*; the verb is proper of plucking fruit. The important allusion is to 5.536–537 *puniceum curva decerpserat arbore pomum / sumptaque pallenti septem de cortice grana / presserat ore suo,* of the fateful acceptance of the pomegranate by Persephone in the underworld; the pomegranate imagery will recur at the very end of the present book, as Ovid connects the eschatology of the close of the first two acts of his three act epic.

650   aurea poma manu; nullique videnda nisi ipsi

videnda: Venus must be seen by no one; the goddess almost makes it seem as if this should be a difficult task for an immortal. *Videnda* is the future participle passive/gerundive, the so-called passive periphrastic construction that expresses obligation or necessity. Bömer's commentary lists parallel passages of the phenomenon of the immortal who appears only to certain individuals, as he or she will.

poma: There are two useful comprehensive studies of the motif of the apple in classical literature; Littlewood's paper "The Symbolism of the Apple in Greek and Roman Literature" in *Harvard Studies in Classical Philology* 72 (1968), 147–181 (a very detailed and often cited major study of the topic), and, for those with German, also Brazda's Bonn dissertation of 1977, "Zur Bedeutung des Apfels in der antiken Literatur."

651   Hippomenen adii docuique quis usus in illis.

Hippomenen: Greek accusative form.

adii: Another divine epiphany, as the goddess approaches the mortal.

docui: With a hint of the idea of Venus as *praeceptor amoris.*

quis usus in illis: Cf. 731. *Quis* is an interrogative adjective.

652   signa tubae dederant, cum carcere pronus uterque

Bömer's commentary considers the influence here of the traditions of both Greek athletics and the Roman circus games; also the influence of the crucial narrative of the foot race (with Nisus and Euryalus) in Virgil, *Aeneid* 5. That foot race is intimately tied in with the Virgilian program of ethnographic reflection on the nature of the future Rome, born from Troy.

carcere: The starting gate, as it were. The construction here is another example of *cum inversum.*

pronus: Atalanta and Hippomenes assume the stance of runners at the starting line.

653   emicat et summam celeri pede libat harenam;

libat: The verb vividly describes how the swift foot of each contestant just grazes the sands of the race course. The singular verbs with 652 *uterque* help to serve to make the two contestants almost shade into one, as the dramatic race commences. The image is striking; M reads *summa celeris pendebat harena*, which gives easier but perhaps less dramatic sense.

harenam: Cf. the scene of Adonis' death at 716.

654   posse putes illos sicco freta radere passu

Ovid's comparison of Atalanta and Hippomenes is inspired by Virgil's description of Camilla at the end of *Aeneid* 7.808–809 *illa vel intactae segetis per summa volaret / gramina nec teneras cursu laesisset aristas.*

putes: Potential subjunctive.

sicco: The reading *celeri* is from diplography or "double writing" after 653; the point is that the running is so swift that if they were on water the feet would not become wet.

radere: The variant reading *laedere* was likely inspired by a reminiscence of *Aeneid* 7.809 *laesisset*—but the point in Virgil is that the beautiful and swift Camilla can skim over the surface of the standing grain without touching and thus potentially harming it.

655   et segetis canae stantes percurrere aristas.

percurrere: The prefix describes the progress "through" the standing ears of grain.

656   adiciunt animos iuveni clamorque favorque

Once again, the main literary influence is the reaction of the crowds during the games of *Aeneid* 5, in particular the ship race and the cheering occasioned by the vicissitudes of the Virgilian regatta. The funeral games in Virgil have their own ethnographic associations; this race will mark a change in Atalanta's life, just as Camilla's entry in war changed hers in the eleventh *Aeneid*.

animos: "Strength," "courage," or even "resolve." The alliteration of *adiciunt animos* reflects the action of the crowd as they applaud the contestants.

clamorque favorque: The repeated connectives help to craft an evocation of the crowd's repeated cheering and vigorous, vocal support for the young suitor.

657   verbaque dicentum nunc, nunc incumbere tempus;

dicentum: Genitive plural; the crowd favors the handsome young competitor in his attempt to surpass the swift girl.

nunc, nunc: Repetition once again evokes the extreme sense of excitement of the race, especially for the spectators.

658   Hippomene, propera! nunc viribus utere totis;

The excitement of the race is sustained; the precise influence of the fragmentary Hesiodic *Catalogue* on the race narrative is difficult to determine, but the Ovidian narrative ultimately refashions its archaic source in light of later, especially Virgilian intertexts.

utere: With ablative *viribus ... totis.*

659   pelle moram, vinces! dubium, Megareius heros

Megareius: Adjectival form of the name Megareus (= the father of Hippomenes). The emphasis on the varied names (cf. 660 *Schoeneia*) reflects the concerns of the poet with onomastics and related questions of ethnography.

heros: In striking balance with 660 *virgo.*

660   gaudeat an virgo magis his Schoeneia dictis.

virgo: With special emphasis on the status of the girl as she runs the race that will result in her being won by the lustful Hippomenes.

Schoeneia: Both Atalanta and Hippomenes are identified by patronymics.

661   o quotiens, cum iam posset transire, morata est

posset: Imperfect subjunctive in a concessive *cum-* clause (Bömer notes in his commentary that it could also be a *cum-* adversative, but the difference is not very great).

662   spectatosque diu vultus invita reliquit!

spectatosque . . . vultus: With emphasis yet again on how vision and the sustained gaze plays a key part in the erotic experience. *Vultus* is a poetic plural.

invita: A subtle and important indicator of Atalanta's mood regarding her handsome young suitor.

663   aridus e lasso veniebat anhelitus ore,

Shackleton Bailey posited a lacuna of perhaps two verses before the present line, or before 661 above; the detail about the panting breath of the runner does come swiftly and suddenly, though it is possible that this is a deliberate technique of the equally breathless narrative of the race.

aridus . . . anhelitus: The rhythm and alliteration nicely convey something of the panting of the exhausted runner. At first it is not entirely clear whose breath is coming short and hard.

lasso . . . ore: Bömer notes that the adjective is used with *os* only here.

veniebat: Probably a frequentative imperfect; the heavy breathing keeps coming hard and fast as the race intensifies; possibly with inceptive force—the hard sprint is beginning to take its toll even on the experienced, gifted runner.

664   metaque erat longe; tum denique de tribus unum

meta: The goal or finish line of the race.

longe: "Far off."

665   fetibus arboreis proles Neptunia misit.

proles Neptunia: An epic, heroic onomastic for the young runner once again articulates the young man's divine favor; he will win, though the victory will prove less than fortuitous. Reed notes the double solemnity of this epic periphrasis with the *fetus arborei*; the tone may be a deliberate reflection of the splendor of the moment, as Hippomenes employs his divine machinery in pursuit of his amatory goal.

666   obstipuit virgo nitidique cupidine pomi

virgo: The poet narrator once again emphasizes Atalanta's virginal state.

nitidi: Cf. 647 *nitet.* Atalanta is distracted by the loveliness of the magical apple; the attraction will lead to her doom.

667   declinat corpus aurumque volubile tollit.

declinat: She bends her course to reach for the tantalizing golden fruit; with the use of the verb Bömer compares 7.88.

volubile: The adjective underscores the point of how the golden fruit can roll and thus deter the runner from the course.

668   praeterit Hippomenes; resonant spectacula plausu.

resonant: "Resounds" or "echoes back."

spectacula: From the language of the Roman circus and the games, though not exclusively so or anything like a technical term (indeed, cf. Virgil, *Aeneid* 6.37 for a very different use of the noun).

669   illa moram celeri cessataque tempora cursu

celeri ... cursu: Echoing 653 *celeri pede.*

cessataque tempora: The time that she spent in the delay to retrieve the magical fruit. The plural is poetic; Bömer discusses parallels for the transitive use of the verb. The alliterative effect of this verse and the next wonderfully conveys something of the hard and fast correction of Atalanta's delay (*celeri ... cessata. cursu ... corrigit*).

670   corrigit atque iterum iuvenem post terga relinquit;

The first apple failed to do the trick for Hippomenes.

atque iterum: The elision neatly conveys the repetition of the action, as Atalanta once again flies past Hippomenes.

terga: Poetic plural (as often).

671   et rursus pomi iactu remorata secundi

The swift description of the action is fitting to the context; at once Venus narrates how the second apple was used in vain.

remorata: "Having been delayed again." The subject is Atalanta.

secundi: The adjective can mean "favorable" (cf. the sense of a favorable wind as one that "follows" a naval vessel); in this case the apple will once again delay Atalanta, but the third fruit will be needed to win the contest.

672   consequitur transitque virum. pars ultima cursus

consequitur: The force of the prefix is to underscore the neck and neck moment of pursuit just before Atalanta surpasses Hippomenes.

virum: Significantly, Hippomenes is now a *vir*, not a *iuvenis*; cf. 675 *iuvenaliter*.

673   restabat. nunc inquit ades, dea muneris auctor

The asyndeton or lack of connectives allows the verse to reflect the hurried nature of the final prayer of Hippomenes to the goddess before he might lose race, girl, and life.

ades: Cf. 4 *adfuit*, of the divine epiphany of Hymenaeus. The goddess' help to the lovestruck young man will not lead to a happy union.

muneris: The "boon" by which Hippomenes may aspire to win Atalanta. The language once again emphasizes the key part played in the whole drama by Venus, an involvement that goes back to the goddess' central role in the Pygmalion story. The variant reading *numinis* of M and S does not lend nearly as good a sense.

auctor: Cf. the previous uses of the same image at 83, 199, and 214; the word may have metapoetic associations.

674   inque latus campi, quo tardius illa rediret,

quo: "Where." The last part of the course is a flat plain, and Atalanta cannot make up the lost time as easily; the implication may be that she does better than Hippomenes in the inclines that characterized the rest of the course.

675   iecit ab obliquo nitidum iuvenaliter aurum.

Hippomenes throws the apple in the manner of a youth (*iuvenaliter*); the description may imply a hint of petulance and playful impishness.

obliquo: Cf. 712.

nitidum: "Shining" or "gleaming"; the apple will distract Atalanta in the same way that the yellow vesture of Chloreus fatally tempted Virgil's Camilla.

676   an peteret, virgo visa est dubitare; coegi

visa est: The meaning may be literal; Atalanta may have been seen by the audience to pause (and the pause may well be thought to have contributed to the loss).

coegi: To be construed closely with the force of 677 *adieci* and 678 *impedii*; the heavy first person singular perfect indicatives active underscore Venus' manipulation of the situation.

677   tollere et adieci sublato pondere malo

It may have been one thing for the goddess to compel Atalanta to fetch the apple; it is quite another to add weight to the apple. The text makes it clear that Atalanta was something of a victim of Venus; the immediate comparison is to Myrrha (and cf. 629).

pondere: Cf. 179.

malo: Ablative after *sub-*.

678   impediique oneris pariter gravitate moraque.

impediique oneris: The elision reflects the scenario, as the action of the goddess in weighing down the apple slows down the swift girl. M has the reading *impeditique*, which gives a less balanced description of the verbal action.

pariter: The added weight of the apple and the delay occasioned by the retrieval were equally responsible for the girl's defeat.

679   neve meus sermo cursu sit tardior ipso,

A line of charming sense and spirit; Venus needs to end the story quickly so as to match the finish of the sprint. The book now moves relatively swiftly to its own conclusion, which will come in the aftermath of the race with the Adonis coda.

680   praeterita est virgo, duxit sua praemia victor.

praeterita est virgo: The synaloepha or merging of the two syllables into one expresses effectively and with subtle power how the maiden is defeated at last.

sua: The reflexive possession carries special force.

praemia: Cf. 571 and 581; once again, the plural is probably poetic.

victor: Cf. 598 *victrix.*

681   dignaque cui grates ageret, cui turis honorem

ageret: The subject is Hippomenes.

turis honorem: The genitive is essentially one of specification; the goddess expects offerings of incense on her altar in thanksgiving for her service; cf. 683.

682   ferret, Adoni, fui? nec grates immemor egit

Cf. 290–291, of the very different reaction of Pygmalion to the goddess' help in his romantic endeavors.

ferret ... fui: Venus practically spits out her indignant sentiments in the matter of how Hippomenes has failed to honor her.

683   nec mihi tura dedit. subitam convertor in iram

The verse may betray a hint of childishness on the part of the goddess, as she repeats her craving for incense.

subitam ... iram: "Sudden" or "immediate anger"; the goddess was at once transformed into a vision of rage.

684   contemptuque dolens ne sim spernenda futuris

dolens: Venus is seriously aggrieved by the slight to her dignity. Reed comments on the parallelism of Juno from *Aeneid* 1, with the anger of the goddess that was directed at the Trojan exiles.

spernenda: The future passive participle in a passive periphrastic construction expressing obligation or necessity.

685   exemplo caveo meque ipsa exhortor in ambos.

exemplo caveo: Bömer notes that the expression is without extant parallel; the ablative is one of means—Venus will warn with an example.

meque ipsa: The elision effectively links the two references to the goddess; the effect of the strong emphasis on self is to highlight the goddess' solipsistic self-absorption and the contrast with the two doomed lovers. The nominative of the intensive works much better than the variant reading of the accusative *ipsam.*

ambos: A key final word; in the Orphic/Ovidian narrative Atalanta has been cast as the innocent.

686   templa, deum Matri quae quondam clarus Echion

templa: With 687 *abdita,* as the poet narrator unfolds his brief but rich description of the sacred precinct that Atalanta and Hippomenes are about to invade all unwittingly.

deum Matri: Cybele. Reed offers a convenient summary of the different traditions of the transformation of Atalanta. For the *templa* cf. also 691, as the poet underscores the sanctity of the locale. *Deum =* genitive plural.

clarus: "Famous" or "renowned."

687   ex voto, nemorosis abdita silvis,

nemorosis: "Full of groves"; the forest is especially dense. With *silvis* the phrase is pleonastic, as Bömer notes.

abdita: "Hidden."

688   transibant, et iter longum requiescere suasit.

The situation is identical to that which brought Venus and Adonis to the place of rest that has been the locus of the story of the race and the golden apples.

requiescere suasit: Bömer notes that the use of the infinitive with *suadere* is old (Terence), though not especially common (four other examples in Ovid).

689   illic concubitus intempestiva cupido

illic: "There, in that (very) spot."

intempestiva: "Untimely." The root of the adjective is the notion of time and indeed season; *tempestas* can refer to a storm (cf. English "tempest"), or simply a season or time of the year. With the untimely lust that helps to spell doom for Hippomenes and Atalanta cf. the passion of Meleager for Atalanta during the Calydonian boar hunt that helps to inspire his slaying of his uncles and thus works to seal his own death.

690   occupat Hippomenen, a numine concita nostro.

The goddess incites the one who had ignored her; Atalanta will again be an innocent victim of her partner.

concita nostro: Bömer compares 6.158 *divino concita motu*; the passion (689 *cupido*) is engendered by the divine power of the indignantly enraged and affronted goddess.

691 luminis exigui fuerat prope templa recessus,

luminis exigui: The hollow is of but the poorest light; the sexual tryst will be concealed, though not from the goddess. The passage is reminiscent of the poet narrator's description of how the celestial lights recoiled from the sight of Myrrha's illicit and perverse union with her father Cinyras. The variant reading *liminis* gives much weaker sense; the alternative *numinis* cannot be defended.

prope templa: The key detail: Hippomenes and Atalanta will be driven by the goddess to desecrate a holy place. Cf. 686.

692 speluncae similis, nativo pumice tectus,

There may be a deliberate reminiscence of the cave that witnessed the commencement of the ill-fated union of Aeneas and Dido. Bömer collects the instances of additional parallel passages where caves are the locus of erotic involvements.

pumice: Pumice, or indeed any volcanic rock. The description of the sacred space is designed to highlight its great antiquity and rough circumstance; its age has rendered it so venerable that it is left more or less in the condition in which more recent generations found it.

693 religione sacer prisca, quo multa sacerdos

Nearly every word of the verse is invested with solemnity and sanctity.

religione ... prisca: "Ancient" or even "hallowed religious practice"; Hippomenes is driven by the goddess to profane a place of exceptionally sacred associations.

quo: Of direction as well as location.

694 lignea contulerat veterum simulacra deorum;

lignea: The wood implies not the material value of the statues of the divinities, but rather the antiquity of the images. Bömer observes here that the adjective does not appear elsewhere in Ovid, or at all in Virgil or Horace; twice in Propertius. "The rustic ideal," as Reed comments ad loc.; the idea is that the statues contain the immortals, as it were, and serve essentially as conduits for their divine power.

veterum: These are the elder gods, as it were, possibly the Titans of old (see Reed here); the poet's point is to evoke a primeval spirit of mystery and eerie magic in this remote haunt, a place where the young couple could have expected privacy from the world of mortals—but not from the sanctity of a place dedicated so long ago to such ancient powers.

695   hunc init et vetito temerat sacraria probro.

init: The subject is Hippomenes; the singular is telling in terms of the relative guilt of the partners in crime.

temerat: The verb conveys a sense of recklessness and disregard for the sanctity of the precinct that serves to highlight the crime of the young newlyweds.

sacraria: Poetic plural, the force of which is to aggrandize the crime of Hippomenes: he has committed a sacrilege on a grand scale, admittedly at the behest of the goddess he offended.

probro: The basic meaning is any sort of insult or reproach that can be uttered or thrown forth; the word can have a particular force in connection to functions that pertain to the body (*OLD s.v.* 3b). In this case the adjective *vetito* serves to underscore and highlight just how forbidden the sexual act of Atalanta and Hippomenes is in context. With *vetito* there may be something of a tautological sense that serves only to underscore the wrongness of the act and the doom that is attendant on its consummation. *Probrum* is a strong word, which appears nowhere else in the epic (as Bömer observes); cf. *Ars Amatoria* 3.716 (of Procris), with Gibson's note.

696   sacra retorserunt oculos, turritaque Mater

retorserunt: The verb is especially strong to describe the shocked reaction of the sacred images to the desecration of the sacred space.

turrita: "Towered"; Cybele was often depicted with a crown of towers. Bömer notes that the goddess and her accoutrements were so well known that there is no explicit need to identify her here by name.

697   an Stygia sontes dubitavit mergeret unda;

Stygia … unda: The Stygian wave, appropriately enough, effectively envelops the line that describes the goddess' consideration of plunging the guilty pair into the underworld river. There may also be an allusion to the Stygian *stips* of 313 that is blamed for Myrrha's perverse passion for her father. Cf. also 13 and 65.

Venus' work is done; the desecration of her own sacred place is the business of Cybele to avenge.

sontes: "The guilty."

698   poena levis visa est. ergo modo levia fulvae

The poet returns to the theme of how metamorphosis occupies some mysterious middle ground between life and death—and that it may well be worse than the latter.

levia: With 699 *colla*; Bömer notes that the collocation is without parallel, perhaps rather surprisingly.

fulvae: The key color is mentioned yet again. Bömer notes parallels for *fulvus* of the *iubae* of lions, though the association may be original to Ovid.

699   colla iubae velant, digiti curvantur in ungues,

The metamorphosis is swift and sudden; the lovers will be transformed into lions.

curvantur: The verb balances 701 *verruntur.*

700   ex umeris armi fiunt, in pectora totum

armi: The forearms of the beasts.

totum: With 701 *pondus;* the enjambment neatly conveys something of the heaviness of the weight that is now subject to animal metamorphosis.

701   pondus abit, summae cauda verruntur harenae;

summae ... harenae: Rather a striking change from the image of 653–655.

verruntur: The basic meaning of the verb is to "sweep"; in this case the ground is brushed, as it were, by the trailing tails of the lions.

harenae: Properly "sand," and by extension dirt or dust; the image of the arena, however, is present, and will recur as the locus for Adonis' death. See Reed here for comment on the irony, if not "punitive correction," of the detail about the speed of Atalanta and Hippomenes above at 653.

702   iram vultus habet, pro verbis murmura reddunt,

Something of the anger of the goddesses involved in the whole matter of the punishment will live on in the ferocious nature of the lions.

murmura: Cf. 382.

703   pro thalamis celebrant silvas aliisque timendi

Atalanta, fittingly, returns to the forest whence she came.

celebrant: "They frequent/haunt." The verb is in stark contrast to the sense of *celebrare* and its compounds in relation to religious festivals; the lions of Cybele perform their own devotional service to the goddess by drawing her chariot.

timendi: Future passive participle/gerundive in a passive periphrastic construction expressing obligation or necessity; Bömer notes the concessive force.

704   dente premunt domito Cybeleia frena leones.

The pair of lions is yoked for service in driving Cybele's chariot.

dente ... domito: The yoking of the lions has the effect of taming their ferocious and deadly teeth; these lions pose little threat.

Cybeleia: For the use of the adjective in place of a possessive genitive see Bömer.

705   hos tu, care mihi, cumque his genus omne ferarum

The narrative returns to the immediate scene of the divine lover and her mortal plaything.

hos ... his: The repeated demonstratives emphasize the sort of animals Venus wants her lover to flee (707 *effuge*).

genus omne ferarum: "The whole race of wild animals." From the leonine example Venus extrapolates a thesis that applies to all manner of fierce beasts.

706   quod non terga fugae, sed pugna pectora praebet

pugna, etc.: The alliteration strikingly conveys the imagined sound of the imagined beast when confronted.

praebet: Singular after *genus omne*; Tarrant notes that the variant plural reading *praebent* may be right, though the meaning is of course the same either way.

707   effuge, ne virtus tua sit damnosa duobus.

An effective irony with which to end the tale; the *virtus* of Hippomenes, after all, had defeated his beloved Atalanta.

virtus tua: "Virtue," which is literally the quality of being a *vir.*

708   illa quidem monuit iunctisque per aera cycnis

The poet indulges in a deliberate contrast between the fearsome conveyance of the great mother goddess and Venus' swan chariot.

709   carpit iter; sed stat monitis contraria virtus.

carpit: A delicate verb; the swans almost "pluck" the path back to Cyprus (cf. 718).

710   forte suem latebris vestigia certa secuti

suem: The same as the *trux aper* of 715. The accusative is better than the variant genitive reading *suis.*

vestigia certa: "Certain/sure tracks."

711   excivere canes, silvisque exire parantem

silvis: Separative ablative; the beast is preparing to depart the woods.

parantem: The boar is about to make its dash when Adonis strikes.

712   fixerat obliquo iuvenis Cinyreius ictu;

obliquo: Cf. 675. The shaft is hurled slant-wise at the beast.

Cinyreius: Just before his doom is met, the young Adonis is described with reference to his father/grandfather; the association is baleful given the circumstances of his conception.

713   protinus excussit pando venabula rostro

pando ... rostro: "Flat ... snout."

venabula: "Hunting spears."

714   sanguine tincta suo trepidumque et tuta petentem

The scene is not dissimilar to that of the Calydonian boar hunt in Book 8 where Ovid had introduced Atalanta.

trepidumque et tuta petentem: The synaloepha (whereby two syllables are merged into one) may reflect something of the speed with which Adonis seeks safety in vain and to no avail.

715   trux aper insequitur totosque sub inguine dentes

trux: The boar is especially fierce now that it has been wounded and rendered angry; cf. the monstrous boar of Book 8. With the boar cf. Ovid's *nec minus est confusa Veus moriente Tibullo / quam iuveni rupit cum ferus inguen aper* (*Amores* 3.15–16), with J. Reed's "Ovid's Elegy on Tibullus and Its Models," in *Classical Philology* 92.3 (1997), 260–269, 263, where the elegiac poet Tibullus is explicitly associated with Adonis. In a metapoetic sense, the slaying of Adonis by the boar is a vivid enactment of the seeming conflict (or at least tension) between epic and elegiac verse. The verse opens with the quality of the boar that is most important in the context; this animal has no concern for the handsome young hunter except as a possible victim of animalistic ferocity.

inguine: The boar attacks the "groin"; there may be a pointedly sexualized reference given the relationship between Adonis and Venus.

totos: The detail underscores the severity of the wound; the entirety of the boar's natural weapon is sunk into Adonis.

716   abdidit et fulva moribundum stravit harena.

fulva: Cf. the tawny manes of the lions at 698; also on 733. *Fulva ... harena* is an ablative of place where; the young hunter falls on the tawny sand almost as if he were a victim of a gladiatorial contest in the arena (which took its name from the sand that was used to absorb the blood of the vicims of the games).

stravit: From *sternere.*

717   vecta levi curru medias Cytherea per auras

vecta: With Cytherea (from the verb *vehere*).

levi curru: Again, with likely intentional comparison to the swift course of Atalanta and Hippomenes. The ablative = of means.

medias . . . auras: Bömer notes that the poet narrator does not indicate where exactly the goddess has been; cf. 708 ff.

718   Cypron olorinis nondum pervenerat alis;

olorinis . . . alis: "On the wings of swans." The lovely descriptor helps to craft an image of the serene peace of the heavens that is at striking variance with the scene unfolding in the woods.

pervenerat: The prefix underscores how the goddess had not yet successfully made it completely back home to Cyprus (cf. 709).

719   agnovit longe gemitum morientis et albas

agnovit: Almost the same as *cognovit*, as Bömer observes; the point may be the emphasis on direction toward something (in this case, the goddess) that is implied by the prefix.

longe: "From afar." The goddess is able to recognize the voice of her beloved even from a significant distance through the air.

gemitum: Cf. the groan of the executed suitors of Atalanta at 599. The variant reading *gemitus* (plural) may well be correct, though the question may be no more than whether one is to imagine the death agony of Adonis to be especially brief and/or especially intense.

albas: With 720 *aves*; = the swans that convey her chariot.

720   flexit aves illuc, utque aethere vidit ab alto

illuc: "There, to that place."

aethere: The ethereal heaven of the immortals, lofty (*alto*) and removed from the gory results of human recklessness.

ab: The anastrophe of the preposition works alongside the elision of *utque aethere* to convey syntactically something of the rapidity and speed with which the goddess responds to the lover.

721   exanimem inque suo iactantem sanguine corpus,

The poet effectively describes the grisly death agonies of the dying hunter. All the emphasis is on the dying body, and so the line is framed by it: *exanimem ... corpus.*

iactantem: The verb is used here to make vividly real the death throes of the mortally wounded Adonis. Reed compares *Heroides* 3.49–50 and *Metamorphoses* 5.59.

722   desiluit pariterque sinum pariterque capillos

desiluit: "She leaped down."

pariter: The adverb is repeated to highlight the equality of the violent action of lament and grief.

723   rupit et indignis percussit pectora palmis.

indignis: "Unworthy," because the goddesses' hands should not be occupied with beating her breast in grief.

pectora palmis: The line-end is Catullan; cf. c. 64.351; also Virgil, *Aeneid* 1.481 (of the Trojan women).

The heavy alliteration of the end of the line effectively describes the goddess' physical self-abuse; Bömer lists other similar passages of lament that display the same effect.

724   questaque cum fatis at non tamen omnia vestri

questa: From *queri.*

fatis: Adonis must die; some things, however, are permitted to the goddess in her moment of loss. The conjunction *at* once again introduces a strong contrast that serves to introduce the climactic floral metamorphosis of the book.

at: The reading is in question (Korn conjectured *sed,* but *at* accomplishes the same thing better and with fewer paleographical problems); *et* is not particularly difficult to construe, but the force of the strong adversative gives better sense.

725   iuris erunt, dixit; luctus monimenta manebunt

The floral metamorphosis that the goddess will effect in memory of her beloved may well be considered to have been a part of fated destiny; it may be a matter only of *seeming* to the goddess that she is somehow defeating fate.

726   semper, Adoni, mei, repetitaque mortis imago

Adoni: Vocative.

repetitaque mortis imago: A rather mysterious phrase that likely describes the sacral, ritual reenactment of the death of Adonis. A fragment of Sappho (140A Lobel-Page) preserves a ritual lament for the slain lover of the goddess. The wild boar of Calydon was slain by Atalanta and Meleager in Book 8; the boar of 10 slays the goddess' favorite, and this time there is no successful quest to vanquish the monstrosity.

727   annua plangoris peraget simulamina nostri.

Not only the memory of the young victim of the boar, but also the grief of the goddess who loved the doomed hunter will be commemorated each year.

simulamina: Any kind of imitation or mimetic event; the word is extremely rare and was likely invented by Ovid; Reed draws attention here to the association with 14 *simulacra*; cf. too the *firmamina* in the context of Myrrha's tree; also the images of the divinities that avert their gaze from the desecration of the sacred precinct by Hippomenes and Atalanta.

728   at cruor in florem mutabitur. an tibi quondam

cruor … florem: With deliberate antithesis (introduced once again by the strong adversative *at*); the immediate comparison is to the similar fate of Hyacinthus (another tetrasyllabic name beginning with a rough breathing). The etiology of the anemone or wind flower is heralded here; the flower takes its name from the Greek for "wind."

an: Introducing a rather indignant rhetorical question; the key, main verb = 730 *licuit*.

729   femineos artus in olentes vertere mentas,

Fittingly, the poet will introduce *Persephone* somewhat by surprise at the end of this second third of his epic, just as the story of her abduction by Pluto came in the last book of the first third.

mentas: "Mints." The story of Menta or "Mint" is fairly obscure (the poet's main point is to reintroduce the goddess to the narrative); according to the geographer Strabo (8.3.14), she was a lover of Hades who was trampled underfoot by Persephone and transformed into mint leaves. The Greek imperial epic poet Oppian (*Halieutica* 3.486 ff.) also has her as a sexual partner of Hades; after the abduction of Persephone, she complains about her altered status and is trampled not by the new mistress of the dead, but rather by Demeter. Persephone appears at the beginning and end of this book that is so concerned with matters eschatological; here she may appear in something of the vindictive role of a goddess who is rather suited for her status as queen of the infernal regions. An underworld nymph indeed: "eine Unterweltsnymphe, eine Gestalt aus der Persephone-Sage" (Bömer). It is possible that the story was as obscure to Ovid's audience as it is to us.

730   Persephone, licuit, nobis Cinyreius heros

Persephone: We return to something of the situation of the opening of the book, where the underworld goddess was a player in the drama of Orpheus and Eurydice; here hell's queen is invoked rather in the manner of Juno's complaint about Minerva from the opening scenes of the *Aeneid*—will Venus not be able to do what the implicitly lesser goddess Persephone was permitted to accomplish in the matter of Mint?

nobis: With 731 *invidiae* in a double dative construction.

heros: With deliberate force; Venus wishes to memorialize her Adonis as a hero, notwithstanding the details of 714. There is something rather ridiculous about the whole matter; the poet (through his Orphic narrator) has crafted a less than flattering image of the would-be hunter of big game.

Cinyreius: A reminder, so close to the end, of the incest that was responsible for the birth of the hunter whose death will so soon be immortalized with its own floral metamorphosis.

731   invidiae mutatus erit? sic fata cruorem

invidiae: Dative of reference.

fata: With a hint of the notion of "fate" that the verb implies; the verb = *fari.*

cruorem: Ovid artfully balances the end of this verse and the start of the next with two strikingly juxtaposed terms that serve to describe the sanitizing and beautification of the gore as it is transformed into an anemone.

732   nectare odorato sparsit, qui tactus ab illo

odorato: Cf. 729 *olentes.* The blood and gore is sprinkled with the food of the immortals in an effort to render something of Adonis eternal and undying. Bömer links the present scene with Homer, *Iliad* 23.186 ff., where Aphrodite assists in preserving the body of Hector from disfigurement at the hands of Achilles; the parallel does not exist, but the sense is indeed the same. *Nectare odorato* = an ablative of means; she sprinkled the gore with the nectar.

tactus: An interesting textual crux; the reading of M = *tractus*, while Housman conjectured *tinctus* (*fortasse recte*).

733   intumuit sic, ut fulvo perlucida caelo

fulvo: Cf. 716. A dramatic reappearance of the signal color near the end of the book, as in a final simile it describes the locus for the rising of the Adonis *bulla*, a word that in part may have been chosen here because it could be used of a part of a plant. The sky (or mud!) in which the *bulla* is accustomed to rise is the same color we have seen intimately associated with important symbols and marks of both ethnographic and philosophical significance. "The yellow Italian sky," as Anderson calls it, is exactly the same as the image at *Aeneid* 12.792, just before the great ethnographic revelations of Jupiter to Juno. The book neatly begins and closes with a shade of yellow; cf. Hymenaeus' *croceus*-colored cloak and the *fulvum caelum* here, and, too, the use of *croceus* by Virgil in *Aeneid* 11 to describe the cloak of Camilla's prey Chloreus—who embodies the spirit of the old Troy.

perlucida: Cf. Catullus, c. 64.4 *perluciduli ... lapidis*; Ps.-Tibullus, c. 3.12.13; Horace, c. 1.18.3 *perlucidior vitro*; *Heroides* 15.157; *Metamorphoses* 2.586; 3.161 (of a *gemma* and of a *fons* respectively). The prefix expresses the high quality of the pellucidity of the *bulla*, and the emphasis on how one can essentially see *through* the object in question.

caelo: Or *caeno* (so Merkel?). The passage is a difficult one; Melville (1986) openly calls his Oxford translation "free" because of the "uncertain" text. Doubtless it is no coincidence that a *bulla* (734) recurs near the end of the book—the word is rare (especially in verse), and the stories of Cyparissus and Adonis can be linked, though in the latter the young man is violently killed, while in the former he wastes away, as it were, with grief for a violently slain animal. So are we to imagine that Ovid closes his book on a note of mud or one of sky and heaven? (Anderson does well to ask the question.) The key to interpretation likely rests with the *bulla*. Roman youths of aristocratic upbringing wore the *bulla* until they reached manhood (cf. the poet's concern in the stories of Hippomenes, Adonis, etc. for the difference between a *vir* and a *iuvenis*); when the youth reached manhood his childhood *bulla* was consecrated to the Lares (Cicero, *Verrine* 2.1.58; Persius, s. 5.30; Juvenal, s. 13.33). In the case of Adonis—and of Cyparissus and his deer, for that matter—the surrender of the *bulla* never really comes; death intercedes before the ornament can be offered to the household gods, and the youths remain forever frozen in time, as it were. The *bulla* can be said to be surrendered by death, while the association with the *bulla* can likewise be said to last forever precisely because the youth dies young: the token of youth becomes an eternal reminder of the life cut off before it had reached full development (cf. Eurydice and the interception of her *crescentes annos* at 24). The *bulla* of Cyparissus' deer was clearly an ornament that evoked the jewelry of Roman youths; the *bulla* of the simile here is a feature of the natural world, a bubble of some sort that evokes the aristocratic Roman ornament all the same—and invests it with an effectively transient quality. The world of Troy is transient in the light of the future Rome; on the philosophical level, promises of rebirth and renewal may prove groundless in the light of what some might call a Lucretian correction. See further von Glinski (2012: 41–42) (who reads *caeno*), and who observes that "the challenge to interpret this strange sight remains."

The image of the *bulla* rising up in the sky may also distantly presage the image of the Caesarian comet that comes near the end of the poem's last third, in the final metamorphosis of Book 15. The poet may also be playing with the idea that through verse the youth frozen in time receives a sort of immortality; cf. the end of Book 15 here too, with its questions about the truth of the *praesaga vatum* and the (implicit) lies of the poet Orpheus: bubbles as harbingers of apotheosis. It is possible, too, that regardless of whether we imagine heaven or mud in this passage, the point is on the association of the *bulla* with the Attis-like Adonis—in other words, with an eminently Phrygian or Trojan image that offers a comment on the ethnography of the future Rome from the songs of Orpheus—an image that may not come to decisive fruition until the end of Book 11 of the poem, where the Trojan Aesacus will fail in his pursuit of the nymph Hesperia (i.e., Italy)—who, like Orpheus' Eurydice, will fall prey to a serpent's bite.

734   surgere bulla solet; nec plena longior hora

bulla: Cf. 114. The earlier *bulla* was a tangible adornment of the deer (however ludicrous the image); the present *bulla* is part of a descriptive simile.

plena: Not now of pregnancy or the carrying of a child, but rather of the metaphorical fullness of the hour. The alternative vision that Orpheus presents will not last long, as it were. *Plena . . . hora* = ablative of degree of difference; there was a delay of not longer than a full hour before the metamorphosis was effected.

735   facta mora est, cum flos de sanguine concolor ortus,

facta mora est: The goddess had had either no time or all too little in which to delay in helping Hippomenes (643); now there is a pause of no more than an hour before the epiphany of the new flower.

concolor: "Having the same color throughout"; the anemone is blood-red. Cf. the *bicolor myrtus* of 98 that is sacred to Venus.

ortus: From *oriri.*

736   qualem quae lento celant sub cortice granum

The line is powerfully and deliberately spondaic; the poet wishes the audience to pause over the detail that connects the present scene with the Persephone lore of the close of the first third of the epic; the dactylic rhythm of the following lines seals the contrast and effect, and comes as the narrator arrives at the climactic point of the exceedingly brief and fragile life of the wind flower.

qualem ... granum: A wonderful trick; the *granum* envelops the line, though in reality it is the *cortex* that is responsible for envelopment, the *cortex* that here is encircled by that which in botanical life it encircles. The effect is to add still more to the strangeness and wonder of the image, as Ovid invites the audience to linger and reflect at the close of the book (and, perhaps, with a final hint of the theme of falsehood) Venus wants to memorialize Adonis, after all, and memorialized he will be—though with a flower that is doomed to be blown away by the slightest breeze (a final wry comment, to be sure, on the hunting abilities and stamina of the would-be boar slayer).

lento: The bark of the tree is flexible and pliant; there is perhaps a shade of the sense that the pregnancy is long and difficult.

cortice: With reference to the (maternal) Myrrha metamorphosis. Ovid imitates the present passage at *Epistulae ex Ponto* 4.15.8; cf. *Fasti* 4.608.

737   punica ferre solent. brevis est tamen usus in illo;

punica: Pomegranates. The second third of the epic draws to a close with a mention of the fateful underworld fruit from the end of its first act, the fruit that had snared Persephone for the underworld (her story a play on the same themes as the Orpheus and Eurydice tale).

brevis: The goddess imparts something of an immortal boon on Adonis, but the anemone she creates from his blood is exceedingly fragile and delicate—hence the appropriateness of the bubble imagery, and rather a pointed comment on the Orphic lore that lies behind the ideas of rebirth and renewal that are associated with the singer of the tale.

usus in illo: Cf. 651.

738   namque male haerentem et nimia levitate caducum

male haerentem: "Clinging badly"; the phrase is from Livy (*Ab Urbe Condita* 23.24.9.4); there may be a subtle touch of black humor given the mode of Adonis' death.

nimia levitate: "With excessive lightness"; the image of the swift runners is maintained. The phrase is Lucretian; cf. *De Rerum Natura* 3.387; Ovid has it also at *Metamorphoses* 2.163–164 *utque labant curvae iusto sine pondere naves / per mare instabiles nimia levitate feruntur.* Nimia works closely with *male* in the poet's crafting of an image that is something less than optimistic; the fragility of Adonis' life is mirrored in the frail, weak nature of the flower into which his corpse is transformed. The book draws to a close on a wisp of the wind, as it were, an insubstantial note that recalls the ghosts of its opening story.

739   excutiunt idem, qui praestant nomina, venti.

excutiunt: Cf. 426.

nomina: The book ends on an onomastic note. The flower is the anemone, from the Greek for "wind." The etymological detail secures the correct reading here, despite the much better attested *omnia.*

venti: The final word of the book describes the force that is responsible for the shaking and blowing away, as it were, of the fragile flower.

Bibliography and Further Reading

The bibliography on Ovid is immense. What follows represents a mere sampling of the riches available (a few non-Ovidian works are included that are cited in the commentary notes, as well as some editions of related classical works of particular relevance to a study of *Metamorphoses* 10).

Ahl, F. (1985), *Metamorfations: Soundplay and Wordplay in Ovid and Other Classical Poets*. Ithaca: Cornell University Press.

Anderson, W. (1972), *Ovid's Metamorphoses: Books 6–10*. Norman: The University of Oklahoma Press.

Anderson, W. (1977), *Ovidius Metamorphoses*. Leipzig: Teubner.

Barchiesi, A. (1997), *The Poet and the Prince: Ovid and Augustan Discourse*. Berkeley-Los Angeles: The University of California Press.

Barchiesi, A. (2000), *Speaking Volumes: Narrative and Intertext in Ovid and Other Latin Poets*. London: Laterza.

Barchiesi, A., Hardie, P., and Hinds, S., (eds.) (1999), *Ovidian Transformations: Essays on the Metamorphoses and Its Reception*. Cambridge: Cambridge Philosophical Society.

Barkan, L. (1986), *The Gods Made Flesh: Metamorphosis and the Pursuit of Paganism*. New Haven: Yale University Press.

Bömer, F. (1980), *P. Ovidius Naso Metamorphosen: Kommentar X-XI*. Heidelberg: Carl Winter Verlag.

Boyd, B., (ed.) (2002), *Brill's Companion to Ovid*. Leiden: Brill.

Cameron, A. (2004), *Greek Mythography in the Roman World*. Oxford-New York: Oxford University Press.

Clark, J., Coulson, F., and McKinley, K., (eds.) (2011), *Ovid in the Middle Ages*. Cambridge: Cambridge University Press.

Deferrari, R., Barry, M., and McGuire, M. (1939), *A Concordance of Ovid*. Washington: The Catholic University of America Press.

Due, O. (1974), *Changing Forms: Studies in the Metamorphoses of Ovid*. Copenhagen: Museum Tusculanum Press.

Edgeworth, R. (1992), *The Colors of the Aeneid*. New York: Peter Lang.

Fantham, E. (2004), *Ovid's Metamorphoses*. Oxford: Oxford University Press.

Feeney, D. (1991), *The Gods in Epic*. Oxford: Oxford University Press.

Feldherr, A. (2010), *Playing Gods: Ovid's Metamorphoses and the Politics of Fiction*. Princeton: Princeton University Press.

Forbes, P. (1990), *Metamorphosis in Greek Myths*. Oxford: Oxford University Press.

Fränkel, H. (1945), *Ovid: A Poet Between Two Worlds*. Berkeley: The University of California Press.

Fratantuono, L. (2005), "*Posse putes:* Virgil's Camilla, Ovid's Atalanta." In C. Deroux, (ed.), *Studies in Latin Literature and Roman History XII*. Bruxelles: Editions Latomus, 185–193.

Fratantuono, L. (2008), "*Velocem potuit domuisse puellam:* Propertius, Catullus, and Atalanta's Race." In *Latomus*, 67: 342–352.

Fratantuono, L. (2011), *Madness Transformed: A Reading of Ovid's Metamorphoses*. Lanham: Lexington Books.

Frazer, J. (1921), *Apollodorus The Library* (two volumes). Cambridge, Massachusetts: Harvard University Press (Loeb Classical Library).

Galasso, L. (2002), *Ovidio: Opere II: Le Metamorfosi*. Torino: Biblioteca della Pléiade, Einaudi-Gallimard.

Galinsky, K. (1975), *Ovid's Metamorphoses: An Introduction to the Basic Aspects*. Berkeley-Los Angeles: The University of California Press.

Gantz, T. (1993), *Early Greek Myth* (two volumes). Baltimore: The Johns Hopkins University Press.

Gee, E. R. R. (2013), *Aratus and the Astronomical Tradition*. New York: Oxford University Press.

Glare, P. G. G., (ed.) (1982), *The Oxford Latin Dictionary*. Oxford: Oxford University Press.

Hardie, P., (ed.) (2002a), *The Cambridge Companion to Ovid*. Cambridge: Cambridge University Press.

Hardie, P. (2002b), *Ovid's Poetics of Illusion*. Cambridge: Cambridge University Press.

Hill, D. (1999), *Ovid: Metamorphoses IX-XII*. Warminster: Aris and Phillips.

Hinds, S. (1987), *The Metamorphosis of Persephone: Ovid and the Self-Conscious Muse*. Cambridge: Cambridge University Press.

Hinds, S. (1998), *Allusion and Intertext: Dynamics of Appropriation in Roman Poetry*. Cambridge: Cambridge University Press.

Hollis, A. (1970), *Ovid Metamorphoses VIII*. Oxford: Oxford University Press.

Holzberg, N. (2002), *Ovid: The Poet and His Work*. Ithaca: Cornell University Press.

Hunter, R., (ed.) (2005), *The Hesiodic Catalogue of Women*. Cambridge: Cambridge University Press.

Knox, P. (1986), *Ovid's Metamorphoses and the Traditions of Augustan Poetry*. Cambridge: Cambridge University Press.

Knox, P., (ed.) (2006), *Oxford Readings in Ovid*. Oxford: Oxford University Press.

Knox, P., (ed.) (2009), *A Companion to Ovid*. Malden: Wiley-Blackwell.

Mack, S. (1988), *Ovid*. New Haven: Yale University Press.

Martindale, C. (1990), *Ovid Renewed: Ovidian Influences on Literature and Art from the Middle Ages to the Renaissance*. Cambridge: Cambridge University Press.

Melville, A. (1986), *Ovid's Metamorphoses*. Oxford: Oxford University Press (Oxford World's Classics).

Michalopoulos, A. (2001), *Ancient Etymologies in Ovid's Metamorphoses*. Leeds: Francis Cairns.

Murphy, G. (1972), *Ovid Metamorphoses XI*. Oxford: Oxford University Press.

Myers, S. (1994), *Ovid's Causes: Cosmogony and Aetiology in the Metamorphoses*. Ann Arbor: The University of Michigan Press.

Mynors, R. (1990), *Virgil: The Georgics*. Oxford: Oxford University Press.

O'Bryhim, S. (1991), *The Amathusian Myths of Ovid's Metamorphoses, Book 10*. Dissertation at The University of Texas at Austin.

OLD (Oxford Latin Dictionary)—See Glare, P. G. G., (ed.) (1982).

Otis, B. (1970), *Ovid as an Epic Poet*. Cambridge: Cambridge University Press.

Papathomopoulos, M. (1968), *Antoninus Liberalis: Les Métamorphoses*. Paris: Les Belles Lettres.

Reed, J. (1997), *Bion of Smyrna: The Fragments and the Adonis*. Cambridge: Cambridge University Press.

Reed, J. (2013), *Ovidio Metamorfosi Volume V (Libri X-XII).* Fondazione Lorenzo Valla.

Reid, J., (ed.) (1993), *The Oxford Guide to Classical Mythology in the Arts, 1300–1990s.* Oxford: Oxford University Press.

Richardson, N. (1974), *The Homeric Hymn to Demeter.* Oxford: Oxford University Press.

Rimell, V. (2006), *Ovid's Lovers: Desire, Difference, and the Poetic Imagination.* Cambridge: Cambridge University Press.

Segal, C. (1969), *Landscape in Ovid's Metamorphoses: A Study in the Transformation of a Literary Symbol.* Wiesbaden (Hermes Einzelschriften 31).

Segal, C. (1989), *Orpheus: The Myth of the Poet.* Baltimore: The Johns Hopkins University Press.

Solodow, J. (1988), *The World of Ovid's Metamorphoses.* Chapel Hill-London: The University of North Carolina Press.

Tarrant, R. (2004), *P. Ovidii Nasonis Metamorphoses.* Oxford: Oxford University Press (Oxford Classical Texts).

Thomas, R. (1988), *Virgil: The Georgics* (2 volumes). Cambridge: Cambridge University Press.

Thomas, R., and Ziolkowski, J. (2014), *The Virgil Encyclopedia* (three volumes). Malden: Wiley-Blackwell.

Tissol, G. (1997), *The Face of Nature: Wit, Narrative, and Cosmic Origins in Ovid's Metamorphoses.* Princeton: Princeton University Press.

von Albrecht, M., and Zinn, E., (eds.) (1968), *Ovid.* Darmstadt (Wege der Forschung 92).

von Glinski, M. (2012), *Simile and Identity in Ovid's Metamorphoses.* Oxford: Oxford University Press.

West, M. (1966), *Hesiod Theogony.* Oxford: Oxford University Press.

West, M. (1983), *The Orphic Poems.* Oxford: Oxford University Press.

West, M. (1985), *The Hesiodic Catalogue of Women.* Oxford: Oxford University Press.

Wheeler, S. (1999), *A Discourse of Wonders: Audience and Performance in Ovid's Metamorphoses.* Philadelphia: The University of Pennsylvania Press.

White, P. (1993), *Promised Verse: Poets in the Society of Augustan Rome.* Cambridge, Massachusetts: Harvard University Press.

Wilkinson, L. (1955), *Ovid Recalled*. Cambridge: Cambridge University Press.

Ziogas, I. (2013), *Hesiod in Ovid: The Metamorphosis of the Catalogue of Women*. Cambridge: Cambridge University Press.

Ziolkowski, T. (2005), *Ovid and the Moderns*. Ithaca: Cornell University Press.

Index

(Numbers refer to pages, not to line-numbers of the Latin text.)